The Korn Shell

User and Programming Manual

Revised Edition

The Korn Shell

User and Programming Manual

Revised Edition

Anatole Olczak

Published for Addison Wesley Longman Limited by ASP Inc.
ASP Inc., PO Box 23837, San Jose, California 95153, USA
Order Desk (800) 777-UNIX • (510) 531-5615

ADDISON-WESLEY

Harlow, England • Reading, Massachusetts
Menlo Park, California • New York • Don Mills, Ontario
Amsterdam • Bonn • Sydney • Singapore • Tokyo • Madrid
San Juan • Milan • Mexico City • Seoul • Taipei

The Korn Shell User and Programming Manual
Revised Edition
by Anatole Olczak

Copyright © 1991, 1997 ASP Inc.
San Jose California 95153 USA

Published for Addison Wesley Longman Limited by

ASP Inc. PO Box 23837 • San Jose California USA 95153
(800) 777-UNIX • (510) 531-5615

Cover designed by odB Design & Communications, Reading
and printed by The Riverside Printing Co. (Reading) Ltd
Typeset by Meridian Colour Repro Ltd, Pangbourne
Printed and bound in Great Britain by Biddles Ltd, Guildford and King's Lynn

First edition printed in 1991
Second edition printed in 1997. Reprinted 1997

CIP Data available on request

ISBN 0-201-17688-2

To
Jarmila,
Renata, and
Larissa

Table of Contents

Preface .... **xviii**

Acknowledgments xx

Miscellaneous xxi

Conventions xxi

Source Code Listing xxii

Other Publications and Services xxii

Chapter 1: Introduction **1**

Major Features 1

Where to Get the Korn Shell 3

Logging In 4

    Changing the Login Shell 4

Invoking the Korn Shell Separately 5

Using the Korn Shell in Scripts 6

Chapter 2: Korn Shell Basics **7**

Process Execution 7

    Multiple Commands 8

    Continuing Commands 8

    Background Jobs 9

    Pipes 9

    Conditional Execution 10

    Grouping Commands 12

Input/Output Redirection 15

    Redirecting Standard Output 15

        The **noclobber** Option 17

    Redirecting Standard Input 17

    File Descriptors 18

        Redirecting Standard Error 18

        More with File Descriptors 20

    Here Documents 22

        Here Documents and File Descriptors ... 23

    Discarding Standard Output 23

File Name Substitution 25

    The * Character 25

    The ? Character 27

The [ ] Characters 28
The ! Character 29
Matching . Files 30
Complex Patterns 30
    *(*pattern*) 30
    ?(*pattern*) 32
    +(*pattern*) 33
    @(*pattern*) 33
    !(*pattern*) 34
    More Complex Patterns 34
Disabling File Name Substitution 34
Command Substitution 36
Bourne Shell Compatibility 37
Directing File Input 37
Arithmetic Operations 38
Tilde Substitution 38

Chapter 3: Parameters and Variables **41**
Variables 41
Accessing Variable Values 42
Variable Attributes 43
    Lowercase (**–l**) and Uppercase (**–u**) 44
    Readonly (**–r**) 44
    Integer (**–i**) 45
    Right (**–r**) and Left (**–l**) Justify 46
    Autoexport (**–x**) 47
    Removing Variable Attributes 47
    Multiple Attributes 49
    Checking Variable Attributes 49
More with Variables 50
Unsetting Variables 51
Special Parameters 51
The ? Parameter 51
The $ Parameter 52
Other Special Parameters 52

Variable Expansion 53
    $*variable*, ${*variable*} 54
    ${#*variable*} 54
    ${*variable:–word*}, ${*variable–word*} 55
    ${*variable:=word*}, ${*variable=word*} 57
    ${*variable:?word*}, ${*variable:?*} 59
    ${*variable:+word*}, ${*variable+word*} 59
    ${*variable#pattern*}, ${*variable##pattern*} 60
    ${*variable%pattern*}, ${*variable%%pattern*} 61
Array Variables 63
    Array Variable Assignments & Declarations 63
    Array Variable Expansion 64
    Array Variable Attributes 66
    Array Variable Reassignments 67
Quoting 69
    Single Quotes 69
    Double Quotes 70
    Back Quotes 72

Chapter 4: Editing Commands **73**
Terminal Requirements 73
Command History File 74
The **fc** Command 74
    Displaying the Command History File 74
    Editing the Command History File 76
In-Line Editor 78
    Vi Edit Mode 78
        Input Mode 79
        Command Mode 79
        Moving Around the History File 80
        Editing Previous Commands 81
    Displaying Long Command Lines 84
    Emacs/Gmacs Edit Modes 84
        Editing Commands in Emacs/Gmacs Mode 84

Korn Shell User and Programming Manual

Chapter 5: Job Control **89**

    Manipulating Jobs 90

        Checking Job Status... 92

        Killing Jobs.. 92

        Waiting for Jobs.. 93

    Background Jobs and I/O 93

    Job Names 97

    Leaving Stopped Jobs... 98

Chapter 6: Performing Arithmetic **99**

    The **let** Command.. 99

    The ((...)) Command... 102

    Declaring Integer Variables... 102

    Arithmetic Constants.. 104

    Arithmetic Operators.. 105

        −*expression* (Unary Minus) 106

        !*expression* (Logical Negation) 106

        ~*expression* (Bitwise Negation) 106

        expression1 * *expression2* (Multiplication) 107

        expression1 / *expression2* (Division) 107

        expression1 % *expression2* (Modulo) 108

        expression1 + *expression2* (Addition).............. 108

        expression1 − *expression2* (Subtraction)......... 108

        identifier=expression (Assignment) 109

        expression1 << *expression2* (Left shift)........... 109

        expression1 >> *expression2* (Right shift)......... 110

        expression1 <= *expression2* (Less than or equal) 110

        expression1 < *expression2* (Less than)........... 110

        expression1 >= *expression2* (Greater than or equal)..... 111

        expression1 > *expression2* (Greater than) 111

        expression1 == *expression2* (Equal to)........... 111

        expression1 != *expression2* (Not equal to).... 112

        expression1 & *expression2* (Bitwise AND) ... 112

        expression1 ^ *expression2* (Bitwise Exclusive OR)...... 112

        expression1 | *expression2* (Bitwise OR)........ 113

        expression1 && *expression2* (Logical AND) ... 113

expression1 || *expression2* (Logical OR) 114
(*expression*) (Override Precedence) 114
Random Numbers 115

Chapter 7: The Environment **117**
After You Log In 117
The Environment File 118
Environment Variables 118
  The **cd** Command 118
  CDPATH 120
  PATH 121
  TMOUT 121
  Mail 122
    MAILCHECK 122
    MAIL 122
    MAILPATH 122
    New Mail Notification Message 123
    TERM 124
Korn Shell Options 124
  Enabling/Disabling Options 124
    The **ignoreeof** Option 126
    The **markdirs** Option 126
    The **noclobber** Option 127
    The **nounset** Option 127
  Displaying the Current Settings 128
  Command-line Options 130
Aliases 130
  Displaying Current Aliases 132
  Tracked Aliases 133
  Removing Aliases 135
Prompts 135
  Customizing Your Command Prompt 136
Subshells 137
Restricted Shell 139
Privileged Mode 140

Chapter 8: Writing Korn Shell Scripts **141**

Executing Korn Shell Scripts 141

Positional Parameters 144

Modifying Positional Parameters 146

The **exit** Command 148

The [[...]] Command 149

Checking Strings 150

Checking Patterns.. 151

Checking File Attributes 151

Checking Integer Attributes 155

The ! Operator 157

Compound Expressions 157

&& - The AND Operator 158

|| - The OR Operator................................ 158

[[...]] vs **test** and [...] 160

Checking File Descriptors 160

Control Commands.. 161

The **case** Command 161

Specifying Patterns with **case** 162

The **for** Command.. 164

Other **for** Syntax.................................... 167

The **if** Command 168

Other **if** Syntax: **else** 170

Other **if** Syntax: **elif** 172

if/elif vs **case** 174

The **while** Command 174

The **until** Command................................ 176

Nested Loops 178

Breaking Out of Loops 179

The **continue** Command 181

The **select** Command 182

Other **select** Syntax 187

The **select** Menu Format 187

Comments 188

Table of Contents

Input/Output Commands 189

The **print** Command 190

Escape Characters 190

print Options 193

The **echo** Command 196

The **exec** Command 196

The **read** Command 198

Reading Input from Files.............................. 201

The **IFS** Variable 203

More with **read** 204

Reading Input Interactively 206

The **REPLY** variable 208

Miscellaneous Programming Features 208

The . Command... 208

Functions.. 209

Returning Function Exit Status 210

Scope & Availability 211

Using Functions in Korn Shell Scripts 211

Function Variables.. 212

Displaying Current Functions 213

Auto-loading Functions 213

FPATH. 214

Removing Function Definitions 214

Traps 215

Ignoring Signals 216

Resetting Traps 216

Exit & Function Traps 216

Debugging with trap... 217

Trap Signal Precedence 218

Debugging Korn Shell Scripts 218

Enabling Debug Options 218

Debugging Example 219

Debugging with **trap** 222

Parsing Command-line Arguments 223

More with Here Documents 224

Co-Processes... 227

Chapter 9: Miscellaneous Commands **231**

The **:** Command 231

The **eval** Command 232

The **export** Command 234

The **false** Command 235

The **newgrp** Command 235

The **pwd** Command 236

The **readonly** Command 236

The **set** Command 237

The **time** Command 239

The **times** Command 239

The **true** Command 239

The **ulimit** Command 240

The **umask** Command 241

The **whence** Command 242

Appendix A: Sample .profile File **245**

Appendix B: Sample Environment File **247**

Appendix C: C Shell Functionality **249**

Directory Functions 249

Miscellaneous Commands 255

The **.logout** File 255

The **chdir** Command 255

The **logout** Command 256

The **setenv** Command 256

The **source** Command 257

Appendix D: Sample Korn Shell Scripts **259**

Display Files - **kcat** 259

Interactive uucp - **kuucp** 261

Basename - **kbasename** 263

Dirname - **kdirname** 264

Display Files with Line Numbers - **knl** 265

Find Words - **match** 266

Simple Calculator - **kcalc** 268

Table of Contents

Search for Patterns in Files - **kgrep** 269

Calendar Program - **kcal** 274

Appendix E: Korn Shell Quick Reference 291

Appendix 7: Korn Shell Man Pages 327

Index 383

Korn Shell User and Programming Manual

List of Tables:

2.1: Command Execution Format 14
2.2: Some I/O Redirection Operators 19
2.3: File Descriptors 21
2.4: Redirect Operators and File Descriptors 24
2.5: Basic Pattern Matching Characters 31
2.6: Other File Name Patterns 35
2.7: Tilde Substitution 39

3.1: Assigning Values to Variables 43
3.2: Assigning Values/Attributes to Variables 45
3.3: Setting Variable Attributes 48
3.4: Some Preset Special Parameters 55
3.5: Variable Expansion Formats 62
3.6: Array Variables 67

4.1: Vi Input Mode Commands 81
4.2: Some Vi Command Mode Commands 82
4.3: Some Emacs/Gmacs In-Line Editor Commands 87

5.1: Job Control Commands 96
5.2: Job Names 97

6.1: Arithmetic Operators 101

7.1: Some Korn Shell Environment Variables 125
7.2: Some Korn Shell Options 129
7.3: Preset Aliases 134

8.1: [[...]] String Operators 152
8.2: Some [[...]] File Operators 154
8.3: [[...]] Integer Operators 156
8.4: Other [[...]] Operators 159
8.5: **print** Escape Characters 193
8.6: **print** Options 195

Table of Contents

8.7: **read** Options 207
8.8: Some Frequently Used Signals 217
8.9: Korn Shell Debugging Options 220
8.10: Co-Processes 229

9.1: **ulimit** Options 259

Preface

Acknowledgements
Miscellaneous
Conventions
Source Code Listing
Other Publications and Services

The **Korn Shell User and Programming Manual** is designed to be a reference and learning tool for a range of users - from the novice with some experience to the pro who is familiar with both the Bourne and C shells. It contains complete technical information, as well as hands-on examples and complete programs to help guide you and illustrate all the features of the Korn shell. This book assumes that you are familiar with the basic UNIX commands, and understand file system concepts. You should also be able to login to a system, and enter basic commands.

If you are an experienced user, you may want to skip Chapter 1 and the first half of Chapter 2. The first seven chapters deal primarily with interactive use, while Chapter 8 and 9 cover the programming concepts.

The goal of this book to teach you the Korn Shell, and this is done by walking you through examples. So by the time you are finished reading the book, you'll be comfortable with it, and writing your own Korn shell scripts.

But don't just read the book. The best way for you to learn about the Korn shell is to type in the examples yourself. Then do some experimentation on your own by either modifying the examples or coming up with your own commands.

Chapter 1 contains an overview of the major features in the Korn shell. It covers where to get it, how your login shell is configured, and setting up the Korn shell to co-exist with other shells while you are on the learning curve. It also includes brief descriptions of other related shells, including the Windowing Korn Shell (**wksh**), Born Again Shell (**bash**), MKS ksh, and the public domain Korn shell (**pdksh**).

Chapter 2 covers the Korn shell basics: how commands can work together to do other things, and some basic shortcuts to improve productivity, and Korn shell I/O. You'll also be introduced to file name, command, and tilde substitution: important concepts that are the basis of much of the Korn shell.

Chapter 3 teaches you about Korn shell variables, variable attributes, and parameters. You'll learn about all the different types of variable expansion, including the substring features. Array variables and quoting are also discussed in detail.

Chapter 4 discusses the Korn shell command history mechanism and vi and emacs in-line editors. Here you will learn how to call up previous commands and manipulate them.

Chapter 5 shows you how to manage and manipulate multiple processes using the job control mechanism, a feature almost directly copied from the C shell.

In Chapter 6, you will learn how to perform arithmetic with the Korn shell. It contains sections on multi-base arithmetic, declaring integer-type variables, and random numbers, along with examples for each type of arithmetic operator.

Chapter 7 will show you how to set up your own customized environment: from setting up the prompt how you like it, to configuring your personal email. Korn shell options, environment variables, aliases, the **.profile** file, and subshells are also covered.

In Chapter 8, you are taught how to write programs using the many Korn shell commands and features. Executing and debugging scripts, input/output commands, positional parameters, flow control commands such as **case, for, if, select, while,** and **until** are also discussed. Step-by-step examples are included, and complete usable scripts are built from the bottom up. For those experienced UNIX programmers, important differences between the Korn and Bourne shells are discussed, and something else new to UNIX shell programming - performance. You'll learn a few tricks that can speed up execution of your Korn shell scripts.

Chapter 9 covers miscellaneous commands, such as **readonly, ulimit,** and **whence,** and Korn shell functions.

Appendix A and B include a sample ready-to-use profile and environment file.

Appendix C contains the Korn shell versions of a number of C shell commands and functions.

Appendix D contains the source code listing for a number of handy ready-to-run Korn shell scripts, including an interactive calendar program.

Appendix E contains the Korn shell man pages.

Appendix F contains a Korn Shell Quick Reference section and more examples.

Acknowledgments

Thanks to David Korn for developing the Korn shell, Steven Bourne for the Bourne shell, and Bill Joy for the C shell. Other thanks to Mike Veach and Pat Sullivan for contributing to the development of the Korn shell. and Mark Horton, Bill Joy (again), and Richard Stallman for developing the vi and emacs editors which were used in the development of the Korn shell.

Special thanks to Peter Collinson, Cynthia Duquette, Ian Jones, Peter Kettle, Heather Prenatt, the ASP staff, Aspen Technologies, O'Reilly & Associates (who reviewed the initial draft of this book before publishing their own Korn shell book!), James Lamm and others for reviewing drafts of this book.

Miscellaneous

The information and material has been tested and verified to the best of our ability. This does not mean that it is always 100% correct! Subtle differences and variations may exist between implementations and features may have changed. Add of course there may even be bugs or mistakes! Please send us any comments or suggestions for future editions, along with information about your environment. Email can be sent to:

info@aspinc.com

You can also call or fax us. We will send you the next edition free if we use any of your comments or suggestions.

Conventions

For readability sake, the default **$** prompt is used in the examples in this publication. Control characters are given as **Ctl** followed by the character in boldface. For example, **Ctl-d** specifies **Control-d** and is entered by pressing the **d** key while holding down the **Control** key. Special keys, like carriage-return and backspace, are enclosed in <>'s. For example, <RETURN> specifies the carriage-return key. Long command lines are continued onto the next line using the \ character. It is assumed it is understood that <RETURN> (sometimes labeled on some keyboards as <ENTER>) is pressed when you enter a command.

Source Code Listing

If you would like the source code listing to the Korn shell scripts listed in the appendices, send us a request via email or visit our web site at:

www.aspinc.com.

Other Publications and Services

ASP offers a full line of technical reference manuals, guides, and quick reference cards for UNIX, Tcl, JavaScript, Java, HTML, X Windows, C /C++, Netnews/Usenet and other topics. They are specifically designed for the professional who needs easy-to-access reference information to increase productivity. Please call or email for more information:

ASP, Inc.
PO Box 23837
San Jose California USA 95153
(510) 531-5615
(800) 777-UNIX
web: www.aspinc.com
email: info@aspinc.com

Chapter 1:
Introduction

Major Features
Where to Get the Korn Shell
Which Version Do You Have?
Logging In
Invoking the Korn Shell
Separately

The Korn shell is an interactive command and programming language that provides an interface to the UNIX and other systems. As an interactive command language, it is responsible for reading and executing the commands that you enter at your terminal. As a programming language, its special commands allow you to write sophisticated programs. It also provides the ability to customize your working environment.

Major Features

The Korn shell offers compatibility with the Bourne shell, while providing a more robust programming language and command interpreter. It also contains some features of the C shell. The major features of the Korn shell are:

• **Improved performance.** Programs written in the Korn shell can run faster than similar programs written in the Bourne or C shells.

• **Bourne shell compatibility.** Programs written for the Bourne shell can run under the Korn shell without modification.

- **Command-line editing.** Instead of backspacing or retyping, commands can be edited in **vi, emacs,** or **gmacs** mode.

- **Command history.** Commands are stored in a history file, which can then be modified and re-executed or just re-executed as is. The commands are saved, up to a user-specified limit, across multiple login sessions.

- **Enhanced I/O facilities.** File descriptors and streams can be specified. Multiple files can be opened at the same time and read. Menus can be formatted and processed more easily.

- **Added data types and attributes.** Variables can now have a type, as well as size and justification attributes.

- **Integer arithmetic support.** Integer arithmetic can be performed in any base from two to thirty-six using variables and constants. A wide range of arithmetic operators is supported, including bitwise operators.

- **Arrays.** One-dimensional arrays can be used.

- **Improved string manipulation facilities.** Substrings can be generated from the value of strings. Strings can be converted to upper or lower case.

- **Regular expressions.** Better support of regular expressions in variable expansion and filename wildcards has been added.

- **Job control.** The Korn shell job control feature is virtually the same as that of the C shell. Programs can be stopped, restarted, or moved to and from the background. Programs can be identified for **kill** with their job numbers.

- **Aliases.** Programs, and Korn shell scripts, along with their options can be aliased to a single name.

• **New options and variables.** These have been added to provide more control over environment customization.

• **Functions.** Increases programability by allowing code to be organized in smaller, more manageable units, similar to procedures in other languages. Functions also allow Korn shell programs to be stored in memory.

• **Enhanced directory navigation facilities.** The previous directory, and home directory of any user can be referred to without using pathnames. Components of previous pathnames can be manipulated to generate new pathnames.

• **Enhanced debugging features.** More robust diagnostic facilities have been provided, and functions can be traced separately.

• **Other miscellaneous features.** New test operators, special variables, special commands, control commands, command-line options, and security features have also been added.

Where To Get the Korn Shell

The Korn shell is included as an optional shell, along with the Bourne and C shells by most vendors, including Sun for Solaris, SCO for UnixWare, Hewlett-Packard for HP-UX, DEC for Digitial UNIX, and others. It is also available as an unbundled product by many vendors.

The Windowing Kon Shell (**wksh**) is a full version of the Kornshell with graphical user interface extensions for the X Window System. It is available for System V Release 4 based systems, Solaris, and UnixWare.

Public domain Korn shell (**pdsh**) has many features of the Korn shell, as well as the C shell and is available (via source code) from the **comp.sources.unix** newsgroup.

Mortice Kern Systems sells a version of the Korn shell for MS-DOS & Windows. There are also a number of shareware shells that have Korn shell-like functionality.

Logging In

A number of things happen before you see the **login**: prompt on your terminal. After you enter the login name, the **login** program is started. It finishes the process of logging you in by prompting for a password, checking the **/etc/passwd** file, and finally starting up your login shell. Your login shell is specified in the **/etc/passwd** file like this:

```
larissa:*:101:12::/home/larissa:/bin/sh
renata:*:102:101::/home/renata:/bin/ksh
```

For **larissa**, the login shell is **/bin/sh**, while for **renata** it is **/bin/ksh**.

Changing the Login Shell

To make the Korn shell your default login shell, have your system administrator change it to **/bin/ksh** or the pathname of wherever the Korn shell binary is located, or run the **chsh** command (if available on your system). Until that is done, you can still run the Korn shell by simply invoking:

```
$ ksh
```

This will give you a Korn subshell. To get back to your login shell, type **Ctl-d** (**Control-d**). If you get an error message complaining about ksh not being found, you can try to find it by executing:

```
$ find / —name ksh —print
/usr/local/bin/ksh
```

Once you've found it, add the directory in which it was found to your

PATH variable. If you're using the Bourne shell, it would be done like this:

```
$  PATH=$PATH:/usr/local/bin
$  export PATH
$  ksh
```

while for the C shell:

```
%  set path=($path /usr/local/bin)
%  ksh
```

You could also invoke the Korn shell with the full pathname:

```
$  /usr/local/bin/ksh
```

More about the **PATH** variable is explained later in **Chapter 7**.

Invoking The Korn Shell Separately

If you would like to use the Korn shell, but keep your login shell the same, you can avoid conflicts between the two shells by putting all of your Korn shell environment and startup commands in the environment file. This is specified by the **ENV** variable, which could be set in your Bourne shell **.profile** file like this:

```
$  grep ENV $HOME/.profile
ENV=$HOME/.kshrc
```

or in the C shell **.login** file:

```
$  grep ENV $HOME/.login
setenv ENV $HOME/.kshrc
```

This way, when you invoke the Korn shell, it will know where to look
and find the environment settings. Here are some basic commands that
should be in the environment file:

```
$ cat $HOME/.kshrc
SHELL=/usr/local/bin/ksh
EDITOR=vi
export SHELL EDITOR
```

The **EDITOR** variable specifies the editor to use for command-line
editing. Here it is set to **vi**, but it can also be set to **emacs** or **gmacs**.
This will be covered in detail later in **Chapter 7**.

Using The Korn Shell in Scripts

For those experienced users that are ready to dive into writing some
Korn shell scripts, but do not have their login shells configured for the
Korn shell, make sure to add this to the top of your Korn shell script to
make sure that it is executed by the Korn shell:

```
#!/bin/ksh
```

Use the full pathname of **ksh** if it is not located in **/bin**.

Chapter 2:
Korn Shell Basics

Process Execution
Input/Output Redirection
File Name Substitution
Command Substitution
Tilde Substitution

This chapter covers some of the basic features of the Korn shell. If you've worked with the Bourne and/or C shells, then most of the **Process Execution** section will be a review of what you are already familiar with. The **Input/Output Redirection** section shows how you can use the special Korn shell I/O operators with regular commands to perform more sophisticated programming tasks. The last three sections in this chapter, **File Name Substitution**, **Command Substitution**, and **Tilde Substitution** show you how these powerful features can be used as shortcuts to help simplify your work.

Process Execution

This section provides a quick overview of how the Korn shell interacts with UNIX.

Multiple Commands

Multiple commands can be given on the same line if separated with the
; character. Notice that the command prompt is not displayed until the
output from all three commands is displayed:

```
$ pwd ; ls dialins ; echo Hello
/home/anatole
dialins
Hello
$
```

This is also useful when you want to run something more complex
from the command line, like rename all the files in the current directory
using flow control commands:

```
$ for i in $(ls); do mv $i $i.bak; done
```

The **for** loop command is covered in more detail in **Chapter 8**.

Continuing Commands

If a command is terminated with a \ character, it is continued on the
next line. Here, the **echo** arguments are continued onto the next line:

```
$ echo a b \
> c
a b c
```

This is often used to make Korn shell scripts mode readable. Refer to
Appendix D for some good examples. The **echo** command itself can be
continued onto the next line by using the \ character:

```
$ ec\
> ho a b c
a b c
```

Background Jobs

Commands terminated with a **&** character are run in the background.
The Korn shell does not wait for completion, so another command can
be given, while the current command is running in the background. In
this example, the **ls** command is run in the background while **pwd** is
run in the foreground:

```
$ ls —lR /usr > ls.out &
[1] 221
$ pwd
/home/anatole/bin
```

This feature is discussed in detail in **Chapter 5**.

Pipes

The output of a command can be directed as the input to another
command by using the I symbol. Here, a pipe is used to see if **root** is
logged on by connecting the output of **who** to **grep**:

```
$ who I grep root
root   console   Sep 12 22:16
```

It can also be used to count the number of files in a directory by
connecting the **ls** and **wc** commands. This shows that there are eleven
files in the current directory:

```
$ ls I wc —1
11
```

You can also have multiple pipes to connect a series of commands
together. The name of each unique user that is logged on is displayed
using this command:

```
$ who I cut —f1 —d' ' I sort —u
anatole
```

You could even add another pipe to give you just the count of unique users:

```
$ who | cut -f1 -d' ' | sort -u | wc -l
3
```

Conditional Execution

The Korn shell provides the **&&** and **||** operators for simple conditional execution. First you need to know that when programs finish executing, they return an exit status that indicates if they ran successfully or not. A zero exit status usually indicates that a program executed successfully, while a non-zero exit status usually indicates that an error occurred.

If two commands are separated with **&&**, the second command is only executed if the first command returns a zero exit status. Here, the **echo** command is executed, because **ls** ran successfully:

```
$ ls temp && echo "File temp exists"
temp
File temp exists
```

Now, file **temp** is removed and the same command is run again:

```
$ rm temp
$ ls temp && echo "File temp exists"
ls: temp: No such file or directory
```

If two commands are separated with **||**, the second command is only executed if the first command returns a non-zero exit status. In this case, the **echo** command is executed, because **ls** returned an error:

```
$ ls temp || echo "File temp does NOT exist"
ls: temp: No such file or directory
File temp does NOT exist
```

Remember that basic conditional execution using these operators only works with two commands. Appending more commands to the same command-line using **;** does not cause these to also be conditionally executed. Here, the **touch temp** command is executed, regardless if **ls temp** failed or not. Only the **echo** command is conditionally executed:

```
$ ls temp || echo "File temp does NOT exist"; \
touch temp
ls: temp: No such file or directory
File temp does NOT exist
```

The next section talks about how you can conditionally execute more than one command by using { }'s or ( )'s. As you can see, the **&&** and **||** operators can come in handy. There are certainly many situations where they can be more efficient to use than the **if** command.

There is one more type of logic you can perform using these operators. You can implement a simple **if** command by using the **&&** and **||** operators together like this:

command1 **&&** *command2* **||** *command3*

If *command1* returns true, then *command2* is executed, which causes *command3* to not be executed. If *command1* does not return true, then *command2* is not executed, which causes *command3* to be executed. Confusing, right? Let's look at a real example to make sense out of this. Here, if the file **temp** exists, then one message is displayed, and if it doesn't exist, the another message is displayed:

```
$ touch temp
$ ls temp && echo "File temp exists" || echo \
File temp does NOT exist
temp
File temp exists
```

Now we remove file **temp** and run the same command:

```
$ rm temp
$ ls temp && echo "File temp exists" || echo \
"File temp does NOT exist"
ls: temp: No such file or directory
File temp does NOT exist
```

Although compact, this format may not be considered as readable as the **if** command. We look at comparing the **&&** and || operators to the **if** command later in **Chapter 8**.

Grouping Commands

Multiple commands can be grouped together using {} or (). Commands enclosed in {} are executed in the current shell. This is useful for when you want to combine the output from multiple commands. Here is file **temp**:

```
$ cat temp
The rain in Spain
falls mainly on the plain
```

Let's say we want to add a header to the output, then line-number the whole thing with the **nl** command (or **pr −n** if you don't have **nl**). We could try it like this:

```
$ echo "This is file temp:" ; cat temp | nl
This is file temp:
1   The rain in Spain
2   falls mainly on the plain
```

Only the output from **cat temp** was line numbered. By using {}'s, the output from both commands is line numbered:

```
$ { echo "This is file temp:"; cat temp ; } | nl
1   This is file temp:
2   The rain in Spain
3   falls mainly on the plain
```

There must be whitespace after the opening {, or else you get a syntax error. One more restriction: commands within the {}'s must be terminated with a semi-colon when given on one line. This keeps commands separated so that the Korn shell knows where one command ends, and another one begins.

This means that commands can be grouped within {}'s even when separated with newlines like this:

```
$ { pwd ; echo "First line"
> echo "Last line"
> }
/usr/spool/smail
First line
Last line
```

Another use for this feature is in conjunction with the **&&** and ||
operators to allow multiple commands to be conditionally executed.
This is similar to the example from the previous section. What we
want this command to do is check if file **temp** exists, and if it does,
display a message, then remove it. Unfortunately, the way it is written,
rm temp is executed regardless if it exists or not.

```
$ rm temp
$ ls temp && echo "temp exists.removing";rm temp
ls: temp: No such file or directory
rm: temp: No such file or directory
```

Table 2.1: Command Execution Format

command1 ; *command2*
> execute *command1* followed by *command2*

command **&**
> execute *command* asynchronously in the
> background; do not wait for completion

command1 | *command2*
> pass the standard output of *command1* to
> standard input of *command2*

command1 **&&** *command2*
> execute *command2* if *command1* returns zero
> (successful) exit status

command1 || *command2*
> execute *command2* if *command1* returns non-
> zero (unsuccessful) exit status

command |**&**
> execute *command* asynchronously with its
> standard input and standard output attached to the
> parent shell; use **read –p/print –p** to manipulate
> the standard input/output (see **Chapter 8**)

command \
> continue *command* onto the next line

{ *command* ; }
> execute *command* in the current shell

(*command*)
> execute *command* in a subshell

By using { }'s, both the **echo** and **rm** commands are only executed if **temp** exists:

```
$ touch temp
$ ls temp && { echo "temp exists..removing" ;
> rm temp ; }
temp
temp exists..removing
```

Commands enclosed in ( ) are executed in a subshell. This is discussed in detail in **Chapter 7**.

Input/Output Redirection

The Korn shell provides a number of operators than can be used to manipulate command input/output and files. For example, you can save command output to a file. Or instead of typing in the input to a command, it can be taken from a file. The following sections describe some of the features of Korn shell I/O redirection.

Redirecting Standard Output

The standard output of a command is by default directed to your terminal. By using the > symbol, the standard output of a command can be redirected to a file, instead of your terminal. In this example, the standard output of the **echo** command is put into the file **p.out**:

```
$ echo "Hello" > p.out
$ cat p.out
Hello
```

If the file doesn't exist, then it is created. Otherwise, the contents are usually overwritten. Usually, but not always. If you have the **noclobber** option set (discussed in the next section), or the file attributes (permissions and/or ownership) do not permit writing, the file will not be overwritten. If we change permission on **p.out** and try to direct output to it again, we get an error message:

```
$ chmod 444 p.out
$ echo "Hello again" > pwd.out
/bin/ksh: p.out: cannot create
```

We'll see in the next section how to force overwriting of existing files using a variation of the > redirect operator.

You can also use the > command to create an empty file:

```
$ > tmp
$ ls —s tmp
0 tmp
```

This is equivalent to **touch tmp**.

Standard output can be appended to a file by using the >> redirect operator. Here, the output of **find** is appended to **deadfiles.out**:

```
$ echo "Dead File List" > junk.out
$ find . —name dead.letter —print >>junk.out
$ find . —name core —print >>junk.out
$ cat junk.out
Dead File List
./mail/dead.letter
./bin/core
```

Standard output is closed with the >&— redirect operator:

```
$ echo "This is going nowhere" >&—
$
```

This feature can be used in a Korn shell script to close the output of a group of commands instead of redirecting the output of each command individually.

The noclobber Option

To prevent redirecting output to an existing file, set the **noclobber** option. By default, this feature is usually disabled, but can be enabled with the **set –o noclobber** command:

```
$ ls > file.out
$ set -o noclobber
```

Now when we try to redirect output to **file.out**, an error message is returned:

```
$ ls > file.out
/bin/ksh: file.out: file already exists
```

The **>|** operator is used to force overwriting of a file, even if the **noclobber** option is enabled. Here, **file.out** can now be overwritten, even though the **noclobber** option is set:

```
$ ls >| file.out
```

Redirecting Standard Input

Standard input to a command is redirected from a file using the **<** operator. This feature can be used to read in a mail message from a file, instead of typing it in:

```
$ mail dick jane spot < mlist
```

This could also be implemented using a pipe:

```
$ cat mlist | mail dick jane spot
```

In both cases, file **mlist** becomes the standard input to **mail**.

Standard input can be closed with the <&– redirect operator. Here, the standard input to the **wc** command is closed:

```
$ cat mlist | wc -l <&-
0
```

Not really exciting. This useful when manipulating file descriptors with the **exec** command, which is discussed later in **Chapter 8**.

File Descriptors

File descriptors are used by processes to identify their open files. The Korn shell automatically assigns file descriptor 0 to standard input for reading, file descriptor 1 to standard output for writing, and file descriptor 2 to standard error for reading and writing. The file descriptors 3 through 9 can be used with I/O redirection operators and are opened, closed, and/or copied with the **exec** command, which is discussed later in **Chapter 8**.

Redirecting Standard Error

Most UNIX commands write their error messages to standard error. As with standard output, standard error is by default directed to your terminal, but it can be redirected using the standard error file descriptor (2) and the > operator. For example, the **ls** command displays a message on standard error when you attempt to display information about a non-existent file:

```
$ ls tmp
tmp not found
```

Now, if you do an **ls** on an existent and non-existent file on the same command-line, a message about the non-existent file goes to standard error, while the output for the existent file goes to standard output:

Table 2.2: Some I/O Redirection Operators

<file   redirect standard input from *file*

>file   redirect standard output to *file*. Create *file* if non-existent, else overwrite.

>>file   append standard output to *file*. Create *file* if non-existent.

>|file   redirect standard output to *file*. Create *file* if non-existent, else overwrite even if **noclobber** is enabled.

<>file   open *file* for reading and writing as standard input

<&-   close standard input

>&-   close standard output

```
$ ls tmp t.out
tmp not found
t.out
```

By using the **2>** operator, the standard error of the same command is redirected to **ls.out**. The standard output is still displayed directly to your terminal:

```
$ ls tmp t.out 2>ls.out
t.out
$ cat ls.out
tmp not found
```

There can be no space between the **2** and **>** symbol, otherwise the **2** is interpreted as an argument to the command.

More with File Descriptors

The **>&***n* operator causes output to be redirected to file descriptor *n*. This is used when you want to direct output to a specific file descriptor. To send the output of the **echo** command to standard error, just add **>&2** to the command-line:

```
$ echo This is going to standard error >&2
This is going to standard error
```

In the next command, the standard error and output are sent to **ls.out** by specifying multiple redirections on the same command line. First, **>&2** causes standard output to be redirected to standard error. Then, **2>ls.out** causes standard error (which is now standard output and standard error) to be sent to **ls.out**:

```
$ ls tmp t.out >&2 2>ls.out
$ cat ls.out
tmp not found
t.out
```

This command causes output to be redirected to both standard output and standard error:

```
$ { echo "This is going to stdout" >&1 ; \
echo "This is going to stderr" >&2 ; }
This is going to stdout
This is going to stderr
```

If the output of the last command was redirected to a file using the > operator, then only the standard output would be redirected. The standard error would still be displayed on your terminal.

```
$ { echo "This is going to stdout" >&1 ; \
echo "This is going to stderr" >&2 ; } >out
This is going to stderr
$ cat out
This is going to stdout
```

Table 2.3: File Descriptors

0	standard input
1	standard output
2	standard error
3–9	unassigned file descriptors

The *n>&m* operator causes the output from file descriptors *n* and *m* to be merged. This operator could be used in the previous command to direct both the standard output and standard error to the same file.

```
$ { echo "This is going to stdout" >&1 ; \
echo "This is going to stderr" >&2 ; } >out 2>&1
$ cat out
This is going to stdout
This is going to stderr
```

If you wanted the standard output and standard error appended to the output file, the >> operator could be used:

```
$ { echo "This is going to stdout again" >&1 ; \
echo "This is going to stderr again" >&2 ; } \
>>out 2>&1
$ cat out
This is going to stdout
This is going to stderr
This is going to stdout again
This is going to stderr again
```

As seen in the previous example, multiple file descriptor redirections can also be specified. To close the standard output and standard error of this **ls** command:

```
$ ls tmp t.out >&- 2>&-
$
```

The **print** and **read** commands have special options that allow you to redirect standard output and input with file descriptors. This is discussed in **Chapter 8**.

Here Documents

Here documents is a term used for redirecting multiple lines of standard input to a command. In looser terms, they allow batch input to be given to programs and are frequently used to execute interactive commands from within Korn shell scripts. The format for a here document is:

> *command << word*
> or
> *command <<-word*

where lines that follow are used as standard input to *command* until *word* is read. In the following example, standard input for the **cat** command is read until the word **END** is encountered:

```
$ cat >> .profile <<END
> export TERM=sun-cmd
> export ORACLE_HOME=/apps/oracle
> END
```

The other variation, *command <<- word*, deletes leading tab characters from the here document. It is often used over the first variation to produce more readable code when used within larger scripts. A good use for here documents is to automate **ftp** file transfers.

This snippet of code could be used within a larger script to automatically **ftp** code to or from another server.

```
$ ftp <<- END
open aspsun
user anonymous
cd /usr/pub
binary
get ksh.tar.Z
quit
END
```

Here Documents and File Descriptors

Here documents can also be used with file descriptors. Instead of reading multiple lines from standard input, multiple lines are read from file descriptor *n* until *word* is read.

command n<<word
or
command n<<-word

Discarding Standard Output

The **/dev/null** file is like the system trash bin. Anything redirected to it is discarded by the system.

```
$ ls >/dev/null
```

This is not the same as:

```
$ ls >&-
```

which closes standard output.

Table 2.4: Redirect Operators and File Descriptors

$<\&n$ redirect standard input from file descriptor n

$>\&n$ redirect standard output to file descriptor n

$n<file$ redirect file descriptor n from *file*

$n>file$ redirect file descriptor n to *file*

$n>>file$ redirect file descriptor n to *file*. Create *file* if non-existent, else overwrite.

$n>|file$ redirect file descriptor n to *file*. Create *file* even if **noclobber** is enabled.

$n<\&m$ redirect file descriptor n input from file descriptor m

$n>\&m$ redirect file descriptor n output to file descriptor m

$n<>file$ open *file* for reading and writing as file descriptor n

$n<<word$

         redirect to file descriptor n until *word* is read

$n<<-word$

         redirect to file descriptor n until *word* is read; ignore leading tabs

$n<\&-$ close file descriptor n for standard input

$n>\&-$ close file descriptor n for standard output

print –**u**n *args*

         redirect arguments to file descriptor n. If n is greater than **2**, it must first be opened with **exec**. If n is not specified, the default file descriptor argument is **1** (standard output).

read –**u**n *args*

         read input line from file descriptor n. If n is greater than **2**, it must first be opened with **exec**. If n is not specified, the default file descriptor argument is **0** (standard input).

File Name Substitution

File name substitution is a feature which allows strings to be substituted for patterns and special characters. This provides greater flexibility and saves a lot of typing time. Most frequently this feature is used to match file names in the current directory, but can also be used to match arguments in **case** and [[...]] commands.

The syntax for file name substitution is not the same as regular expression syntax used in some UNIX commands like **ed**, **grep**, and **sed**. The examples in the following sections assume that the following files exist in the current directory:

```
$ ls —a
.            .molog   abc        dabkup3     mobkup1
..           a        dabkup1 dabkup4     mobkup2
.dalog   ab       dabkup2 dabkup5
```

The * Character

The * character matches any zero or more characters. This is probably the most frequently used pattern matching character. If used alone, * substitutes the names of all the files in the current directory, except those that begin with the "." character. These must be explicitly matched. Now, instead of typing in each individual file name to the **cat** command:

```
$ cat dabkup1 dabkup2 dabkup3 dabkup4 ...
. . .
```

You can do this:

```
$ cat *
. . .
```

The * character can also be used with other characters to match only certain file names. Let's say we only wanted to list the monthly backup files. We could do it like this:

```
$ ls m*
mobkup1      mobkup2
```

The **m*** matches any file name in the current directory that begins with
m, which here would be **mobkup1** and **mobkup2**. This command lists
file names that end in **2**:

```
$ ls *2
dabkup2      mobkup2
```

This command lists file names that contain **ab**. Notice that **ab** and **abc**
are also listed:

```
$ ls *ab*
ab           dabkup1      dabkup3      dabkup5
abc          dabkup2      dabkup4
```

Remember that file name substitution only works with files in the
current directory. To match file names in subdirectories, the / character
must be explicitly matched. This pattern would match file names
ending in **.Z** from any directories one-level under the current directory:

```
$ ls */*.Z
bin/smail.Z     bin/calc.Z        bin/testsh.Z
```

To search the next level of directories, another /* would need to be
added.

```
$ ls */*/*.Z
bin/fdir/foo.Z
```

Be careful, because on some systems, matching files names in
extremely large directories and subdirectories will generate an
argument list error.

Don't forget that the "." character must be explicitly matched. Here, the . files in the current directory are listed:

```
$ echo .*
. .. .dalog .malog
```

The ? Character

The **?** character matches exactly one character. It is useful when the file name matching criteria is the length of the file name. For example, to list two-character file names in the current directory, **??** could be used.

```
$ echo ??
ab
```

What if you wanted to list the file names in the current directory that had at three or more characters in the name. The **???** pattern would match file names that had exactly three characters, but not more. You could try this:

```
$ echo ??? ???? ?????  . . .
```

but that is not correct either. As you probably already guessed, the pattern to use would be **???***, which matches files names with three charaacters, followed by any zero or more characters. Let's try it:

```
$ echo ???*
abc dabkup1 dabkup2 dabkup3 dabkup4 dabkup5
mobkup1 mobkup2
```

If you only wanted to list the **dabkup***, you could you the following pattern:

```
$ echo dabkup?
dabkup1 dabkup2 dabkup3 dabkup4 dabkup5
```

The [] Characters

The [] characters match a single, multiple, or range of characters. It is useful for when you want to match certain characters in a specific character position in the file name. For example, if you wanted to list the file names in the current directory that began with **a** or **m**, you could do it like this:

```
$ ls a* m*
a           ab          abc         mobkup1   mobkup2
```

or do it more easily using []:

```
$ ls [am]*
a           ab          abc         mobkup1   mobkup2
```

This command lists file names beginning with **d** or **m**, and ending with any number **1** through **5**:

```
$ echo [dm]*[12345]
dabkup1         dabkup3         dabkup5         mobkup2
dabkup2         dabkup4         mobkup1
```

You could do the same thing using a range argument instead of listing out each number:

```
$ echo [dm]*[1-5]
dabkup1         dabkup3         dabkup5         mobkup2
dabkup2         dabkup4         mobkup1
```

In the range argument, the first character must be alphabetically less than the last character. This means that [c–a] is an invalid range. This also means that pattern [0–z] matches any alphabetic or alphanumeric character, [A–z] matches any alphabetic character (upper and lower case), [0–Z] matches any alphanumeric or upper case alphabetic character, and [0–9] matches any alphanumeric character.

Multiple ranges can also be given. The pattern [a–jlmr3–7] would match files names beginning with the letters **a** through **j**, **l**, **m**, **r**, and **3** through **7**.

The ! Character

The **!** character can be used with [] to reverse the match. In other words, [!a] matches any character, except **a**. This is another very useful pattern matching character, since frequently you want to match everything except something. For example, if the current directory contained these files:

```
$ ls
a           abc         dabkup2     dabkup4   mobkup1
ab          dabkup1     dabkup3     dabkup5   mobkup2
```

and we wanted to list all of the file names, except those that started with **d**, we could do this:

```
$ ls [0-ce-z]*
a           abc         mobkup2
ab          mobkup1
```

or it could be done more easily using [!d]:

```
$ ls [!d]*
a           abc         mobkup2
ab          mobkup1
```

Multiple and range arguments can also be negated. The pattern [!lro]* would match strings not beginning with **l**, **r**, or **o**, *[!2–5] would match strings not ending with **2** through **5**, and *.[!Z] would match strings not ending in **.Z**.

Matching . Files

Certain characters like "." (period) must be explicitly matched. This command matches the file names **.a**, **.b**, and **.c**:

```
$ ls .[a-c]
.a   .b   .c
```

To remove all the files in the current directory that contain a ".", except those that end in **.c** or **.h**:

```
$ rm *.[!ch]
```

Complex Patterns

The latest version of the Korn shell also provides other matching capabilities. Instead of matching only characters, entire patterns can be given. For demonstration purposes, let's assume that we have a command called **match** that finds words in the on-line dictionary, **/usr/dict/words**. It's like the **grep** command, except that Korn shell patterns are used, instead of regular expression syntax that **grep** recognizes. The source code for **match** is listed in **Appendix D**.

*(pattern)

This format matches any zero or more occurrences of *pattern*. You could find words that contained any number of consecutive **A**'s:

```
$ match *(A)
A
AAA
AAAAAAAA
```

Table 2.5: Basic Pattern-Matching Characters

?	match any single character
*	match zero or more characters, including null
[*abc*]	match any character or characters between the brackets
[*x*−*z*]	match any character or characters in the range *x* to *z*
[*a*−*ce*−*g*]	match any character or characters in the range *a* to *c*, *e* to *g*
[!*abc*]	match any character or characters not between the brackets
[!*x*−*z*]	match any character or characters not in the range *x* to *z*
.	strings starting with **.** must be explicitly matched

Multiple patterns can also be given, but they must be separated with a |
character. Let's try it with **match**:

```
$ match *(A|i)
A
AAA
AAAAAA
i
ii
iii
iiiiii
```

This pattern matches **anti**, **antic**, **antigen**, and **antique**:

```
$ match anti*(c|gen|que)
anti
antic
antigen
antique
```

This format is also good for matching numbers. The **[1–9]*([0–9])** pattern matches any number **1–9999999*** (any number except **0**).

?(*pattern*)

This format matches any zero or one occurrences of *pattern*. Here we look for one, two, and three letter words beginning with **s**:

```
$ match s?(?|??)
s
sa
sac
sad
...
```

Here are some more patterns using this format:

```
1?([0-9])
```
matches
```
1, 10, 11, 12, ..., 19
```

```
the?(y|m|[rs]e)
```
matches
```
the, they, them, there, these
```

+(*pattern*)

This format matches one or more occurrences of *pattern*. To find any words beginning with **m** followed by any number of **iss** patterns:

```
$ match m+(iss)*
miss
mississippi
```

Here is another pattern using this format. It matches any number.

```
+([0-9])
matches
0-9999999*
```

@(*pattern*)

This format matches exactly one occurrence of *pattern*. Let's look for words beginning with **Ala** or **Cla**:

```
$ match @([AC]la)*
Alabama
Alameda
Alamo
Alaska
Claire
Clara
Clare
...
```

Now for another number-matching pattern. This one matches any number **0–9**:

```
@([0-9]
matches
0, 1, 2, 3, ..., 9
```

!(*pattern*)

This format matches anything except *pattern*. To match any string that does not end in **.c**, **.Z**, or **.o**:

```
!(*.c|*.Z|*.o)
```

or any string that does not contain digits:

```
!(*[0-9]*)
```

More Complex Patterns

The complex file patterns can be used together or even nested to generate even more sophisticated patterns. Here are a few examples:

```
@([1-9])+([0-9])
matches
1-9999999*

@([2468]|+([1-9])+([02468]))
matches any even numbers
2, 4, 6, 8, ...

@([13579]|+([0-9])+([13579]))
matches any odd numbers
1, 3, 5, 7, ...
```

Disabling File Name Substitution

File name substitution can be disabled by setting the **noglob** option using the **set** command:

```
$ set -o noglob
or
$ set -f
```

Table 2.6: Other File Name Patterns

?(*pattern-list*)
> match zero or one occurrence of any *pattern*

*(*pattern-list*)
> match zero or more occurrences of any *pattern*

+(*pattern-list*)
> match one or more occurrence of any *pattern*

@(*pattern-list*)
> match exactly one occurrence of any *pattern*

!(*pattern-list*)
> match anything except any *pattern*

pattern-list
> multiple patterns must be separated with a |
> character

The **–o noglob** and **–f** options for the **set** command are the same. Once file name substitution is disabled, pattern-matching characters like *, ?, and] lose their special meaning:

```
$ ls a*
a* not found
$ ls b?
b? not found
```

Now we can create some files that contain special characters in their names.

```
$ touch *a b?b c-c d[]d
$ ls
*a  b?b  c-c  d[]d
```

Within [...] patterns, a \ character is used to remove the meaning of the special pattern-matching characters. This means that the [*\?]* pattern would match file names beginning with * or ?.

Command Substitution

Command substitution is a feature that allows output to be expanded from a command. It can be used to assign the output of a command to a variable, or to imbed the output of a command within another command. The format for command substitution is:

$(*command*)

where *command* is executed and the output is substituted for the entire $(*command*) construct. For example, to print the current date in a friendly format:

```
$ echo The date is $(date)
The date is Fri Jul 27 10:41:21 PST 1996
```

or see who is logged on:

```
$ echo $(who -q) are logged on now
root anatole are logged on now
```

Any commands can be used inside $(...), including pipes, I/O operators, metacharacters (wildcards), and more. We can find out how many users are logged on by using the **who** and **wc -l** commands:

```
$ echo $(who | wc -l) users are logged on
There are 3 users logged on
```

Bourne Shell Compatibility

For compatibility with the Bourne shell, the following format for command substitution can also be used:

> `` `command` ``

Using `` `...` `` command substitution, we could get the names of the files in the current directory like this:

```
$ echo `ls` are in this directory
NEWS asp bin pc are this directory
```

If you wanted a count of the files, a pipe to **wc** could be added:

```
$ echo There are `ls | wc -l` files here
There are 4 files here
```

Directing File Input

There is also a special form of the $(...) command that is used to substitute the contents of a file. The format for file input substitution is:

> $(<*file*)

This is equivalent to **$(cat** *file*) or `` `cat *file*` ``, except that it is faster, because an extra process does not have to be created to execute the **cat** command. A good use for this is assigning file contents to variables, which we will talk about later in **Chapter 3**.

Arithmetic Operations

Another form of the $(...) command is used to substitute the output of arithmetic expressions. The value of an arithmetic expression is returned when enclosed in double parentheses and preceded with a dollar sign.

> $(($(*arithmetic-expression*)))

Here are a few examples.

```
$ echo $((3+5))
8
$ echo $((8192*16384%23))
9
```

Performing arithmetic is discussed in detail in **Chapter 6**.

Tilde Substitution

Tilde substitution is used to substitute the pathname of a user's home directory for ~*user*. Words in the command line that start with the tilde character cause the Korn shell to check the rest of the word up to a slash. If the tilde character is found alone or is only followed by a slash, it is replaced with the value of the **HOME** variable. This is a handy shortcut borrowed from the C shell. For example, to print the pathname of your home directory:

```
$ echo ~
/home/anatole
```

or to list its contents:

```
$ ls ~/
NEWS          bin          pc
asp           mail         src
```

Table 2.7: Tilde Substitution

~	replaced with **$HOME**
~*user*	replaced with the home directory of *user*
~–	replaced with **$OLDPWD** (previous directory)
~+	replaced with **$PWD** (current directory)

If the tilde character is followed by a login name file, it is replaced with the home directory of that user. Here we change directory to the **tools** directory in **smith**'s home directory:

```
$ cd ~smith/tools
$ pwd
/home/users/admin/smith/tools
```

If the tilde character is followed by a + or –, it is replaced with the value of **PWD** (current directory) and **OLDPWD** (previous directory), respectively. This is not very useful for directory navigation, since **cd ~+** leaves you in the current directory. The **cd ~–** command puts you in the previous directory, but the Korn shell provides an even shorter shortcut: **cd –** does the same thing. This is discussed in **Chapter 9**.

Chapter 3: Variables and Parameters

Variables
Variable Expansion
Array Variables
Quoting

Variables and parameters are used by the Korn shell to store values. Like other high-level programming languages, the Korn shell supports data types and arrays. This is a major difference with the Bourne and C shells, which have no concept of either.

Variables

Korn shell variable names can begin with an alphabetic (**a–Z**) or underscore character, followed by one or more alphanumeric (**a–Z, 0–9**) or underscore characters. Other variable names that contain only digits (**0–9**) or special characters (**!, @, #, %, *, ?, $**) are reserved for special parameters set directly by the Korn shell.

To assign a value to a variable, you can simply name the variable and set it to a value. For example, to assign **abc** to variable **X**:

```
$ X=abc
```

The **typeset** command can also be used to assign values, but unless you are setting attributes, it's a lot more work for nothing. If a value is not given, the variable is set to null. Here, **X** is reassigned the null value:

```
·$ X=
```

This is not the same as being undefined. As we'll see later, accessing the value of an undefined variable may return an error, while accessing the value of a null variable returns the null value.

Accessing Variable Values

To access the value of a variable, precede the name with the **$** character. There can be no space between **$** and the variable name. In this example, **CBIN** is set to **/usr/ccs/bin**.

```
$ CBIN=/usr/ccs/bin
```

Now you can just type **$UUDIR** instead of the long pathname:

```
$ cd $CBIN
$ pwd
/usr/ccs/bin
```

Here is a new command to go along with this concept: **print**. It displays its arguments on your terminal, just like **echo**.

```
$ print Hello world!
Hello world!
```

Here we use **print** to display the value of **CBIN** :

```
$ print $CBIN
/usr/ccs/bin
```

Table 3.1: Assigning Values to Variables

variable=	declare *variable* and set it to null
typeset *variable=*	declare *variable* and set it to null
variable=value	assign *value* to *variable*
typeset *variable=value*	
	assign *value* to *variable*

Variable Attributes

Korn shell variables can have one or more attributes that specify their internal representation, access or scope, or the way they are displayed. This concept is similar to a data type in other high-level programming languages, except that in the Korn shell it is not as restrictive. Variables can be set to integer type for faster arithmetic operations, read-only so that the value cannot be changed, left/right justified for formatting purposes, and more. To assign a value and/or attribute to a Korn shell variable, use the following format with the **typeset** command:

> **typeset** *−attribute variable=value*
> or
> **typeset** *−attribute variable*

Except for **readonly**, variable attributes can be set before, during, or after assignment. Functionally it makes no difference. Just remember that the attribute has precedence over the value. This means that if you change the attribute after a value has been assigned, the value may be affected.

The Lowercase (–l) and Uppercase (–u) Attributes

These attributes cause the variable values to be changed to lower or
uppercase. For example, the lowercase attribute and uppercase value
ASPD are assigned to variable **MYSYS**:

```
$ typeset -l MYSYS=ASPD
```

Despite the fact that **MYSYS** was assigned uppercase **ASPD**, when
accessed, the value is displayed in lowercase:

```
$ print $MYSYS
aspd
```

This is because the attribute affects the variable value, regardless of the
assignment. Variable attributes can also be changed after assignment.
If we wanted to display variable **MYSYS** in uppercase, we could just
reset the attribute:

```
$ typeset -u MYSYS
$ print $MYSYS
ASPD
```

The Readonly (–r) Attribute

Once the readonly attribute is set, a variable cannot be assigned another
value. Here, we use it to set up a restricted **PATH**:

```
$ typeset -r PATH=/usr/rbin
```

If there is an attempt to reset **PATH**, an error message is generated:

```
$ PATH=$PATH:/usr/bin:
/bin/ksh: PATH: is read only
```

We'll come back to this in a few pages. Unlike other variable
attributes, once the **readonly** attribute is set, it cannot be removed.

Table 3.2: Assigning Values/Attributes to Variables

typeset −*attribute variable=value*
> assign *attribute* and *value* to *variable*

typeset −*attribute variable*
> assign *attribute* to *variable*

typeset +*attribute variable*
> remove *attribute* from *variable*

The Integer (−i) Attribute

The integer attribute (**−i**) is used to explicitly declare integer variables. Although it is not necessary to set this attribute when assigning integer values, there are some benefits to it. We'll cover this later in **Chapter 6**. In the meantime, **NUM** is set to an integer-type variable and assigned a value:

```
$ typeset −i NUM=1
$ print $NUM
1
```

We could also assign **NUM** the number of users on the system using command substitution like this:

```
$ typeset −i NUM=$(who | wc −1)
$ print $NUM
3
```

There is one restriction on integer variables. Once a variable is set to integer type, it can't be assigned a non-integer value:

```
$ typeset −i NUM=abc
/bin/ksh: NUM: bad number
```

The Right (–r) and Left (–l) Justify Attributes

The right and left justify attributes cause variable values to be justified within their width and are be used to format data. Here, variables **A** and **B** are set to right-justify with a field width of **7** characters. Notice that integer values are used, even though the integer attribute is not set.

```
$ typeset -R7 A=10 B=10000
$ print :$A:
:    10:
$ print :$B:
: 10000:
```

If the field width is not large enough for the variable assignment, the value gets truncated. Variable **X** is assigned a seven-character wide value, but the field width is set to **3**, so the first four characters are lost:

```
$ typeset -R3 X=ABCDEFG
$ print $X
EFG
```

If a field width is not given, then it is set with the first variable assignment. Variable **Y** is assigned a three-character wide value, so the field width is set to **3**.

```
$ typeset -L Y=ABC
$ print $Y
ABC
```

Without explicitly resetting the field width, a subsequent assignment would be restricted to a three-character wide value:

```
$ Y=ZYXWVUT
$ print $Y
ZYX
```

Chapter 3: Variables and Parameters

The Autoexport (–x) Attribute

This is another useful attribute. It allows you to set and export a variable in one command. Instead of

```
$ typeset X=abc
$ export X
```

you can do this:

```
$ typeset -x X=abc
```

We could use this attribute to add the **/lbin** directory to the **PATH** variable and export it all in one command:

```
$ typeset -x PATH=$PATH:/lbin
```

Removing Variable Attributes

Except for readonly, variable attributes are removed with the **typeset** +*attribute* command. Assuming that the integer attribute was set on the **NUM** variable, we could remove it like this:

```
$ typeset +i NUM
```

and then reassign it a non-integer value:

```
$ NUM=abc
```

Once the readonly attribute is set, it cannot be removed. When we try to do this with the **PATH** variable that was previously set, we get an error message:

```
$ typeset +r PATH
/bin/ksh: PATH:  is read only
```

Table 3.3: Some Variable Attributes

typeset –i *var*	Set the type of *var* to be integer
typeset –l *var*	Set *var* to lower case
typeset –L *var*	Left justify *var*; the field width is specified by the first assignment
typeset –L*n* *var*	Left justify *var*; set field width to *n*
typeset –LZ*n* *var*	
	Left justify *var*; set field width to *n* and strip leading zeros
typeset –r *var*	Set *var* to be readonly (same as the **readonly** command)
typeset –R *var*	Right justify *var*; the field width is specified by the first assignment
typeset –R*n* *var*	Right justify *var*; set field width to *n*
typeset –RZ*n* *var*	
	Right justify *var*; set field width to *n* and fill with leading zeros
typeset –t *var*	Set the user-defined attribute for *var*. This has no meaning to the Korn shell.
typeset –u *var*	Set *var* to upper case
typeset –x *var*	Automatically export *var* to the environment (same as the **export** command)
typeset –Z *var*	Same as **typeset –RZ**

Chapter 3: Variables and Parameters

The only way to reassign a readonly variable is to unset it first, then assign a value from scratch.

Multiple Attributes

Multiple attributes can also be assigned to variables. This command sets the integer and autoexport attributes for **TMOUT**:

```
$ typeset —ix TMOUT=3000
```

To set and automatically export **ORACLE_SID** to uppercase **prod**:

```
$ typeset —ux ORACLE_SID=prod
$ print $ORACLE_SID
PROD
```

Obviously, some attributes like left and right justify are mutually exclusive, so they shouldn't be set together.

Checking Variable Attributes

Attributes of Korn shell variables are listed using the **typeset** — *attribute* command. For example, to list all the integer type variables and their values:

```
$ typeset —i
ERRNO=0
MAILCHECK=600
PPID=177
RANDOM=22272
SECONDS=4558
TMOUT=0
```

To list only the names of variables with a specific attribute, use the **typeset** +*attribute* command.

More with Variables

You can do other things with variables, such as assign them the value
of another variable, the output of a command, or even the contents of a
file. Here **Y** is assigned the value of variable **X**:

```
$ X=$HOME
$ Y=$X
$ print $Y
/home/anatole
```

Variables can be assigned command output using this format:

> *variable*=**$**(*command*)
> or
> *variable*=`command`

The second format is provided for compatibility with the Bourne shell.
Here, **UCSC** is set to its internet ID by assigning the output of the **grep**
and **cut** commands:

```
$ UCSC=$(grep UCSC /etc/hosts | cut -f1 -d" ")
$ print $UCSC
128.114.129.1
```

Variables can also be assigned the contents of files like this:

> *variable*=**$**(<*file*)
> or
> *variable*=`cat file`

The first format is equivalent to *variable*=**$**(**cat** *file*). The second
format is much slower, but is provided for compatibility with the
Bourne shell. Here, the **FSYS** variable is set to the contents of the
/etc/fstab file:

```
$ FSYS=$(</etc/fstab)
$ print $FSYS
/dev/roota / /dev/rootg /usr
```

Notice that the entries were displayed all on one line, instead of each on separate lines as in the file. We'll talk about this in the **Quoting** section later in this chapter.

Unsetting Variables

Variable definitions are removed using the **unset** command. The **TMOUT** variable is not being used, so let's unset it:

```
$ unset TMOUT
```

Now to check and see:

```
$ print $TMOUT

$
```

This is not the same as being set to null. As we'll see later in this chapter, variable expansion may be performed differently, depending on whether the variable value is set to null.

Special Parameters

Some special parameters are automatically set by the Korn shell and usually cannot be directly set or modified.

The ? Parameter

The **?** parameter contains the exit status of the last executed command. In this example, the **date** command is executed. It ran successfully, so the exit status is **0**:

```
$ date +%D
05/24/96
$ print $?
0
```

Notice that there was no output displayed from the **date** command. This is because the **>&-** I/O operator causes standard output to be closed. The next command, **cp ch222.out /tmp**, did not run successfully, so **1** is returned:

```
$ cp ch222.out /tmp
ch222.out: No such file or directory
$ print $?
1
```

When used with a pipe, **$?** contains the exit status of the last command in the pipeline.

The $ Parameter

The **$** parameter contains the process id of the current shell.

```
$ print $$
178
```

It is useful in creating unique file names within Korn shell scripts.

```
$ touch $0.$$
$ ls *.*
ksh.218
```

Other Special Parameters

The **–** parameter contains the current options in effect. The output of the next command shows that the **interactive** and **monitor** options are enabled:

```
$ print $-
im
```

To display the error number of the last failed system call, use the **ERRNO** variable. Here, an attempt to display a non-existent file returns an error, so **ERRNO** is checked for the error number:

```
$ cat tmp.out
tmp.out: No such file or directory
$ print $ERRNO
2
```

This is system dependent, so it may not be available on your system. Check your documentation or **/usr/include/sys/errno.h** for more information.

Variable Expansion

Variable expansion is the term used for the ability to access and manipulate values of variables and parameters. Basic expansion is done by preceding the variable or parameter name with the **$** character. This provides access to the value.

```
$ UULIB=/usr/lib/uucp
$ print $UULIB
/usr/lib/uucp
```

Other types of expansion can be used to return portions or the length of variables, use default or alternate values, check for mandatory setting, and more.

For the sake of convenience, the term *variable* will refer to both variables and parameters in the following sections that discuss variable expansion.

$*variable*, ${*variable*}

This is expanded to the value of *variable*. The braces are used to
protect or delimit the variable name from any characters that follow.
The next example illustrates why braces are used in variable expansion.
The variable **CA** is set to **ca**:

```
$ CA=ca
```

What if we wanted to reset **CA** to **california**? It could be reset to the
entire value, but to make a point, let's try using the current value like
this:

```
$ CA=$CAlifornia
$ print $CA

$
```

Nothing is printed, because without the braces around the variable **CA**,
the Korn shell looks for a variable named **$CAlifornia**. None is found,
so nothing is substituted. With the braces around variable **CA**, we get
the correct value:

```
$ CA=${CA}lifornia
$ print $CA
california
```

Braces are also needed when attempting to expand positional
parameters greater than 9. This ensures that both digits are interpreted
as the positional parameter name.

${#*variable*}

This is expanded to the length of *variable*. In this example, **X** is set to
a three-character string, so a length of **3** is returned:

Table 3.4: Some Preset Special Parameters

?	exit status of the last command
$	process id of the current Korn shell
–	current options in effect
!	process id of the last background command or co-process
ERRNO	error number returned by most recently failed system call (system dependent)
PPID	process id of the parent shell

```
$ X=abc
$ print ${#X}
3
```

Whitespace in variable values is also counted as characters. Here the whitespace from the output of the **date** command is also counted:

```
$ TODAY=$(date)
$ print ${#TODAY}
28
```

${*parameter*:–*word*}, ${*parameter*–*word*}

This is expanded to the value of *variable* if it is set and not null, otherwise *word* is expanded. This is used to provide a default value if a variable is not set. In the following example, the variable **X** is set to **abc**. When expanded using this format, the default value **abc** is used:

```
$ X=abc
$ print ${X:-cde}
abc
```

After **X** is unset, the alternate value **cde** is used:

```
$ unset X
$ print ${X:-cde}
cde
```

Notice that the value of **X** remains unchanged:

```
$ print $X

$
```

Let's say we needed a command to get the user name. The problem is that some people have it set to **USER**, while others have it set to **LOGNAME**. We could use an **if** command to check one value first, then the other. This would be quite a few lines of code. Or we could use this form of variable expansion to have both values checked with one command. Here, if **USER** is set, then its value is displayed, otherwise the value of **LOGNAME** is displayed.

```
$ print USER=$USER, LOGNAME=$LOGNAME
USER=anatole, LOGNAME=AO
$ print ${USER:-${LOGNAME}}
anatole
```

Now we unset **USER** to check and make sure that **LOGNAME** is used:

```
$ unset USER
$ print ${USER:-${LOGNAME}}
AO
```

But what if both **USER** and **LOGNAME** are not set? Another variable could be checked like this:

```
$ print ${USER:-${LOGNAME:-${OTHERVAR}}}
```

Chapter 3: Variables and Parameters

But to demonstrate other ways that the alternate value can be expanded, let's just use some text.

```
$ unset USER LOGNAME
$ print ${USER:-${LOGNAME:-USER and LOGNAME \
not set!}}
USER and LOGNAME not set!
```

In this version, the output of the **whoami** command is used:

```
$ print ${USER-${LOGNAME:-$(whoami)}}
anatole
```

For compatibility with the Bourne shell, it could also be given as:

```
$ echo ${USER:-${LOGNAME:-`whoami`}}
anatole
```

Remember that the alternate value is only used and not assigned to anything. The next section shows how you can assign an alternate value if a default value is not set. The other format, **${*variable*−*word*}**, causes the variable value to be used, even if it is set to null:

```
$ typeset X=
$ print ${X-cde}

$
```

${*variable*:=*word*}, ${*variable*=*word*}

This is expanded to the value of *variable* if set and not null, otherwise it is set to *word*, then expanded. In contrast to the variable expansion format from the previous section, this format is used to assign a default value if one is not already set. In the next example, the variable **LBIN** is set to **/usr/lbin**. When expanded using this format, the default value **/usr/lbin** is used:

```
$ LBIN=/usr/lbin
$ print ${LBIN:=/usr/local/bin}
/usr/lbin
```

After **LBIN** is unset, this form of variable expansion causes **LBIN** to be assigned the alternate value, **/usr/local/bin**:

```
$ unset LBIN
$ print ${LBIN:=/usr/local/bin}
/usr/local/bin
```

Notice that **LBIN** is now set to **/usr/local/bin**.

```
$ print $LBIN
/usr/local/bin
```

Command substitution can also be used in place of *word*. This command sets the **SYS** variable using only one command:

```
$ unset SYS
$ print ${SYS:=$(hostname)}
aspd
```

The other format, **${*variable=word*}**, causes the variable value to be used, even if it is set to null. Here **LBIN** is not assigned an alternate value. If := was used instead of =, then **LBIN** would be set to **/usr/local/bin**:

```
$ LBIN=
$ print ${LBIN=/usr/local/bin}

$
```

${*variable*:?*word*}, ${*variable*:?}, ${*variable*?*word*}, ${*variable*?}

This is expanded to the value of *variable* if it is set and not null, otherwise *word* is printed and the Korn shell exits. If *word* is omitted, **"parameter null or not set"** is printed. This feature is often used in Korn shell scripts to check if mandatory variables are set. In this example, variable **XBIN** is first unset. When expanded, the default error is printed:

```
$ unset XBIN
$ : ${XBIN:?}
/bin/ksh: XBIN: parameter null or not set
```

The **?** as the *word* argument causes the default error message to be used. You could also provide your own error message:

```
$ print ${XBIN:?Oh my God, XBIN is not set!}
/bin/ksh: XBIN: Oh my God, XBIN is not set!
```

The other formats, **${*variable*?*word*}** and **${*variable*?}**, cause the variable value to be used, even if it is set to null.

${*variable*:+*word*}, ${*variable*+*word*}

This is expanded to the value of *word* if *variable* is set and not null, otherwise nothing is substituted. This is basically the opposite of the **${*variable*:–*word*}** format. Instead of using *word* if *variable* is not set, *word* is used if *variable* is set. In the first example **Y** is set to **abc**. When expanded, the alternate value **def** is displayed because **Y** is set:

```
$ Y=abc
$ print ${Y:+def}
def
```

Here, **Y** is unset. Now when expanded, nothing is displayed:

```
$ unset Y
$ print ${Y:+def}

$
```

Like the **${*variable*:−*word*}** format, the alternate value is only used and not assigned to the variable. **Y** is still set to null:

```
$ print $Y

$
```

The other format, **${*variable*+*word*}**, causes the variable value to be used, even if it is set to null:

```
$ Y=
$ print ${Y+def}
def
```

${*variable#pattern*}, ${*variable##pattern*}

This is expanded to the value of variable with the smallest (#) or largest (##) part of the left matched by *pattern* deleted. What these expansion formats allow you to do is manipulate substrings. To demonstrate the basic functionality, **X** is set to a string that contains a recurring pattern: **abcabcabc**.

```
$ X=abcabcabc
```

When expanded to return the substring that deletes the smallest left pattern **abc**, we get **abcabc**:

```
$ print ${X#abc*}
abcabc
```

while the substring that deletes the largest left pattern **abc** is **abcabcabc**, or the entire string:

```
$ print ${X##abc*}

$
```

We could use this concept to implement the Korn shell version of the UNIX **basename** command. The pattern in this command causes the last directory to be returned if variable **X** is set to a full pathname:

```
$ X=/usr/spool/cron
$ print ${X##*/}
cron
```

${*variable%pattern*}, ${*variable%%pattern*}

This is expanded to the value of *variable* with the smallest (%) or largest (%%) part of the right matched by *pattern* deleted. This is the same as the parameter expansion format from the previous section, except that patterns are matched from the right instead of left side. It could also be used to display file names without their .*suffixes*:

```
$ X=file.Z
$ print ${X%.*}
file
```

Here, any trailing digits are stripped:

```
$ X=chap1
$ print ${X%%[0-9]*}
chap
$ X=chap999
$ print ${X%%[0-9]*}
chap
```

The pattern in this command causes it to act like the UNIX **dirname** command. Everything except the last directory is returned if variable **X**

Table 3.5: Variable Expansion Formats

${#*variable*}
>   length of *variable*

${*variable*:–*word*}
>   value of *variable* if set and not null, else print
>   *word*

${*variable*:=*word*}
>   value of *variable* if set and not null, else *variable*
>   is set to *word*, then expanded

${*variable*:+*word*}
>   value of *word* if *variable* is set and not null, else
>   nothing is substituted

${*variable*:?}
>   value of *variable* if set and not null, else print
>   "*variable*: **parameter null or not set**"

${*variable*:?*word*}
>   value of *variable* if set and not null, else print
>   value of *word* and exit

${*variable*#*pattern*}
>   value of *variable* without the smallest beginning
>   portion that matches *pattern*

${*variable*##*pattern*}
>   value of *variable* without the largest beginning
>   portion that matches *pattern*

${*variable*%*pattern*}
>   value of *variable* without the smallest ending
>   portion that matches *pattern*

${*variable*%%*pattern*}
>   value of *variable* without the largest ending
>   portion that matches *pattern*

is set to a full pathname.

```
$ X=/usr/spool/cron
$ print ${X%/*}
/usr/spool
```

Array Variables

One-dimensional arrays are supported by the Korn shell. Arrays can have a maximum of 512 elements, although some versions may allow more. Array subscripts start at 0 and go up to 511 (or the maximum element minus one). Any variable can become a one-dimensional array by simply referring to it with a subscript. Here, variable **X** is set to **A**:

```
$ X=A
```

By explicitly assigning **X[1]** a value, variable **X** is transformed into an array variable:

```
$ X[1]=B
```

The original assignment to variable **X** is not lost. The first array element (**X[0]**) is still assigned **A**.

Array Variable Assignments & Declarations

Arrays can be assigned values by using normal variable assignment statements, the **set –A** command, or the **typeset** command:

> *variable*[**0**]=*value variable*[**1**]=*value* . . . *variable*[*n*]=*value*
> or
> **set –A** *variable value0 value1* . . . *valuen*
> or
> **typeset** *variable*[**0**]=*value variable*[**1**]=*value* . . . \
> *variable*[*n*]=*value*

The only difference between the formats, is that with the **set** command format, the values are assigned to the array variable sequentially starting from element zero. In the other formats, the array elements can be assigned values in any order. This example assigns the week day names to the array variable **DAY** using normal variable assignment format:

```
$ DAY[0]=Mon DAY[1]=Tue DAY[2]=Wed   \
DAY[3]=Thu DAY[4]=Fri DAY[5]=Sat DAY[6]=Sun
```

The same variable can be assigned values using the **set** command:

```
$ set -A DAY Mon Tue Wed Thu Fri Sat Sun
```

or the **typeset** command:

```
$ typeset DAY[0]=Mon DAY[1]=Tue DAY[2]=Wed \
DAY[3]=Thu DAY[4]=Fri DAY[5]=Sat DAY[6]=Sun
```

Not all the elements of an array need to exist. You can assign values to non-successive elements of an array. Here, the first and fourth elements of the **TEST** array are assigned values.

```
$ typeset TEST[0]=a TEST[3]=b
```

Array Variable Expansion

Array variables are expanded in the same manner as normal variables and parameters: using the **$** character. Without a subscript value, an array variable refers to the first element, or element **0**.

```
$ print $DAYS is the same as $DAY[0]
Mon is the same as Mon
```

To access the value of a specific array variable element use a subscript. Array variable names and subscripts must be enclosed in braces for proper expansion:

```
$ print ${DAY[3]} ${DAY[5]}
Thu Sat
```

If an element does not exist, nothing is substituted:

```
$ print ${DAY[25]}

$
```

All the elements of an array can be accessed by using the * or @ as the subscript value. They both return the same value. These examples print the values of all the elements of the **DAY** array variable:

```
$ print ${DAY[*]}
Mon Tue Wed Thu Fri Sat Sun
$ print ${DAY[@]}
Mon Tue Wed Thu Fri Sat Sun
```

The number of elements of an array variable is returned by using the # in front of the array variable name and using * or @ as the subscript value. Let's try it with **DAY**:

```
$ print ${#DAY[*]}
7
$ print ${#DAY[@]}
7
```

Arithmetic expressions can be used to return a subscript value. This example prints the fifth element of the **DAY** array variable. Remember that array subscripts start with **0**, so the third array element has a subscript of **2**, and the fifth element has a subscript of **4**:

```
$ print ${DAY[4/2]}
Wed
$ print ${DAY[7-6+5-4+3-2+1]}
Fri
```

Variable expansion can also be used to generate a subscript value.

```
$ X=6
$ print ${DAY[$X]}
Sun
```

Array Variable Attributes

As with ordinary variables, attributes can be assigned to array-type variables. Arrays can also be declared, and assigned values and attributes with the **typeset** command:

typeset *–attribute variable*[**0**]*=value variable*[**1**]*=value* . . .

Once set, attributes apply to all elements of an array. This example sets the uppercase attribute for the **DAY** array variable using the **typeset –u** command:

```
$ typeset –u DAY
```

Now all the element values are displayed in upper case:

```
$ print ${DAY[*]}
MON TUE WED THU FRI SAT SUN
```

Array element attributes can be set before or after assignment. Here, **XVAR** is initially assigned lowercase **aaa**, **bbb**, and **ccc**:

```
$ set –A XVAR aaa bbb ccc
$ print ${XVAR[*]}
aaa bbb ccc
```

Now, the uppercase, left-justify, two-character-wide attributes are set and the new element values are displayed. Notice that the third character from each element has been dropped, and the value is now in uppercase:

Chapter 3: Variables and Parameters

Table 3.6: Array Variables

${*array*}, $*array*	array element zero
${*array*[*n*]}	array element *n*
${*array*[*n***+2**]}	array element *n***+2**
${*array*[**$i**]}	array element **$i**
${*array*[*]}, ${*array*[@]}	all elements of an array
${#*array*[*]}, ${#*array*[@]}	number of array elements
${#*array*[*n*]	length of array element *n*

```
$ typeset —uL2 XVAR
$ print ${XVAR[*]}
AA BB CC
```

Array Variable Reassignments

Besides using regular *array-element*[*n*]=*value* or **typeset** *array-element*[*n*]=*value* syntax to reassign values, array variables can also have their values reassigned with the **set +A** command:

> **set +A** *variable value0 value1* . . .

This is helpful when you don't want to reassign values to all the elements of an array. In this example, the array variable **X** is assigned six values:

```
$ set —A X one two three d e f
$ print ${X[*]}
one two three d e f
```

Using the **set +A** command, the first three elements are reassigned **a**, **b**, and **c**:

```
$ set +A X a b c
$ print ${X[*]}
a b c d e f
```

Notice that values of the fourth, fifth, and sixth elements have not been affected.

Quoting

Quotes are used when assigning values containing whitespace or special characters, to delimit parameters and variables, and to assign command output.

There are three types of quotes: single quotes, double quotes, and back quotes. Single and double quotes are similar, except for the way they handle some special characters. Back quotes are used for command output assignment.

Look what happens when you try to perform a variable assignment using a value that contains whitespace without enclosing it in quotes:

```
$ GREETING=Hello world
/bin/ksh: world:   not found
$ print $GREETING

$
```

No assignment is made. To assign **Hello world** to **GREETING**, you would need to enclose the entire string in quotes, like this:

```
$ GREETING='Hello world'
$ print $GREETING
Hello world
```

Single Quotes

Single quotes are also used to hide the meaning of special characters like $, *, \, !, ", ` and /. Any characters between single quotes, except another single quote, are displayed without interpretation as special characters:

```
$ print '* $ \ ! ` / "'
* $ \ ! ` / "
```

This also means that variable and command substitution does not take place within single quotes (because $ and `` lose their special meaning). If you want to access the value of a variable, use double quotes instead of single quotes (discussed in the next section). So, instead of displaying **/home/anatole**, we get **$HOME**:

```
$ print '$HOME'
$HOME
```

and instead of the date, we get `**date**`:

```
$ print 'Today is `date`'
Today is `date`
```

Korn shell command substitution $(...) also doesn't work in single quotes, because of the $ character. You may be thinking what good are single quotes anyway? Well, there are still some good uses for them. You could print a menu border like this:

```
$ print '*******************MENU*****************'
*******************MENU*****************
```

or use the $ character as the dollar symbol:

```
$ print 'Pass GO — Collect $200'
Pass GO — Collect $200
```

You couldn't do that with double quotes! Actually there are quite a few good uses for single quotes. They can be used to print a double-quoted string:

```
$ print '"This is in double quotes"'
"This is in double quotes"
```

or just to surround plain old text that has embedded whitespace. This improves readability by separating the command from the argument. Variables can be set to null with single quotes:

```
$ X=''
```

Single quotes are also used to assign values to aliases and **trap** commands, and prevent alias substitution, but we'll get to that later.

Double Quotes

Double quotes are like single quotes, except that they do not remove the meaning of the special characters **$**, **`**, and ****. This means that variable and command substitution is performed.

```
$ DB="$HOME:`pwd`"
$ print $DB
/home/anatole:/tmp
```

Double quotes also preserve embedded whitespace and newlines. Here are some examples:

```
$ print "Line 1
> Line 2"
Line 1
Line 2
$ print "A                      B"
A                 B
```

Chapter 3: Variables and Parameters

The > is the secondary prompt, and is displayed whenever the Korn shell needs more input. In this case, it waits for the closing double quote:

```
$ ADDR="ASP,Inc
> PO Box 23837
> San Jose CA 95153 USA
> (800)777-UNIX * (510)531-5615"
```

Without double quotes around **ADDR**, we get this:

```
$ print $ADDR
ASP,Inc PO Box 23837 San Jose CA 95153 USA (800)
777-UNIX * (510)531-5615
```

Not quite what we wanted. Let's try it again:

```
$ print "$ADDR"
ASP,Inc
PO Box 23837
San Jose CA 95153 USA
(800)777-UNIX * (510)531-5615
```

There are also other uses for double quotes. You can set a variable to null:

```
$ NULL=""
$ print $NULL

$
```

or display single quotes.

```
$ print "'This is in single quotes'"
'This is in single quotes'
```

If you really wanted to display the **$**, **`**, ****, or **"** characters using double quotes, escape them with a backslash like this:

```
$ print "\$HOME is set to $HOME"
$HOME is set to /home/anatole
$ print "\`=back-quote \\=slash \"=double-quote"
`=back-quote \=slash "=double-quote
```

Back Quotes

Back quotes are used to assign the output of a command to a variable. This format, from the Bourne shell, is accepted by the Korn shell but considered obsolescent. This command sets the variable **SYS** to the system name:

```
$ SYS=`uuname -l`
$ print $SYS
aspd
```

Chapter 4:
Editing
Commands

Terminal Requirements
Command History File
The fc Command
In-Line Editor

One of the major features of the Korn shell is the ability to manipulate current and previous commands using the built-in editors and the **fc** command.

If you make a mistake on the current command line, instead of having to backspace to fix it, or killing the entire line and starting over, you can use the in-line editor to make the correction much more quickly and efficiently.

If you want to re-execute a command, instead of having to type it in all over again, you can use the command re-entry feature to call it back up. You can even make changes to it before re-executing!

Terminal Requirements

The in-line editor and command re-entry features require that the terminal accepts <RETURN> as carriage return without line-feed, and the space character to overwrite the current character on the screen and move right. Some terminals (ADM and HP 2621) may require special settings. For more information, see **Appendix E**.

Command History File

The Korn shell stores the commands that you enter at your terminal in a file, called the command history file. This file is specified by the **HISTFILE** variable. If not set, the default is **$HOME/.sh_history**.

The number of commands accessible via the command history file is specified by the **HISTSIZE** variable. If not set, the last 128 commands are saved, starting from your most recent command. The command history file operates on a first-in, last-out basis, so that as new commands are entered, the oldest commands are not accessible.

There are two ways to access the command history file: using the **fc** command, or the in-line editor. These are discussed in the following sections.

The fc Command

The **fc** command allows you to list, or edit and re-execute history file commands. It is the simplest interface to the command history file provided with the Korn shell. The **fc** command also allows you to manipulate the history file using your own choice of editors.

Displaying the Command History File

The command history file can be displayed using the **fc** command in a number of ways: with or without command numbers, using a range of line numbers, in reverse order, and more. The format for displaying the command history file with the **fc -l** command is:

    fc —l[nr] [*range*]

where the **-n** option causes the command numbers to not be displayed, and the **-r** option specifies reverse order (latest commands first). The range of commands to list is given as:

n1 [*n2*]	display list from command *n1* to command *n2*. If *n2* is not specified, display all the commands from current command back to command *n1*.
−*count*	display the last *count* commands
string	display all the previous commands back to the command that matches *string*

If no *range* argument is given, the last sixteen commands are listed. Let's look at the last five commands:

```
$ fc −l −5
250      set
251      vi /etc/env
252      . /etc/env
253      set
254      alias
255      functions
```

The **history** command is equivalent to **fc −l**. It is much easier to remember than **fc −l**, especially for C shell users. The last command could also be given like this. Notice that the order is reversed.

```
$ history −r −5
255      functions
254      alias
253      set
252      . /etc/env
251      vi /etc/env
250      set
```

By using a string instead of a count argument, we could search backward for a specific command.

```
$ history −r set
258      fc −lr set
257      fc −ln −10
256      fc −l 250 265
```

```
255     functions
254     alias
253     set
```

The argument **set** could also be given as **s**, or **se**, since partial strings are also matched. This means that the string **f** would match **functions** and **fc**, while **fu** would only match **functions**.

Editing the Command History File

Besides displaying the command history file, it can also be edited using the **fc** command with the following format:

> **fc** [–e *editor*] [–r] [*range*]
> or
> **fc** –e – [*old=new*] [*command*]

where the **–e** *editor* option is used to specify an editor. If not given, the value of the **FCEDIT** variable is used, and if not set, the default **/bin/ed** is used. The **–r** option reverses the order of the commands, so that the latest commands are displayed first. The first format allows you to edit a list of commands before re-executing. The range of commands to edit is given as:

n1 n2	edit list from command *n1* to command *n2*
n	edit command *n*
–n	edit the last *nth* command
string	edit the previous command that matches *string*

If no range argument is given, the last command is edited. The second format listed allows you to edit and re-execute a single command, where *old=new* specifies to replace the string *old* with *new* before re-executing, and *command* specifies which command to match. The *command* can be given as:

n	edit and re-execute command number *n*
−n	edit and re-execute the last *nth* command
string	edit and re-execute the most previous command that matches *string*

If no *command* argument is given, the last command is edited. Command **173** could be edited and re-executed like this:

```
$ fc −e − 173
```

Another way to do this is with the **r** command. It is the same as the **fc −e −** command. Using **r**, the last command could also be given as:

```
$ r 173
```

As you can see, using the **r** command is easier to use (and remember) than the **fc −e −** command. What else can be done with this command? The substitution feature is used to make minor changes to a previous command. Let's start with **print Hello**:

```
$ print Hello
Hello
```

We could change **Hello** to something else like this.

```
$ r Hello=Goodbye print
print Goodbye
Goodbye
```

The next section covers an easier way to edit and re-execute commands using the in-line editor.

In-Line Editor

In-line editing provides the ability to edit the current or previous commands before executing them. There are three in-line editing modes available: **emacs**, **gmacs**, and **vi**. The in-line editing mode is specified by setting the **EDITOR** or **VISUAL** variables, but if neither variables are set, the default is **/bin/ed**. The in-line editing mode can also be specified with the **set –o** command like this:

```
$ set -o option
```

where *option* can be **emacs**, **gmacs**, or **vi**. This is usually specified in your **$HOME/.profile** file.

The size of the editing window is specified by the **COLUMNS** variable. The default is **80**, unless **COLUMNS** is set. Some systems use the window size as the default. The size of your command prompt also affects the width of the editing window.

In the examples in the following sections, the **Before** column shows what was displayed at the prompt, the **Command** column lists the edit mode command, and the **After** column displays the result. The underbar character (_) represents the cursor. Control characters are given as **Ctl** followed by the character in boldface. For example, **Ctl-h** specifies **Control-h** and is entered by pressing the **h** key while holding down the **Control** key.

Vi Edit Mode

If you know the UNIX **vi** text editor, then learning how to use the vi in-line editor is relatively easy. The vi in-line editor is a subset of the **vi** editor program, so most of the commands are the same.

In vi edit mode, there are two operating modes: input and command. Operating in and out of input mode is virtually the same. Commands are entered and executed just as if you were not using the in-line editor. As soon as you press the <ESCAPE> key, you are put in command mode. This is where you can enter your vi commands to access and edit commands from the history file, or current command line.

Input Mode

Once the vi edit mode is set, you are placed in input mode. If the vi mode is set in your **.profile** file, then you are automatically in input mode whenever the Korn shell starts up. As stated in the previous section, operating in and out of vi input mode is virtually the same.

The next example shows some of the basic vi input mode commands. We start with "**print Hi again world**". The **Ctl-w** commands delete the strings **world**, and **again**, then the **Ctl-h** command deletes **i**. The @ command kills the entire line, and we get a new command prompt.

Before	Command	After
$ print Hi again world_	Ctl-w	$ print Hi again _
$ print Hi again _	Ctl-w	$ print Hi _
$ print Hi _	Ctl-h	$ print Hi_
$ print Hi_	Ctl-h	$ print H_
$ print H_	Ctl-h	$ print _
$ print _	@	$ _

The *Erase* and *Kill* characters can be set with the **stty** command.

Command Mode

When you press the <ESCAPE> key in vi input mode, you are put in command mode. This is where the **vi** commands can be given to edit a single command from the history file. Editing commands can be given until the <RETURN> key is pressed, then the result is executed. To cancel current editing, press the <ESCAPE> key again. If you enter an invalid command, or a search command fails, the Korn shell will cause your terminal to beep or flash.

Table 4.2 lists the basic commands available in command mode. A complete listing of the commands can be found in Appendix E.

Moving Around the History File

In this example, we navigate through the command history file using some basic vi edit mode commands. Assume that these are the last two commands that were executed:

```
$ history -2
339      pwd
340      date
341      history -2
```

At the command prompt, the <ESCAPE> key is pressed to enter command mode, then a series of **k** commands are given to successively retrieve the previous command. The **j** command is given to retrieve the next commands, until we get to the **date** command. After the <RETURN> key is pressed, **date** is executed.

Before	Command	After
$ _	<ESCAPE>k	$ history -2
$ history -2	k	$ date
$ date	k	$ pwd
$ pwd	j	$ date
$ date	<RETURN>	

Of course, a more efficient way to retrieve the **date** command would be with a single backward search command, <ESCAPE>/**da**<RETURN>. Notice that **da** is used to match **date**.

Table 4.1: Vi Input Mode Commands

Ctl-h, **#**, <BACKSPACE>
        delete the previous character (system dependent)

Ctl-d   terminate the shell

Ctl-x, **@**   kill the entire line (system dependent)

<RETURN>   execute the current line

****   escape the next *Erase* or *Kill* character

Ctl-v   escape the next character

Ctl-w   delete the previous word

```
Before          Command               After

$ _             <ESCAPE>/da<RETURN> $ date
$ date          <RETURN>
```

Editing Previous Commands

In the next example, we want to change the word **Hello** to **Goodbye** in the **print** command. The <ESCAPE> key is pressed to enter command mode. Then the **k** command retrieves the last command, and the **h** command moves the cursor left one character. The **b** command is given to move the cursor back one word, to the beginning of **world**. Another **b** command is given, and the cursor is at the beginning of **Hello**. Now the **cw** command is used to change the word **Hello**, and we can type over the new word **Goodbye**. When we are finished typing, the <RETURN> is pressed, and the result is executed.

Table 4.2: Some Vi Command Mode Commands

h, <BACKSPACE>	
	move left one character
l, <SPACE>	
	move right one character
b	move left one word
B	move left one word; ignore punctuation
w	move right one word
W	move right one word; ignore punctuation
e	move to the end of the next word
E	move to end of next word; ignore punctuation
^	move to beginning of the line
$	move to end of line
f*c*	move right to character *c*
F*c*	move left to character *c*
a	add text after the current character
A	append text to end of the current line
i	insert text left of the current character
r*c*	replace current character with *c*
x	delete the current character
u	undo the last text modification command
k	get previous command from history file
j	get next command from history file
/*string*	search backward in the history file for command that matches *string*
?*string*	search forward in the history file for command that matches *string*
.	repeat the last text modification command
~	toggle the case of the current character

Before	Command	After
$ print Hello world_	<ESCAPE>	$ print Hello world
$ print Hello world	h	$ print Hello world
$ print Hello world	b	$ print Hello world
$ print Hello world	b	$ print Hello world
$ print Hello world	cwGoodbye	$ print Goodbye world
$ print Goodbye world	<RETURN>	

There are a number of ways that the same results could have been achieved. The cursor could have been moved back to **Hello** using **FH** (move left to character H), and then deleted using **dw** (delete word). **Goodbye** could have then been inserted using the **i** (insert) command.

Let's say we want to just add an exclamation point to the **print Hello world** command. Instead of typing it all over again, we enter <ESCAPE> for command mode and **k** to get the last command. Then the **$** command moves the cursor to the end of the line, and the **a!** command appends the **!** character. After the <RETURN> key is pressed, **print Hello world!** is displayed.

Before	Command	After
$ _	<ESCAPE>k	$ print Goodbye world
$ print Hello world	$	$ print Hello world
$ print Hello world	a!	$ print Hello world!_
$ print Hello world!_	<RETURN>	

Here, a typo is spotted in the **chmod** command. Instead of backspacing fourteen times to make the correction, or killing the entire line and typing over, we enter command mode by pressing <ESCAPE>. The **^** command moves the cursor to the beginning of the line, and **e** (end of word) moves it to the **s** character, where we want to make the correction. The **rd** command (replace current character with **d**) is given, followed by <RETURN> to execute.

Before	Command	After
$ chmos 777 /tmp/foo_	<ESCAPE>	$ chmos 777 /tmp/fo<u>o</u>
$ chmos 777 /tmp/fo<u>o</u>	^	$ <u>c</u>hmos 777 /tmp/foo
$ <u>c</u>hmos 777 /tmp/foo	e	$ chmo<u>s</u> 777 /tmp/foo
$ chmo<u>s</u> 777 /tmp/foo	rd	$ chmo<u>d</u> 777 /tmp/foo
$ chmo<u>d</u> 777 /tmp/foo	<RETURN>	

Displaying Long Command Lines

For lines longer than the window width, a mark is displayed at the end of the line to indicate the position. Only part of the command is displayed. The text position markers can be:

>   line extends to the right of the edit window
<   line extends to the left of the edit window
*   line extends on both sides of the edit window

Moving around the command line makes different parts of the command line visible. If the cursor is moved past the last character, the line is redisplayed with the cursor in the middle of the screen. The **COLUMNS** variable setting, and the size of your command prompt also affect the width of the editing window.

Emacs/Gmacs Edit Modes

Like the vi in-line editor, the emacs/gmacs in-line editor is also basically a subset of the same text editors. However, there are a few commands in the emacs/gmacs in-line editors that are not in the regular program.

This only difference between the emacs and gmacs editors is the way **Ctl-t** is handled. In emacs mode, **Ctl-t** transposes the current and next character. In gmacs mode, **Ctl-t** transposes the previous two characters.

Chapter 4: Editing Commands

Table 4.3 lists the basic commands available in emacs/gmacs edit mode. **Appendix E** contains a complete listing of the commands.

Editing Commands in Emacs/Gmacs Mode

Before we look at some emacs/gmacs in-line editor command examples, here are the last three commands from the history file:

```
$ history −r −n −3
history −r −n −3
grep ksh /etc/passwd
print $PATH
cd /usr/etc/yp
```

In the following example, the **Ctl-n** and **Ctl-p** commands are used to get the next and previous commands from the history file. Assuming that **history −r −n −3** just completed execution, the **Ctl-p** command brings it back, and another **Ctl-p** goes back to **grep**. To get back to the **cd** command, the **Ctl-r** command is given. The <RETURN> key is pressed, and the current directory is changed to **/usr/etc/yp**.

<u>Before</u>	<u>Command</u>	<u>After</u>
$ _	Ctl-p	$ history -n -3_
$ history -n -3_	Ctl-p	$ grep x /etc/passwd_
$ grep x /etc/passwd_	Ctl-rcd	$ cd /usr/etc/yp_
$ cd /usr/etc/yp_	<RETURN>	

In the next example, we want to make a correction to the current command line. The **Ctl-b** commands moves the cursor one character left, then **Esc-b** moves the cursor one word left. The **Ctl-d** command deletes character **C**, and **Ctl-]E** moves forward to the next **E** character. The <RETURN> key is pressed, and the result is executed.

Before	Command	After
`$ print AB CD EF_`	Ctl-b	`$ print AB CD EF`
`$ print AB CD EF`	Esc-b	`$ print AB CD EF`
`$ print AB CD EF`	Ctl-d	`$ print AB D EF`
`$ print AB D EF`	^]E	`$ print AB D EF`
`$ print AB D EF`	\<RETURN\>	

What about inserting text? To add characters to the command line, in emacs/gmacs mode, you just type them in. Characters are inserted before the cursor. Here we get the last command using **Ctl-p**. Then we move to the beginning of the line using **Ctl-a**, and to the next word with **Esc-f**. **Ctl-k** deletes to the end of the line, and we insert **hello** by typing it in. To display **hello**, we just press \<RETURN\>.

Before	Command	After
`$ _`	Ctl-p	`$ print AB D EF_`
`$ print AB D EF_`	Ctl-a	`$ print AB D EF`
`$ print AB D EF`	Esc-f	`$ print_AB D EF`
`$ print AB D EF`	Ctl-k	`$ print_`
`$ print_`	hello	`$ print hello_`
`$ print hello_`	\<RETURN\>	

This example shows another way in which a command can be edited using emacs/gmacs mode. The **Ctl-a** command moves the cursor to the beginning of the line, and **^]s** moves to the **s** character. The **Ctl-d** command deletes **s**, then **d** is typed in. The \<RETURN\> key is pressed, and the command is run.

Before	Command	After
`$ chmos 777 /tm/foo_`	Ctl-a	`$ chmos 777 /tmp/foo`
`$ chmos 777 /tm/foo`	^]s	`$ chmos 777 /tmp/foo`
`$ chmos 777 /tm/foo`	Ctl-d	`$ chmo_777 /tmp/foo`
`$ chmo_777 /tm/foo`	d	`$ chmod 777 /tmp/foo`
`$ chmod 777 /tmp/foo`	\<RETURN\>	

Table 4.3: Some Emacs/Gmacs In-Line Editor Commands

Ctl-b	move left one character
Ctl-f	move right one character
Esc-b	move left one word
Esc-f	move right one word
Ctl-a	move to beginning of line
Ctl-e	move to end of line
Ctl-]*c*	move right to character *c*
Ctl-h	delete preceding character
Ctl-x, @	kill the entire line
Ctl-k	delete from cursor to end of line
Ctl-d	delete current character
Esc-d	delete current word
Ctl-w	delete from cursor to mark
Ctl-y	undo last delete (w/**Esc-p**)
Ctl-p	get previous command from history file
Ctl-n	get next command from history file
Ctl-r*string*	search backward in history file for command that contains *string*
Ctl-c	change current character to upper case
Esc-l	change current character to lower case
Esc-p	save to buffer from cursor to mark
Esc-<SPACE>	mark current location
Ctl-l	redisplay current line

Chapter 5:
Job Control

Manipulating Jobs
Checking Job Status
Background Jobs and I/O
Job Names
Leaving Stopped Jobs

The Korn shell provides a job control mechanism that is virtually identical to the C shell version of BSD UNIX. Job control allows programs to be stopped and restarted, moved between the foreground and background, their processing status to be displayed, and more. To enable the job control feature, the **monitor** option must be enabled with the **set** command:

```
$ set —o monitor
or
$ set —m
```

This can be put into the .**profile** file so that job control is automatically enabled at login. On most systems that provide the job control mechanism, this option is automatically enabled for interactive shells. It can be checked by executing the **set —o** command. Let's see if it is set:

```
$ set —o | grep monitor
monitor     on
```

If a command is run in the background, the Korn shell returns a job number and process id. Here, the **find** command is assigned job number **1** and process id **1435**:

```
$ find / —name core —exec rm —rf {} \; &
[1]  1435
```

The next command is assigned job number **2** and process id **1437**:

```
$ cpio —iBcdu < /dev/rmt0 &
[2]  1437
```

When background jobs are completed, a message is given before the next prompt is displayed. This is done so that other work is not interfered with. In this example, the **ls** command is put in the background. Although it finished before the **sleep** command, the completion message is not displayed until **sleep** is finished:

```
$ ls —x > ls.out &
[3]  1438
$ sleep 30
[3]  + Done      ls —x > ls.out &
$
```

Manipulating Jobs

Jobs running in the foreground are suspended by typing **Ctl-z** (**Control-z**). So instead of waiting for the long-running **split** command to complete, it is interrupted using **Ctl-z**:

```
$ split —5000  hugefile
Ctl-z
[3]  + Stopped  split  —5000  hugefile
$
```

Stopped and backgrounded jobs are brought back into the foreground with the **fg** command. If no argument is given, the current (most recently stopped or backgrounded) job is used. The stopped **split** job is brought back into the foreground with **fg**:

```
$ fg
split -5000 hugefile
```

Stopped jobs are put into the background with the **bg** command. If no argument is given, the most recently stopped job is used. In the next example, we want to put the **split** job back in the background. It is currently running in the foreground, so it must first be suspended with **Ctl-z** again:

```
$ fg
split -5000 hugefile
Ctl-z
```

Now, it can be put into the background using **bg**:

```
$ bg
[3] split -5000 hugefile &
```

The **split** job is brought into the foreground with **fg**, and we are back to where we started. This time we use the job number as the argument to **fg**:

```
$ fg %3
split -5000 hugefile
```

Checking Job Status

The status and other information about all jobs is displayed using the **jobs** command. The following **jobs** output shows that there is one stopped job, and two running jobs. The + indicates the current job, and – indicates the previous job:

```
$ jobs
[3]   + Stopped      split  -5000  hugefile
[2]   - Running      find / -name core -print &
[1]     Running      sleep 25 &
```

The **jobs –l** command shows the same information, along with the process ids, while **jobs –p** only gives you the process ids.

```
$ jobs -l
[3]   + 466 Stopped split  -5000  hugefile
[2]   - 465 Running find / -name core -print &
[1]     463 Running sleep 25 &
```

Killing Jobs

Stopped or background jobs are terminated with the **kill** command. Unlike **bg** or **fg**, a job argument must be given. Here, a **sleep** command is put in the background, then killed:

```
$ sleep 100 &
[1] 254
$ kill %1
```

It could also be given as **kill 254**.

Waiting for Jobs

You can make the Korn shell wait for some or all background jobs to complete with the **wait** command. If no argument is given, the Korn shell waits for all background jobs to complete.

Background Jobs and I/O

Jobs being executed in the background will stop if they attempt to read input from your terminal. If you tried to interactively remove **$PUBDIR/junk** in the background, this is what would happen:

```
$ rm -i $PUBDIR/junk &
[2]   +Stopped (tty input) rm -i $PUBDIR/junk &
```

The job is stopped because it needs to prompt you for input. The **rm -i** job is brought back into the foreground with the **fg** command and its' prompt is displayed:

```
$ fg %2
rm -i $PUBDIR/junk
rm: remove /usr/spool/uucppublic/junk? y
```

By default, jobs send their output to your terminal, even while running in the background. Here, the **find** command sends its' output to the terminal, even though it is running in the background:

```
$ find / -name core -print &
[2]   1453
$ /usr/lbin/core
/home/anatole/bin/core
```

That can be annoying, especially if you are in the middle of something else. To avoid this problem, redirect the output of background jobs to a file. Make sure to be careful with the redirection. If you don't redirect standard error, error messages will go to your terminal and not to the output file. Let's kill the **find** job, then restart it and send the output to **c.out**:

```
$ kill %2
[2] + Terminated  find   /-name  core  -print>c.out &
$ find / -name core -print >c.out &
[2]   1453
$ jobs
[2]  -  Running  find / -name core -print &
[1]     Running  sleep 1000 &
```

We can work on something else until we get the completion message.

```
[2]   +Done    find / -name core -print>c.out &
```

There are other ways to deal with job output. Jobs being executed in the background are prevented from generating output by setting **stty tostop**. Let's run the **find** job again with the **tostop** option enabled:

```
$ stty tostop
$ find / -name core -print &
[2]   1460
```

Now when the job has some output, we get this message:

```
[1] + Stopped(tty output) find / -name core -
print &
```

The only way to see the **find** output is to bring the job back into the foreground.

```
$ fg
/usr/lbin/core
/home/anatole/bin/core
```

The **stty tostop** command can be put into your profile file so that background job output is by default disabled.

The **nohup** command can also be used to direct output from background jobs. It causes standard output *and* standard error to be automatically sent to **nohup.out**, or whatever file you give it. One added benefit. The **nohup** command will keep jobs running, even if you log out. Here we run the **find** job again using **nohup**. First we need to enable background job output:

```
$ stty -tostop
$ nohup find / -name core -print &
[2] 1469
$ wait
Sending output to 'nohup.out'
[2] + Done   nohup find / -name core -print &
```

The **find** job output is in **nohup.out**:

```
$ cat nohup.out
/usr/lbin/core
/home/anatole/bin/core
```

Table 5.1: Job Control Commands

bg	put the current stopped job in the background
bg *%n*	put the stopped job *n* in the background
fg	move the current background job into the foreground
fg *%n*	move background job *n* into the foreground
jobs	display the status of all jobs
jobs –l	display the status of all jobs along with their process ids
jobs –p	display the process ids of all jobs
kill *%n*	kill job *n*
kill –l	list all valid signal names
kill *–signal %n*	
	send the specified signal to job *n*
set –m, set –o monitor	
	enable job control; execute background jobs in a separate process group, and report the exit status of background jobs
stty tostop	
	prevent background jobs from generating output
stty –tostop	
	allow background jobs to generate output (default)
wait	wait for all background jobs to complete
wait *%n*	wait for background job *n* to complete
Ctl-z	stop the current job

Table 5.2: Job Names

%*n*	job *n*
%+, %%	current job
%−	previous job
%*string*	job whose name begins with *string*
%?*string*	job that matches part or all of *string*

Job Names

Most people use the job number to refer to a job, because one number is easy to remember. However, jobs can be referred to in a number of other ways: by process id, current/previous job, or all or part of a job name. If we had these jobs:

```
$ jobs −1
[3]  + 466 Stopped      split −5000 hugefile
[2]  − 465 Running      find / −name  −print &
[1]    463 Running      sleep 25 &
```

Then the **split** job could be referred to as %3, %+, %%, 466, %split, or %?sp, the **find** job could be referred to as %2, %−, 465, %find, or %?f, and the **sleep** could be referred to as %1, 463, %sleep, or %?sl.

Leaving Stopped Jobs

The Korn shell displays a warning message if you try to exit from the shell while jobs are stopped.

```
$ stty tostop
$ date &
[1] 541
[1] + Stopped(tty output)        date &
$ exit
You have stopped jobs
```

If you ignore this message and exit, the Korn shell will not attempt to warn you again and any stopped jobs will be terminated.

Chapter 6:
Performing
Arithmetic

*The **let** Command*
The ((...)) Command
Declaring Integer Variables
Arithmetic Constants
Arithmetic Operators
Random Numbers

The Korn shell provides the ability to perform integer arithmetic in any base from two to thirty-six using built-in commands. It executes much faster than using the **expr** command, since it doesn't have to start another process. It can also be used instead of the **test** command for integer comparisons. In addition, all of the operators from the C programming language (except **++**, **––**, and **?:**) are now supported by the Korn shell.

The let Command

Integer arithmetic can be done with the **let** command and arithmetic expressions. The format for the **let** command is:

   let "*arithmetic-expression*"

where arithmetic-expressions can contain constants, operators, and Korn shell variables. Double quotes are used with arithmetic expressions that contain white space or operators that have special meaning to the Korn shell. For example, variable **X** can be set to the sum of 1+1 like this:

```
$ let "X=1 + 1"
$ print $X
2
```

then incremented:

```
$ let "X=X + 1"
$ print $X
3
```

Notice that in arithmetic expressions, regular variables can be referenced by name only, and do not have to be preceded by **$** for substitution to be performed. Both

```
$ let "X=X + 1"
```
and
```
$ let "X=$X + 1"
```

are equivalent. The first format is preferred because parameter expansion does not have to be performed. This causes it to be executed faster.

Arithmetic expressions are made up of constants, variables or any of the arithmetic operators in Table 6.1.

Table 6.1: Arithmetic Operators (in order of precedence)

–	unary minus
!	logical negation
~	bitwise negation
*, /, %	multiplication, division, remainder (modulo)
+, –	addition, subtraction
<<, >>	left shift, right shift
<=, <	less than or equal to, less than
>=, >	greater than or equal to, greater than
==	equal to
!=	not equal to
&	bitwise AND
^	bitwise exclusive OR
|	bitwise OR
&&	logical AND
||	logical OR
=	assignment
*=, /=, %=	
	multiply assign, divide assign, modulo assign
+=, –=	increment, decrement
<<=, >>=	
	left shift assign, right shift assign
&=, ^=, |=	
	bitwise AND assign, bitwise exclusive OR assign, bitwise OR assign
(...)	grouping (used to override precedence rules)

The ((...)) Command

The ((...)) command is equivalent to the **let** command, except that all characters between the ((and)) are treated as quoted arithmetic expressions. This is more convenient to use than **let**, because many of the arithmetic operators have special meaning to the Korn shell. The following commands are equivalent:

```
$ let "X=X + 1"
and
$ ((X=X + 1))
```

Before the Korn shell **let** and ((...)) commands, the only way to perform arithmetic was with **expr**. For example, to do the same increment **X** operation using **expr**:

```
$ X=`expr $X + 1`
```

In tests on a few systems, the **let** command performed the same operation 35-60 times faster! That is quite a difference.

Declaring Integer Variables

As with ordinary variables, integer variables need not be declared. A variable can simply be given an integer value, and then used in an arithmetic expression.

```
$ X=12
$ ((Y=X * 3))
$ print $Y
36
```

However, variables can be explicitly declared integer type by using the **typeset –i** command. The following example sets the **DAYS** and

MONTHS variables to be integer type:

```
$ typeset -i DAYS MONTHS=12
```

There is also another command called **integer**, which is equivalent to **typeset –i**. It could be used to declare the **DAYS** and **MONTHS** variables like this:

```
$ integer DAYS MONTHS=12
```

Variables do not have to be explicitly declared integer type to be used in arithmetic expressions. It may improve performance, but what you really gain with declaring integer variables is stricter type checking on assignments. Integer variables cannot be assigned non-integer values:

```
$ integer I=abc
/bin/ksh: I: bad number
```

Another benefit to declaring integer variables is that arithmetic can be performed directly on integer variables without using the **let** or **((...))** commands, as long as the integer value is being assigned a value. In other words, you can do this:

```
$ integer DAYS="4 + 3"
instead of
$ ((DAYS=4 + 3))
or
$ let "DAYS=4 + 3"
```

This also means that **integer** variables can be assigned values using arithmetic expressions when declared. Let's try it with the **MONTHS** variable:

```
$ integer MONTHS="36 / 3"
$ print $MONTHS
12
```

Arithmetic Constants

The format for arithmetic constants is:

> *number*
> or
> *base#number*

where *base* is a whole number between **2** and **36**, and *number* is any
non-negative integer. If not specified, the default base is **10**. The
arithmetic base of a variable can be set with the **typeset –i***n*
command, or by prepending *base#* to the value. In this example,
variable **X** is set to **5** in base **2** using both formats:

```
$ typeset —i2  X=5
or
$ typeset —i  X=2#101
```

When variable **X** is expanded, the value is written in base **2**:

```
$ print $X
2#101
```

If you want to display the value of **X** in another base, just reset the
base with the **typeset –i***n* command. Here it is reset to base **3**:

```
$ typeset —i3  X
$ print $X
3#12
```

Arithmetic can be performed on numbers with different bases. Here
is an example - **X** is set to **7** in base **2**:

```
$ typeset —i  X=2#111
```

Y is set to **8** in base **5**:

```
$ typeset -i5  Y=8
```

and **Z** is set to base **16**:

```
$ typeset -i16  z
```

Now, **X** and **Y** are added together and the result is put in **Z**:

```
$  Z=X+Y
$ print $z
16#f
```

We could convert the result to octal by resetting the base of **Z** using the **typeset** **-i**n command like this:

```
$ typeset -i8  z
$ print $z
8#17
```

Arithmetic Operators

The following sections contain examples for each of the arithmetic operators available to the Korn shell. Table 6.1 lists all of the arithmetic operators available to the Korn shell in order of precedence.

–expression (Unary Minus)

Evaluates to the negative value of *expression*.

```
$ ((X=-7))
$ ((Y=-X + 2))
$ print - "$X $Y"
-7 9
```

The **print –** command is used so that the negative sign is not interpreted as an argument.

!expression (Logical Negation)

The **!** operator returns **0** (true) for expressions that do not evaluate to zero, or **1** (false) if they do.

```
$ X=0
$ ((X=!X)); print "$X"
1
$ ((X=!X)); print "$X"
0
```

~expression (Bitwise Negation)

Evaluates to the bitwise negated value (one's complement) of *expression*. It returns a value that contains a **1** in each bit position where *expression* contains **0**, and a **0** in each bit position where *expression* contains **1**.

```
$ X=2#011
$ ((X=~X)); print - "$X"
-2#100
```

*expression1 * expression2* (Multiplication)
*expression1 *= expression2* (Multiply assign)

Evaluates to the product of *expression1* multiplied by *expression2*.
The second format assigned the result of the evaluation to *expression1*.

```
$ ((X=5 * 4)); print "$X"
20
$ ((X=3 * 1 * 2 * 4)); print "$X"
24
$ ((X*=2)); print "$X"
48
```

expression1 / expression2 (Division)
expression1 /= expression2 (Divide assign)

Evaluates to the quotient of *expression1* divided by *expression2*. The
second format assigned the result of the evaluation to *expression1*.

```
$ Y=50
$ ((X=Y / 10)); print "$X"
5
$ ((X=21 / 5)); print "$X"
4
$ ((X/=2)); print "$X"
2
```

expression1 % *expression2* (Modulo)
expression1 %= *expression2* (Modulo assign)

Evaluates to the remainder of *expression1* divided by *expression2*.
The second format assigned the result of the evaluation to
expression1.

```
$ ((X=20 % 7)); print "$X"
6
$ ((X=11 % 4)); print "$X"
3
$ ((X%=2)); print "$X"
1
```

expression1 + *expression2* (Addition)
expression1 += *expression2* (Increment)

Evaluates to the sum of *expression1* and *expression2*. The second
format assigned the result of the evaluation to *expression1*.

```
$ ((X=1 + 2)); print "$X"
3
$ ((X=4 + 1 + 3)); print "$X"
8
$ ((X+=1)); print "$X"
9
```

expression1 – *expression2* (Subtraction)
expression1 –= *expression2* (Decrement)

Evaluates to the difference of *expression1* and *expression2*. The
second format assigned the result of the evaluation to *expression1*.

```
$ ((X=3 – 1)); print "$X"
```

```
2
$ ((X=X - 1)); print "$X"
1
$ ((X-=1)); print "$X"
0
```

identifier=expression (Assignment)

Assigns *identifier* the value of *expression*.

```
$ ((X=12)); print "$X"
12
$ Y=7
$ ((X=Y)); print "$X"
2
```

expression1 << expression2 (Left shift)
expression1 <<= expression2 (Left shift assign)

Left shift *expression1* by the number of bits specified in *expression2*.
The second format assigned the result of the evaluation to
expression1.

```
$ typeset -i2 X
$ ((X=2#11 << 1)); print "$X"
2#110
$ ((X=2#110 << 2)); print "$X"
2#11000
$ ((X=2#11000 << 3)); print "$X"
2#11000000
```

expression1 >> *expression2* (Right shift)
expression1 >>= *expression2* (Right shift assign)

Right shift *expression1* by the number of bits from *expression2*. The
second format assigned the result of the evaluation to *expression1*.

```
$ typeset -i2 X
$ ((X=2#10101 >> 2)); print "$X"
2#101
$ ((X=2#101 >> 1)); print "$X"
2#10
$ ((X>>=1)); print "$X"
2#1
```

expression1 <= *expression2* (Less than or equal)

Evaluates to **0** (true) if *expression1* is less than or equal to
expression2, otherwise evaluates to **1** (false).

```
$ ((1 <= 2)) && print "1 is less than 2"
1 is less than 2
$ ((3 <= 2)) || print "3 is not less than 2"
3 is not less than 2
```

expression1 < *expression2* (Less than)

Evaluates to **0** (true) if *expression1* is less than *expression2*, otherwise
evaluates to **1** (false).

```
$ ((1 < 2)); print "$?"
0
$ ((3 < 2)); print "$?"
1
```

expression1 >= *expression2* (Greater than or equal)

Evaluates to **0** (true) if *expression1* is greater than or equal to *expression2*, otherwise evaluates to **1** (false).

```
$ ((3 >= 2)) && print "3 is greater than 2"
3 is greater than 2
$ ((1 >= 2)) || print "1 is not greater than 2"
1 is not greater than 2
```

expression1 > *expression2* (Greater than)

Evaluates to **0** (true) if *expression1* is greater *expression2*, otherwise evaluates to **1** (false).

```
$ ((3 > 2)); print $?
0
$ ((1 > 2)); print $?
1
```

expression1 == *expression2* (Equal to)

Evaluates to **0** (true) if *expression1* is equal to *expression2*, otherwise evaluates to **1** (false).

```
$ ((3 == 3)) && print "3 is equal to 3"
3 is equal to 3
$ ((4 == 3)) || print "4 is not equal to 3"
4 is not equal to 3
```

expression1 != expression2 (Not equal to)

Evaluates to **0** (true) if *expression1* is not equal to *expression2*, otherwise evaluates to **1** (false).

```
$ ((4 != 3)); print "$?"
0
$ ((3 != 3 )); print "$?"
1
```

expression1 & expression2 (Bitwise AND)
expression1 &= expression2 (Bitwise AND assign)

Returns a value that contains a **1** in each bit where there is a **1** in both expressions, and a **0** in every other bit. The second format assigned the result of the evaluation to *expression1*.

```
$ typeset -i2 X
$ ((X=2#11 & 2#10)); print "$X"
2#10
$ ((X=2#101 & 2#111)); print "$X"
2#101
$ ((X&=2#001)); print "$X"
2#1
```

expression1 ^ expression2 (Bitwise Exclusive OR)
expression1 ^= expression2 (Bitwise XOR assign)

Returns a value that contains a **1** in each bit where there is a **1** in only one of the expressions, and a **0** in every other bit. The second format assigned the result of the evaluation to *expression1*.

```
$ typeset -i2 X
$ ((X=2#11 ^ 2#10)); print "$X"
```

```
2#1
$ ((X=2#101 ^ 2#011)); print "$X"
2#110
$ ((X^=2#100)); print "$X"
2#10
```

expression1 | expression2 (Bitwise OR)
expression1 |= expression2 (Bitwise OR assign)

Returns a value that contains a **1** in each bit where there is a **1** in either of the expressions, and a **0** in every other bit. The second format assigned the result of the evaluation to *expression1*.

```
$ typeset -i2 X
$ ((X=2#11 | 2#10)); print "$X"
2#11
$ ((X=2#101 | 2#011)); print "$X"
2#111
$ ((X|=2#1001)); print "$X"
2#1111
```

expression1 && expression2 (Logical AND)

If *expression1* evaluates to **0** (true), *expression2* is evaluated. The value of the entire expression is **0** (true) only if *expression1* and *expression2* are both true. Since both **X** and **Y** are equal to **1**, the entire expression returns **0**, and the **print** command is executed:

```
$ X=1 Y=1
$ ((X==1 && Y==1)) && print "X and Y equal 1"
X and Y equal 1
```

Now only **X** is equal to **1**, so the entire expression returns **1**, and the **print** command is not executed:

```
$ unset Y
$ ((X==1 && Y==1)) && print "X and Y equal 1"
$
```

expression1 || expression2 (Logical OR)

If *expression1* evaluates to non-zero (false), *expression2* is evaluated. The value of the entire expression is **0** (true) if either *expression1* or *expression2* are true. Since **X** is less than **2**, the entire expression returns **0**, and the **print** command is executed:

```
$ X=1  Y=2
$ ((X<2 || Y<5)) && print "X or Y less than 2"
X or Y less than 2
```

Now, neither **X** nor **Y** are less than **2**, so the entire expression returns **1**, and the **print** command is not executed:

```
$ X=2  Y=2
$ ((X<2 || Y<5)) && print "X or Y less than 2"
$
```

(expression) (Override Precedence)

The () operators are used to override precedence rules. In the next expression, normal precedence rules cause the **Y * Z** operation to be performed first:

```
$ X=1  Y=2  Z=3
$ ((TMP=X + Y * Z))
$ print $TMP
7
```

If the expression is rewritten using the precedence override operators, the **X + Y** operation is performed first:

```
$ ((TMP=(X + Y) * Z))
$ print $TMP
9
```

Random Numbers

The Korn shell provides a special variable, **RANDOM**, which is used to generate random numbers in the range from 0 to 32767. It generates a different random number each time it is referenced:

```
$ print $RANDOM
27291
$ print $RANDOM
5386
$ print $RANDOM
6884
```

You can also initialize a sequence of random numbers by setting **RANDOM** to a value. Here, **RANDOM** is set to **7**. When subsequently accessed, the values **2726** and **18923** are returned:

```
$ RANDOM=7
$ print $RANDOM
2726
$ print $RANDOM
18923
```

When **RANDOM** is reset to **7** again, the same numbers are returned:

```
$   RANDOM=7
$  print   $RANDOM
2726
$  print   $RANDOM
18923
```

If **RANDOM** is unset, the special meaning is removed, even if reset.

Chapter 7:
The Environment

After You Log In
The Environment File
Environment Variables
Korn Shell Options
Aliases
Prompts
Subshells
Restricted Shell

Besides executing commands and being a programming language, the Korn shell also provides a number of commands, variables, and options that allow you to customize your working environment.

After You Log In

After you login, the Korn shell performs a number of actions before it displays the command prompt. Usually it first looks for **/etc/profile**. If it exists, it is read in and executed. The **/etc/profile** file contains system-wide environment settings, such as a basic **PATH** setting, a default **TERM** variable, the system **umask** value and more. The Korn shell then reads and executes **$HOME/.profile**. This file contains your local environment settings, such as your search path, execution options, local variables, aliases, and more. A sample profile file is included in **Appendix A**.

The Environment File

Once the profile files are processed, the Korn shell checks the environment file, which is specified by the **ENV** variable. The environment file usually contains aliases, functions, options, variables and other environment settings that you want available to subshells. Besides being processed at login, the environment file is processed each time a new Korn shell is invoked. There is no default value for **ENV**, so if not specifically set, this feature is not enabled. A sample environment file is included in **Appendix B**.

Because the environment file must be opened and read each time a new Korn shell is invoked, performance can be adversely affected by having a large environment file with lots of functions.

Environment Variables

There are a number of variables provided by the Korn shell that allow you to customize your working environment. Some are automatically set by the Korn shell, some have a default value if not set, while others have no value unless specifically set.

Table 7.1 lists some of the Korn shell variables. The following sections cover some of the important variables and how they affect your working environment. All the available variables are listed in the **Appendix E**.

The cd Command

New functionality has been added to the **cd** command. You can change back to your previous directory with:

```
$ cd —
```

It also causes the name of the new current directory to be displayed. Here, we start in **/home/anatole/bin**, then change directory to **/usr/spool/news/lib**:

```
$  cd  /usr/spool/news/lib
```

Now we **cd** back to **/home/anatole/bin:**

```
$ cd —
/home/anatole/bin
```

Another **cd –**, and we are back in **/usr/spool/news/lib**:

```
$ cd —
/usr/spool/news/lib
```

You can also change directories by substituting parts of the current pathname with something else using this format:

```
cd   string1  string2
```

where *string1* in the current pathname is substituted with *string2*. The new current working directory is displayed after the move. In this example, we start in **/usr/spool/uucp**:

```
$  pwd
/usr/spool/uucp
```

By substituting **uucp** with **cron**, we change directory to **/usr/spool/cron**:

```
$ cd  uucp  cron
/usr/spool/cron
```

CDPATH

The **CDPATH** variable is provided to make directory navigation easier. It contains a list of colon-separated directories to check when a full pathname is not given to the **cd** command. Each directory in **CDPATH** is searched from left-to-right for a directory that matches the **cd** argument. A **:** alone in **CDPATH** stands for the current directory. This **CDPATH**:

```
$ print $CDPATH
:/home/anatole:/usr/spool
```

indicates to check the current directory first, **/home/anatole**, then **/usr/spool** when **cd** is not given a full pathname. Instead of typing **cd /usr/spool/uucp**, you could just type **cd uucp**:

```
$ cd uucp
/usr/spool/uucp
```

Or to change directory to **/home/anatole/bin**, you could type **cd bin**:

```
$ cd bin
/home/anatole/bin
```

There is no default for **CDPATH**, so if it not specifically set, this feature is not enabled.

Make sure that only frequently used directories are included, because if **CDPATH** is too large, performance can be adversely affected by having to check so many directories each time **cd** is invoked.

PATH

The **PATH** variable contains a list of colon-separated directories to check when a command is invoked. Each directory in **PATH** is searched from left-to-right for a file whose name matches the command name. If not found, an error message is displayed. A **:** alone in **PATH** specifies to check the current directory. This **PATH** setting specifies to check the **/bin** directory first, then **/usr/bin**,   **/usr/spool/news/bin**, and finally the current directory:

```
$ print $PATH
/bin:/usr/bin:/usr/spool/news/bin:
```

Don't let **PATH** get too large, because performance can be adversely affected by having to check so many directories each time a command is invoked.

If not set, the default value for **PATH** is **/bin:/usr/bin**.

TMOUT

The **TMOUT** variable specifies the number of seconds that the Korn shell will wait for input before displaying a 60-second warning message and exiting. If not set, the default used is **0**, which disables the timeout feature. To set a 10-minute timer, set **TMOUT** to **600**:

```
$ TMOUT=600
```

This variable is usually set by the system administrator in the **/etc/profile** file.

Mail

The Korn shell provides a number of variables that allow you to specify your mailbox file, how often to check for mail, what your mail notification message is, and a search path for mailbox files.

MAILCHECK

The **MAILCHECK** variable specifies how often, in seconds, to check for new mail. If not set, or set to zero, new mail is checked before each new prompt is displayed. Otherwise, the default setting is **600** seconds (10 minutes).

MAIL

The **MAIL** variable contains the name of a single mailbox file to check for new mail. It is not used if **MAILPATH** is set.

MAILPATH

The **MAILPATH** variable contains a colon-separated list of mailbox files to check for new mail and is used if you want to read multiple mailboxes. It overrides the **MAIL** variable if both are set. This **MAILPATH** setting specifies to check two mailbox files, **/home/anatole/mbox** and **/news/mbox**.

```
$ print $MAILPATH
MAILPATH=/home/anatole/mbox:/news/mbox
```

Just so you don't think you can go snooping around someone else's
mailbox, this only works if you have read permission on the mailbox
file.

If **MAILPATH** is not set, there is no default.

New Mail Notification Message

When you get new mail, the Korn shell displays this message on your
terminal right before the prompt:

```
you have mail in mailbox-file
```

You can also create your own mail notification message by appending
a **?** followed by your message to the mailbox files given in
MAILPATH. If you wanted your message to be "**New mail alert**",
then **MAILPATH** would be set like this:

```
$  MAILPATH=~anatole/mbox?'New  mail  alert'
```

What if you had two mailboxes set in **MAILPATH**? How would you
know which one to read? For this reason, the Korn shell has the _
(underscore) variable. When given in the new mail notification
message, it is substituted for the name of the mail box file. This
MAILPATH setting:

```
$  MAILPATH=~anatole/mbox?'Check  $_':\
/news/mbox?'Check  $_'
```

would cause "**Check /home/anatole/mbox**"or "**Check /news/mbox**"
to be displayed if new mail was received in either of the mailboxes.

TERM

The **TERM** variable specifies your terminal type, and is usually set by your system administrator in the global **/etc/profile** file. If it's not set there, then it's probably in your **~/.profile** file. You can tell if it's not set correctly by invoking **vi** on an existent file. If you get garbage on your screen or the **vi** commands are not working correctly, try resetting the **TERM** variable to something else:

```
$ typeset -x TERM=term-type
```

Then try running **vi** again and see what happens.

Korn Shell Options

The Korn shell has a number of options that specify your environment and control execution. There are options that cause background jobs to be run at a lower priority, prevent files from being overwritten with redirection operators, disable filename expansion, specify the **vi**-style in-line command editor, and more.

Table 7.2 lists some of the Korn shell options, along with the default values (these may differ on your system). All of the options are listed in **Appendix E**.

Enabling/Disabling Options

Korn shell options are enabled with the **set** −o*option* or **set** −*option* command. For example, the **noglob** option disables file name substitution and can be set using either of these commands :

Table 7.1: Some Korn Shell Environment Variables

CDPATH	search path for **cd** when not given a full pathname (no default)
COLUMNS	window width for in-line edit mode and **select** command lists (default **80**)
EDITOR	pathname of the editor for in-line editing (default **/bin/ed**)
ENV	pathname of the environment file (no default)
HISTFILE	pathname of the history file (default **$HOME/.sh_history**)
HISTSIZE	number of commands to save in the command history file (default **128**)
HOME	home directory
IFS	internal field separator (default space, tab, newline)
MAIL	name of mail file
MAILCHECK	specifies how often to check for mail (default **600** seconds)
MAILPATH	search path for mail files (no default)
PATH	search path for commands (default **/bin:/usr/bin:**)
PS1	primary prompt string (default **$, #**)
PS2	secondary prompt string (default **>**)
PS3	**select** command prompt (default **#?**)
PS4	debug prompt string (default **+**)
SHELL	pathname of the shell
TERM	specifies your terminal type (no default)
TMOUT	Korn shell timeout variable (default 0)
VISUAL	pathname of the editor for in-line editing

```
$ set -f
or
$ set -o noglob
```

Options can also be enabled by specifying them on the **ksh** command line. Here, a Korn subshell is started with the **emacs** option enabled:

```
$ ksh -o emacs
```

Options can be disabled with the **set +o** *option* or **set** *+option* command. In this example, the **noglob** option is disabled:

```
$ set +o noglob
```

The ignoreeof Option

If this option is enabled, you get this message when you try to log off using **Ctl-d**:

```
$ set -o ignoreeof
$ Ctl-d
Use 'exit' to terminate this shell
```

By default, this option is disabled.

The markdirs Option

When enabled, a trailing **/** is appended to directory names resulting from file name substitution. It's like the **ls -o** or **-F** options, except that you only see the results on file name substitution, not on directory listings. This means that **/** is added to directory names when you do this:

```
$ ls *
```

but not this:

```
$ ls
```

By default, the **markdirs** option is disabled.

The noclobber Option

The noclobber option prevents I/O redirection from truncating or *clobbering* existing files. Let's enable the option and give it a try:

```
$ set —o noclobber
$ ls>ls.out
$ ls>ls.out
/bin/ksh: ls.out: file already exists
```

If **noclobber** is enabled, and you really want to overwrite a file, use the >| operator:

```
$ ls>|ls.out
```

By default, this option is disabled.

The nounset Option

If the **nounset** option is disabled, then the Korn shell interprets unset variables as if their values were null.

```
$ unset X
$ print "X is set to: $X"
X is set to:
```

If enabled, the Korn shell displays an error message when it encounters unset variables and causes scripts to abort:

```
$ set -o nounset
$ unset X
$ print $X
/bin/ksh: X: parameter not set
```

Displaying the Current Settings

The setting of the current options is displayed with the **set -o** command. The first field is the option name, and the second field shows if the option is enabled or disabled:

```
$ set -o
allexport        off
bgnice           on
emacs            off
errexit          off
gmacs            off
ignoreeof        off
interactive      on
keyword          off
markdirs         off
monitor          on
noexec           off
noclobber        off
noglob           off
nolog            off
nounset          off
privileged       off
restricted       off
trackall         off
verbose          off
vi               on
viraw            on
xtrace           off
```

Table 7.2: Some Korn Shell Options

set −a, set −o allexport
  automatically export variables when defined
set −o bgnice
  execute all background jobs at a lower priority
set −o emacs, set −o gmacs
  use **emacs/gmacs** in-line editor
set −o ignoreeof
  do not exit on end of file; use **exit** (default **Ctl-d**)
set −o markdirs
  display trailing **/** on directory names resulting
  from file name substitution
set −m, set −o monitor
  enable job control (system dependent)
set −n, set −o noexec
  read commands without executing them
set −o noclobber
  prevent I/O redirection from truncating existing
  files
set −f, set −o noglob
  disable file name expansion
set −u, set −o nounset
  return error on substitution of unset variables
set −h, set −o trackall
  make commands tracked aliases when first
  encountered
set −o vi use **vi**-style editor for in-line editing
set −x, set −o xtrace
  display commands and arguments as they are
  executed

Command-line Options

Besides the options from the **set** command, the following options can
also be specified on the **ksh** command line:

–c *string*	read and execute the commands from *string*
–i	execute in interactive mode
–r	run a restricted shell
–s	read commands from standard input

These cannot be enabled with the **set** command.

Aliases

Aliases are command name macros used as shorthand for other
commands, especially frequently used ones. This saves a lot of
typing time. Aliases are defined with the **alias** *name=value*
command. For example, we could create an alias for the **print**
command like this:

```
$ alias  p=print
```

Whenever **p** is invoked, **print** is executed:

```
$ p Hello
Hello
```

Make sure to enclose the value in quotes if it contains whitespace.
Here we create an alias **l** that is set to the **ls –Fac** command:

```
$ alias  l="ls –Fac"
```

Now when you type in **l**, **ls –Fac** is executed:

```
$ l
./
../
compress.Z*
func.Z*
test/
uncompress.Z*
.  .  .
```

Alias values can contain any text, including special characters, like wild-cards, pipes, or I/O redirection operators. Let's change alias **l** so that the output is piped to the **more** command:

```
$ alias  l="ls  —Fac  |  more"
```

But what if you wanted to make this a global alias by setting it in the **/etc/profile** file, and some people wanted to use **more**, while others wanted to use **pg**? We could add the **PAGER** variable to the **l** alias, and let each user set **PAGER** to whatever they wanted.

```
$ alias  l="ls  —Fac  |  ${PAGER:-/bin/pg}"
```

Notice that if **PAGER** is not set, the default **/bin/pg** will be used. One last point. Using double quotes cause alias values to be expanded only when the alias is set. This means that if we reset **PAGER** after **l** is defined, it would have no effect on the alias. To have the alias value expanded each time it is invoked, use single quotes like this:

```
$ alias  l='ls  —Fac  |  ${PAGER:-/bin/pg}'
```

Now whenever **PAGER** is redefined, the next time alias **l** is invoked, it uses the new value.

If an alias value ends with a blank, then the next word following the alias is also checked if it an alias. Here we set two aliases: **p** and **h**. When invoked, we get **h** instead of **Hello**.

```
$ alias   p='print'   h=Hello
$ p h
h
```

After the **p** alias is reset with a trailing blank, **h** gets substituted in the next command correctly:

```
$ alias   p='print '   h=Hello
$ p h
Hello
```

Displaying Current Aliases

A list of the current aliases is displayed using the **alias** command without arguments:

```
$ alias
autoload=typeset  -fu
cd=_cd
echo=print  -
functions=typeset  -f
h=Hello
hash=alias  -t  -
history=fc  -l
integer=typeset  -i
l=ls  -Fac  |  more
ls=/usr/bin/ls
mv=/usr/bin/mv
nohup=nohup
p=print
r=fc  -e  -
rm=/usr/bin/rm
```

```
stop=kill -STOP
suspend=kill  -STOP  $$
type=whence -v
vi=SHELL=/bin/sh  vi
```

Exported aliases are displayed using the **alias –x** command.

Tracked Aliases

Tracked aliases are used to associate an alias with the full pathname of a program. When a tracked alias is invoked, instead of searching each directory in **PATH**, the full pathname of the corresponding command is returned from the alias table. This speeds execution by eliminating the path search.

Most implementations of the Korn shell come with a few default tracked aliases. These are usually set to frequently used commands. Tracked aliases and their values can be displayed with the **alias –t** command. Let's see what we've got:

```
$ alias -t
ls=/usr/bin/ls
mv=/usr/bin/mv
rm=/usr/bin/rm
vi=/usr/ucb/vi
```

On this version of the Korn shell, the **ls**, **mv**, **rm**, and **vi** commands are standard tracked aliases. On other implementations, they may be different.

Tracked aliases are basically the same as regular aliases, except that they are defined using the following format:

```
alias -t  name
```

Table 7.3: Preset Aliases

Alias	Value	Definition
autoload	typeset –fu	define an autoloading function
echo	print –	display arguments
functions	typeset –f	display list of functions
hash	alias –t –	display list of tracked aliases
history	fc –l	list commands from history file
integer	typeset –i	declare integer variable
r	fc –e –	re-execute previous command
stop	kill–STOP	suspend job
type	whence –v	display information about commands

Notice that a value is not given, as in normal **alias** –*name=value* syntax. This is because the Korn shell assigns a value automatically by doing a search on **PATH**. In the case of the tracked alias **ls**, the value is set to **/usr/bin/ls**, since **/usr/bin** is the first directory in **PATH** that contains **ls**.

We could set up a tracked alias for the **cp** command like this:

```
$ alias -t cp
```

If the **trackall** option is set (**set –h**, or **set –o trackall**), then the Korn shell attempts to generate tracked aliases for all commands that it encounters for the first time. By default, this option is usually disabled.

Tracked aliases become undefined if the **PATH** variable is unset. However, they continue to be tracked aliases. The next reference to the tracked alias causes the value to be reassigned.

Removing Aliases

Aliases are removed with the **unalias** command. Let's try it with the **l** alias:

```
$ unalias l
```

Now when invoked, it returns an error.

```
$ l
/bin/ksh: l:    not found
```

If you want to prevent an alias from being interpreted as one without having to delete it, just enclose it in single quotes. This is useful for when aliases are named after commands or functions. For example, on systems that alias **cd** to the **_cd** function, the real built-in **cd** command could be invoked like this:

```
$ 'cd'
```

Prompts

There are a number of prompt variables in the Korn shell: **PS1** and **PS2** are two of them. **PS1** contains your primary prompt string and is displayed by the Korn shell when it is ready to read a command. If not specified, the default is **$** for regular users, and **#** for superusers.

PS2 specifies the secondary prompt string and is displayed whenever the Korn shell needs more input. For example, when you enter <RETURN> before a complete command has been given, or continue a command onto the next line with the \ character, the **PS2** variable is displayed. If not specified, the default for **PS2** is the > character.

```
$ print "Here is
> another line"
Here is another line
```

Customizing Your Command Prompt

By default, the command prompt is set to the **$** character. But you could set it to something else by simply reassigning a value to the **PS1** variable. For example, you could have the prompt give you a greeting message like this:

```
$ typeset -x PS1="Good morning  "
```

As soon as you press the <RETURN> key, the prompt is reset.

```
Good morning: pwd
/home/anatole
Good morning:
```

The current command number can be displayed by putting a **!** in the prompt variable **PS1** like this:

```
$ typeset -x PS1="!:Good morning:"
154: Good morning:
```

If you really want to display a **!** in the prompt, use **!!**:

```
$ typeset -x PS1="Hello there!!"
Hello there!
```

Now let's make a fancy prompt that will display the command number and the current working directory. Besides ! for the command number, we'll need the **PWD** variable for the current working directory.

```
$ typeset -x PS1="!:$PWD> "
```

Just to make sure it works, let's change directories:

```
167:/home/anatole>  cd  /tmp
168:/tmp>  cd  /usr/spool/news/comp/sources
169:/usr/spool/news/comp/sources>
```

Don't go overboard with this. If you are using the in-line editor, remember that the prompt size affects the edit window width.

Subshells

Subshells are generated whenever you enclose commands in ()'s, perform command substitution, for background processes, and for co-processes (discussed later in **Chapter 8**). A subshell is a separate copy of the parent shell, so variables, functions, and aliases from the parent shell are available to the subshell. However, subshells cannot change the value of parent shell variables, functions, or aliases. So if we set **LOCALVAR** to a value in the current shell:

```
$ LOCALVAR="This is the original value"
```

then check the value in a subshell, we see that it is defined:

```
$ ( print $LOCALVAR )
This is the original value
```

If we set it in the subshell to another value:

```
$ ( LOCALVAR="This is the new value" )
```

then check the value in the parent shell, we see that **LOCALVAR** is
still set to the original value:

```
$ print $LOCALVAR
This is the original value
```

By default, things like variables, aliases, and functions from the
current environment are not available to separate invocations of the
Korn shell unless explicitly exported or exported in the environment
file. For example, variables are exported with the **typeset −x**
command. Let's look at **LOCALVAR** again. It wasn't exported, so if
we start a new Korn shell, **LOCALVAR** is not defined:

```
$ ksh
$ print $LOCALVAR

$ exit
```

Once exported, it is available to the new Korn shell:

```
$ typeset −x LOCALVAR
$ ksh
$ print $LOCALVAR
This is the original value
```

As with subshells, environment settings are not passed back to the
parent Korn shell. If **LOCALVAR** is set to another value in the
separate Korn shell:

```
$ LOCALVAR="This is the new value"
```

then we exit back to the parent shell, we see that **LOCALVAR** is still set to the original value:

```
$ exit
$ print $LOCALVAR
This is the original value
```

If the **allexport** option is enabled (**set –a**, or **set –o allexport**), variables are automatically exported when defined. By default, this option is disabled.

Aliases can also be exported to separate Korn shells with the **alias –x** command. If we wanted to use the **l** alias in a separate Korn shell, it would have to be exported like this:

```
$ alias –x l
```

Restricted Shell

This is a version of the shell that allows restricted access to UNIX. Running under **rsh** is equivalent to **ksh**, except that the following is not allowed:

- changing directories
- setting the value of **ENV**, **PATH**, or **SHELL** variables
- specifying path or command names containing **/**
- redirecting output of a command with >, >|, <>, or >>

These restrictions apply only after the **.profile** and environment files have been processed.

Privileged Mode

Privileged mode allows execution of the environment and **.profile** files to be controlled. When enabled, the **~/.profile** and environment files are not executed. Instead, **/etc/suid_profile** is read and executed.

The **/etc/suid_profile** file can be configured by the system administrator to control execution of setuid Korn shell scripts, track **su** invocations, set a default readonly **PATH**, log commands, and more.

By default, privileged mode is disable, but is enabled whenever the real and effective user or group ids are not the same.

Besides providing a working environment and executing commands, the Korn shell is also a high-level programming language that can be used to write programs. In Korn shell terminology, these programs are called *scripts*. Korn shell scripts can contain anything that you enter at the command prompt: regular UNIX commands, Korn shell commands, your own programs and scripts, or even commands from other UNIX shells! Unlike many high-level programming languages, Korn shell scripts are interpreted, so they do not have to be compiled. This makes the Korn shell ideal for prototyping.

Executing Korn Shell Scripts

Let's make a Korn shell script out of the **print Hello world** command by putting it into a file like this:

```
$ print "print Hello world" > prhello
```

Before Korn shell scripts can be executed, they must be made executable by setting the execute and read bits with the **chmod** command:

```
$ chmod 755 prhello
or
$ chmod +rx prhello
```

Assuming that the current directory is in the search path **$PATH**, **prhello** can now be executed by simply invoking it by name:

```
$ prhello
Hello world
```

Korn shell scripts can also be executed by invoking them as the first argument to **ksh**:

```
$ ksh prhello
Hello world
```

Now we can use **prhello** like any other command. The output can be directed to a file:

```
$ prhello  >p.out
$ cat p.out
Hello world
```

It can be used with a pipe:

```
$ prhello | wc
1       2      12
```

or with command substitution:

```
$ print "We always say \"$(prhello)\""
We always say "Hello world"
```

By default, Korn shell scripts are run in a separate environment. This means that variables from the current environment are not available to Korn shell scripts unless explicitly exported, and variables defined in Korn shell scripts are not passed back to the parent shell. Just to prove it, here is a demonstration. The **checkvar** Korn shell script does just one thing: it prints the value of **LOCALVAR**.

```
$ cat checkvar
print "LOCALVAR is set to: $LOCALVAR"
```

If **LOCALVAR** is set to something in the current environment, and **checkvar** is run, we see that **LOCALVAR** is not defined:

```
$ LOCALVAR="This is the original value"
$ checkvar
LOCALVAR is set to:
```

If we export **LOCALVAR**, then its' value will be available to **checkvar**:

```
$ typeset -x LOCALVAR
$ checkvar
LOCALVAR is set to: This is the original value
```

To show that Korn shell script environments cannot modify variable values in the parent shell, we'll change **checkvar** to reassign a value to **LOCALVAR**.

```
$ cat checkvar
print "LOCALVAR is set to: $LOCALVAR"
LOCALVAR="This is a new value"
print "The new LOCALVAR is set to: $LOCALVAR"
```

Now when it is run, **LOCALVAR** is set to the new value:

```
$ checkvar
LOCALVAR is set to: This is the original value
The new LOCALVAR is set to:This is a new value
```

Meanwhile, back in the parent shell, **LOCALVAR** has not been affected.

```
$ print $LOCALVAR
This is the original value
```

If the **allexport** option is enabled (**set –a**, or **set –o allexport**), variables are automatically exported when defined. By default, this option is disabled.

Positional Parameters

Positional parameters are special variables used to keep track of arguments to the Korn shell, scripts, and functions. Positional parameter names contain only digits and cannot be set directly using *variable=value* syntax. By default, parameter zero (or **$0**) is set to the name of the shell, script or function.

```
$ print $0
/bin/ksh
```

The remaining parameters **1** to *n* are set to each of the arguments passed to the shell, script or function. For example, if you invoke a Korn shell script called **ptest** and pass the arguments **A**, **B**, and **C**, then in the script **ptest**, **$0** would be set to **ptest**, **$1** to **A**, **$2** to **B**, and **$3** to **C**.

```
$ ptest A B C
```

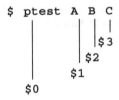

There are three special Korn shell variables that provide information about the current positional parameters. The first is **$#**, and it contains the number of positional parameters. The other two are **$@** and **$***, and they both contain all the positional parameters. So in the above **ptest** example, **$#** would be **3**, and both **$*** and **$@** would be **A B C**. Here is a Korn shell script that manipulates positional parameters. It displays the name of the current script, the number of positional parameters, and the value of each of the positional parameters:

```
$ cat check_params
print "Script name:        $0"
print "Number of args passed: $#"
print "Arguments passed:   $*"
print "Arg 1=$1, Arg 2=$2, Arg 3=$3"
```

If executed with no arguments, this is the output:

```
$ check_params
Script name:            check_params
Number of args passed: 0
Arguments passed:
Arg 1=, Arg 2=, Arg 3=
```

while if executed with the arguments **A** and **B**:

```
$ check_params A B
Script name:            check_params
Number of args passed: 2
Arguments passed:    A B
Arg 1=A, Arg 2=B, Arg 3=
```

Modifying Positional Parameters

By default, **$0** is set to the name of the shell, script or function. It cannot be set or modified. The remaining parameters from **$1** to **$**n can be reassigned with the **shift** command.

The **shift** command, with no arguments, shifts positional parameters left once, so that **$1** takes the value of **$2**, **$2** takes the value of **$3**, and so on. The original value of **$1** is lost.

Let's change the **check_params** script so that it shifts the positional parameters left once:

```
$  cat  check_params
print  "Script  name:                    $0"
print  "Number  of  args  passed: $#"
print  "Arguments  passed:        $*"
print "Arg  1=$1,  Arg  2=$2,  Arg  3=$3"
shift
print  "Number  of  remaining  args  $#"
print  "Remaining  args:          $*"
print  "Arg  1=$1,  Arg  2=$2,  Arg  3=$3"
```

When we run it again with the arguments **A B**:

```
$  check_params  A  B
Script  name:                    check_params
Number  of  args  passed:   2
Arguments  passed:          A  B
Arg  1=A,  Arg  2=B,  Arg  3=
Number  of  remaining  args  1
Remaining  args:              B
Arg  1=B,  Arg  2=,  Arg  3=
```

After the **shift** command, **$1** is set to **B** and **$2** is unset. The original value of **$1** is lost.

The positional parameters can be shifted left more than once by providing an integer argument to the **shift** command: **shift** *n*.

Now let's try something else with positional parameters. Here is a Korn shell script called **kftp**. It uses **ftp** to copy a file to the public directory on **aspsun**.

```
$ cat kftp
ftp <<- END
open aspsun
user anonymous
cd pub
put $1
quit
END
```

To transfer a file to aspsun, we can invoke **kftp** like this:

```
$ kftp n.out
```

and in the script, **$1** gets substituted with **n.out** in the **put** file arguments. We could extend this further to be able to **ftp** files to any system by having a system name given as another command-line argument. Now **$1** is used for the file, and **$2** for the remote system name.

```
$ cat kftp
ftp <<- END
open $2
user anonymous
cd pub
put $1
quit
END
```

To send the file **msg.c** to the public directory on the **unisf** system, **kftp** would be invoked like this:

```
$ kftp msg.c unisf
```

$1 would be substituted with the **msg.c**, and **$2** with **unisf**.

The exit command

In Chapter 2, we learned that UNIX programs return an exit status. And that a zero exit status indicates successful execution, while a non-zero exit status indicates failure. The **exit** command allows you to terminate execution from anywhere in a Korn shell script and return an exit value using this format:

> **exit**
> or
> **exit** *n*

where *n* is the exit status to return. If *n* is not specified, the exit status of the previous command is used. If you don't use **exit**, then scripts finish after the last command is executed.

Take a look at the **kuucp** script:

```
$ cat kuucp
PUBDIR=${PUBDIR:-/usr/spool/uucppublic}
uucp $1 $2!$PUBDIR/$1
print "Copied $1 to $2!$PUBDIR/$1"
```

What happens if an error occurs? For example, if the file argument is entered incorrectly, or it doesn't exist? The **uucp** command will fail, but the status message following will still get displayed. Here is a good place for **exit**. It could be used to terminate execution and return a non-zero exit status if for some reason the **uucp** command failed. To get the exit status, **$?** is checked after **uucp** is run. If it is non-zero, then we display our own error message and exit. Otherwise, the next command is executed and the script terminates successfully.

```
$ cat kuucp
PUBDIR=${PUBDIR:-/usr/spool/uucpublic}
uucp $1 $2!$PUBDIR/$1 2>&-
(($? != 0)) && { print "Got uucp error"; exit 1; }
print "Copied $1 to $2!$PUBDIR/$1"
```

By the way, the **2>&–** just traps the **uucp** error messages. We don't need to see them anymore, since **kuucp** is now doing its own error processing. Now when **kuucp** is run on a non-existent file, this is what happens:

```
$ kuucp nofile unisf
Got uucp error
$ print $?
1
```

The **exit** command does one more thing. If given at the command prompt, it terminates your login shell.

The [[...]] Command

The **[[...]]** command is used to evaluate conditional expressions with file attributes, strings, integers, and more. The basic format is:

[[*expression*]]

where *expression* is the condition you are evaluating. There must be whitespace after the opening brackets, and before the closing brackets. Whitespace must also separate the expression arguments and operators. If the expression evaluates to true, then a zero exit status is returned, otherwise the expression evaluates to false and a non-zero exit status is returned.

If you are familiar with the **test** and [...] commands, then you'll recognize that [[...]] is just a new and improved version of the same commands. It basically functions the same way, except that a number of new operators are available.

Checking Strings

We could use the [[...]] command to check if a variable is set to a certain value. Here, variable **X** is assigned **abc**, then evaluated in this expression:

```
$ X=abc
$ [[ $X = abc ]] && print "X is set to abc"
X is set to abc
```

Using the **test** and [...] commands, the same command could be written as:

```
test "$X" = abc && print "X is set to abc"
or
[ "$X" = abc ] && print "X is set to abc"
```

To check if a variable is set to null, the **-z** option can be used:

```
[[ -z $VAR ]] && print "VAR is set to null"
```

or it could be compared to the null string like this:

```
[[ $VAR = "" ]] && "VAR is set to null"
```

Checking Patterns

The Korn shell also lets you compare strings to patterns. We could check if **X** begins with a 'a' like this:

```
$ X=abc
$ [[ $X = a* ]] && print "$X matches a*"
abc matches a*
```

or if it's a three-character string:

```
$ [[ $X = ??? ]] && print "$X has exactly 3 \
characters"
abc has exactly 3 characters
```

Using the **+([0–9])** pattern, we could check if **X** is set to a number:

```
$ X=123
$ [[ $X = +([0–9]) ]] && print "$X is a \
number"
123 is a number
```

Table 8.1 lists the most commonly used **[[...]]** string operators.

Checking File Attributes

Because manipulating files is so important in programming, the Korn shell provides a whole range of file operators. The most basic operation to perform on a file is to see if it exists, and that can be done using the **–a** operator. This is a new Korn shell file operator. Make sure you don't get it confused with the logical AND operator used by the **test** and **[...]** commands, which is also written as **–a**.

```
$ touch tmp
$ [[ –a tmp ]] && print "File tmp exists"
File tmp exists
```

Table 8.1: [[...]] String Operators

−n *string*	true if length of *string* is not zero
−o *option*	true if *option* is set
−z *string*	true if length of *string* is zero
string1 = *string2*	
	true if *string1* is equal to *string2*
string1 != *string2*	
	true if *string1* is not equal to *string2*
string = *pattern*	
	true if *string* matches *pattern*
string != *pattern*	
	true if *string* does not match *pattern*
string1 < *string2*	
	true if *string1* less than *string2*
string1 > *string2*	
	true if *string1* greater than *string2*

This only indicates that it exists, but not much else. It may be a directory, or a symbolic link, but using this operator, that's all we know. If we wanted more information, the **−f** or **−d** operators could tell us if a file existed *and* was a regular file (**−f**) or if it was just a directory (**−d**). Let's try the **−f** operator on the **tmp** file:

```
$ [[ -f tmp ]] && print "File tmp exists and \
is a regular file"
File tmp exists and is a regular file
```

If we tried the **−d** operator on the **tmp** file, it would evaluate to false, because it isn't a directory:

```
$ [[ -d tmp ]] && print "File tmp exists and \
is a regular file"
$
```

While on a directory it would evaluate to true:

```
$ mkdir tmpdir
$ [[ -d tmpdir ]] && print "Directory tmp \
exists"
Directory tmp exists
```

This conditional command checks if **$FILE** is readable, and if not, prints an error message and exits:

```
[[ -r $FILE ]]||{ print $FILE not readable; \
exit 1; }
```

while this one checks if **$FILE** is writable:

```
[[ -w $FILE ]]||{ print $FILE not writable; \
exit 1; }
```

Here are a couple of new file operators: **−nt** and **−ot**. They compare two files and return true if *file1* is newer than (**−nt**) or older than (**−ot**) *file2*.

```
$ touch tfile2
$ touch tfile1
$ [[ tfile1 -nt tfile2 ]]&&print "tfile1 is \
newer than tfile2"
tfile1 is newer than tfile2
```

Table 8.2: Some [[...]] File Operators

-a *file*   true if *file* exists
-d *file*   true if *file* exists and is a directory
-f *file*   true if *file* exists and is a regular file
-G *file*   true if *file* exists and its group id matches the effective group id of the current process
-L *file*   true if *file* exists and is a symbolic link
-O*file*   true if *file* exists and its user id matches the effective user id of the current process
-r *file*   true if *file* exists and is readable
-s *file*   true if *file* exists and its size is greater than zero
-S *file*   true if *file* exists and is a socket
-u *file*   true if *file* exists and its set user-id bit is set
-w *file*   true if *file* exists and is writable
-x *file*   true if *file* exists and is executable. If *file* is a directory, then true indicates that the directory is searchable.
file1 **-ef** *file2*
     true if *file1* exists and is another name for *file2*
file1 **-nt** *file2*
     true if *file1* exists and is newer than *file2*
file1 **-ot** *file2*
     true if *file1* exists and is older than *file2*

Let's switch the files in the expression and try the **–ot** operator:

```
$ [[ tfile2 —ot tfile1 ]]&&print "tfile2 is \
older than tfile1"
tfile2 is older than tfile1
```

Table 8.2 lists the most commonly used [[...]] file operators.

Checking Integer Attributes

The [[...]] command provides a few integer operators that allow integers to be compared. It is frequently used to check the number of command-line arguments. This expression evaluates to true if there are less than or equal to three positional parameters set:

```
[[ $# —le 3 ]] && print "3 or less args given"
```

The last expression is equivalent to checking if there are less than four positional parameters set:

```
[[ $# —lt 4 ]] && print "Less than 4 args given"
```

The number of users logged on could be checked like this:

```
$ [[ $(who | wc —l) —gt 10 ]] && print "More \
than 10 users are logged on"
More than 10 users are logged on
```

In many cases, the [[...]] integer operators may be sufficient for evaluating expressions that contain integers. To perform other arithmetic operations, use the ((...)) command (discussed in **Chapter 6**). It offers the same arithmetic comparison operators as the [[...]] command, plus many others. Besides offering more arithmetic operators, the ((...)) command provides substantial performance improvements over the [[...]] and **test** commands. The last command

---

Table 8.3: [[...]] Integer Operators

exp1 **–eq** *exp2*
> true if *exp1* is equal to *exp2*

exp1 **–ne** *exp2*
> true if *exp1* is not equal to *exp2*

exp1 **–le** *exp2*
> true if *exp1* is less than or equal to *exp2*

exp1 **–lt** *exp2*
> true if *exp1* is less than *exp2*

exp1 **–ge** exp2
> true if *exp1* is greater than or equal to *exp2*

exp1 **–gt** *exp2*
> true if *exp1* is greater than *exp2*

---

could also be given as:

```
(($(who | wc -l) > 10)) && print "More than \
10  users  are  logged  on"
```

Using an arithmetic expression, the number of command-line arguments can be checked like this:

```
(($# < 4)) && print "Less than 4 args"
```

Table 8.3 lists the most commonly used [[...]] integer operators.

The ! Operator

The ! operator negates the result of any [[...]] expression when used like this:

```
[[ !  expression  ]]
```

For example, to check if **X** is *not* equal to **abc**:

```
$  X=xyz
$  [[ ! $X = abc ]] && print "$X not equals abc"
xyz not equals abc
```

or if a file doesn't exist:

```
$  rm tmp
$  [[ ! -f tmp ]] && print "tmp does NOT exist"
tmp does NOT exist
```

There is one logical operator that can only be implemented with the ! operator. There is no [[...]] file operator that will evaluate to true on a zero-length file.

```
$  >emptyfile
$  [[ ! -s emptyfile ]] && print "emptyfile \
is empty"
emptyfile is empty
```

Compound Expressions

Expressions can also be combined with the **&&** and ǀǀ operators to form compound expressions.

&& - The AND Operator

The **&&** operator is used with the **[[...]]** command to test if multiple expressions are true using this format:

[[*expression1* && *expression2*]]

We could check if two variables were set to specific values like this:

```
$ X=abc Y=def
$ [[ $X = abc && $Y = def ]] && print "X=abc \
and  Y=def"
X=abc  and  Y=def
```

This expression checks if the **noglob** and **noclobber** options are set:

```
[[ -o noglob && -o noclobber ]]
```

Multiple **&&** operators can also be given in one [[...]] command. We could check if three options were set like this:

```
[[ -o noglob && -o noclobber && -o bgnice ]]
```

In some versions of the Korn shell, multiple **&&** operators cannot be given in one [[...]] command unless grouped with parentheses.

|| - The OR Operator

The || operator is used with the **[[...]]** command to test if *expression1* OR *expression2* are true using this format:

[[*expression1* || *expression2*]]

Table 8.4: Other [[...]] Operators

[[*expression1* **&&** *expression2*]]
      true if both *expression1* and *expression2* are true
[[*expression1* || *expression2*]]
      true either *expression1* or *expression2* are true
[[(*expression*)]]
      true if *expression* evaluates to true. The ()'s are
      used to override the precedence rules.
[[!*expression*]]
      true if *expression* evaluates to false

This expression checks if **$FILE** was readable or executable:

```
[[ -r $FILE || -w $FILE ]]
```

while this one checks is either variables were set to your name:

```
[[ $USER=$(whoami) || $LOGNAME=$(whoami) ]]
```

Multiple || operators can also be given in one [[...]] command. We could check if **$FILE** was readable, writable, or executable like this:

```
[[ -r $FILE || -w $FILE || -x $FILE ]]
```

Like with the **&&** operator, in some versions of the Korn shell, multiple || operators cannot be given in one [[...]] command unless grouped with parentheses.

[[...]] vs test and [...]

The **[[...]]** command is preferred to **test** and **[...]**, since many of the errors associated with **test** and **[...]** do not occur. For example, when comparing two variables where one is set to null or unset, the **test** and **[...]** commands return a syntax error if the variable is not surrounded in double quotes. Here, **X** is unset, while **Y** is set to **1**:

```
$ unset X
$ Y=1
```

Without double quotes around the variable names, the **test** and **[...]** commands return a syntax error:

```
$ test $X = $Y && print "X and Y are equal"
/bin/ksh: test: argument expected
or
$ [ $X = $Y ] && print "X and Y are equal"
/bin/ksh: test: argument expected
```

while the **[[...]]** command does not (unless the **nounset** option is enabled):

```
$ [[ $X = $Y ]] && print "X and Y are equal"
```

Checking File Descriptors

On systems that support the **/dev/fd** directory for naming open files, the *files* argument in expressions can be given as **/dev/fd/**n so that the test is applied to the open file associated with file descriptor n. This command checks to see if standard input (file descriptor 0) is readable:

```
$ [[ -r /dev/fd/0 ]] && print "Stdin is \
readable"
Stdin is readable
```

Control Commands

The Korn shell provides a number of control-flow commands typically found in high-level programming languages. The following sections cover these special commands.

The case Command

The **case** command provides multiple-branch capability. It is used to compare a single value against a number of other values. Commands associated with that value are executed when a match is made. The syntax for the **case** command is:

> **case** *value* **in**
>   *pattern1*)   *command*
>   *command* ;;
>   *pattern2*)   *command*
>   *command* ;;
>
>   . . .
>
>   *patternn*)   *command*
>   *command* ;;
> **esac**

where *value* is compared to *pattern1*, *pattern2*, ... *patternn*. When a match is found, the commands associated with that pattern up to the double semi-colons are executed.

The following Korn shell script demonstrates a simple **case** statement.
It successively compares the command-line argument given to **–a**, **–b**,
or **–c** and then prints out which flag was given. First, it checks to make
sure that at least one command-line argument is given:

```
$ cat checkargs
(($#<1)) && {print Not enough args; exit 1; }

case $1 in
    -a )print - "-a flag given" ;;
    -b )print - "-b flag given" ;;
    -c )print - "-c flag given" ;;
esac
$ checkargs -b
-b flag given
$ checkargs -a
-a flag given
```

The **–d** argument is given in the next invocation. It doesn't match any
of the patterns, so nothing is printed:

```
$ checkargs -d
$
```

Specifying Patterns with case

The same patterns used in file name substitution can also be used in
case statements to match patterns. For example, the * pattern is
frequently used to specify a default pattern. It will always match if no
other match is made. Another pattern, **@([1–9])*([0–9])**, will match
any number **1–9999999***. Let's expand the **checkargs** script to
match on any type of argument using some special pattern-matching
characters.

```
$ cat checkargs
case $1 in
    -@([a-z])  )
        print "Lowercase argument given: $1" ;;
    -@([A-Z])  )
        print  "Uppercase  argument  given:  $1"  ;;
    @([1-9])*([0-9])  )
        print "Integer argument given: $1" ;;
    "" )    print "No  argument  given" ;;
    *  ) print "Invalid  argument  given"  ;;
esac
```

Here is sample output:

```
$  checkargs  -a
Lowercase  argument  given:  -a
$  checkargs  99
Integer  argument  given:  99
$  checkargs  -C
Uppercase  argument  given:  -C
$  checkargs  0
Invalid  argument  given
$  checkargs
No  argument  given
```

Notice that the $-@(a-z)$ and $-@(A-Z)$ patterns cause a – followed by only one character to be matched. An argument like **–axyz** would cause the invalid argument message to be printed:

```
$  checkargs  -axyz
Invalid  argument  given!
```

The **–+([A–z]) case** pattern would allow for multiple characters to follow the – character. Multiple **case** patterns can be given, as long as they are separated with a I character. For example, the pattern

```
-a | -b | -c
```

would match **-a**, **-b**, or **-c**. The new Korn shell pattern matching
formats also allow multiple **case** patterns to be given like this:

> ```
> ?(pattern1 | pattern2 | ... | patternn)
> ```
> matches zero or one occurrence of any pattern

> ```
> *(pattern1 | pattern2 | ... | patternn)
> ```
> matches zero or more occurrences of any pattern

> ```
> @(pattern1 | pattern2 | ... | patternn)
> ```
> matches exactly one occurrence of any pattern

> ```
> +(pattern1 | pattern2 | ... | patternn)
> ```
> matches one or more occurrence of any pattern

> ```
> !(pattern1 | pattern2 | ... | patternn)
> ```
> matches all strings except those that match any pattern

The for Command

The **for** command is used to execute commands a specified number
of times. In programming terminology, this iterative execution of
commands is called a *loop*, so you may also hear the **for** command
referred to as a **for** loop. The basic syntax for the **for** command is:

> **for** *variable* **in** *word1 word2 . . . wordn*
> **do**
> > *commands*
>
> **done**

The *commands* are executed once for each *word*, and for each
execution, *variable* is set to *word*. So if there were three words, the

commands would be executed three times, with *variable* set to *word1* in the first execution, *word2* in the second execution, and *word3* in the third and last execution. Here is a simple **for** loop:

```
$ cat floop
integer LOOPNUM=1
for X in A B C
do
    print "Loop $LOOPNUM: X=$X"
    ((LOOPNUM+=1))
done
```

When executed, it prints out the loop number and the value of **X** for each loop.

```
$ floop
Loop 1:  X=A
Loop 2:  X=B
Loop 3:  X=C
```

Remember the **kftp** script that we wrote earlier in this chapter? We could use it with a **for** loop to **ftp** multiple files to a remote system like this:

```
$ for FILE in chap1 chap2 chap3
> do
>   print "Copying $FILE to ukas"
>   kftp $FILE ukas
> done
Copying chap1 to ukas
Copying chap2 to ukas
Copying chap3 to ukas
```

Notice that this **for** loop was run from the prompt, and not from a script. Korn shell control commands are like any other commands, and can be entered at the command prompt. This is useful when you want to run something quickly without having to edit a file.

File name substitution, command substitution, and variable substitution can also be used to generate a list of word arguments for the **for** command. The first line of the previous command could have been given as:

```
for FILE in chap[1-3]
or
for FILE in $(ls chap[1-3])
or
CHAPS=$(ls  chap[1-3])
for FILE in $CHAPS
```

The **$*** and **$@** variables can be used to loop on command-line arguments like this:

for *variable* **in $***
do
    commands
done

This is the same as:

for *variable* **in $1 $2 $3 . . .**
do
    commands
done

This idea could be used to make a Korn shell script that **ftp**'s a variable number of files to **ukas**:

```
$ cat myftp
for FILE in $*
do
    print "Copying $FILE to  ukas"
    kftp $FILE ukas
done
```

Now to **ftp** just one file to **ukas**:

```
$ myftp chap1
Copying chap1 to ukas
```

or all the **chap** files to **ukas**:

```
$ myftp chap*
Copying chap1 to ukas
Copying chap2 to ukas
Copying chap3 to ukas
...
```

With no argument, nothing is displayed:

```
$ myftp
$
```

Other for Syntax

The **for** command can also be used without the list of word arguments:

> **for** *variable*
> **do**
>   *commands*
> done

The *commands* are executed once for each positional parameter, and *variable* is set to each successive positional parameter. It is equivalent to:

> **for** *variable* **in** "$@"
> **do**
>   *commands*
> **done**

The **myftp** script could be modified to use this format and still do the same thing.

```
$ cat myftp
for FILE
do
    print "Copying $FILE to ukas"
    kftp $FILE ukas
done
```

Use this format to enter the **for** command on one line:

> **for** *var* **in** *word1 word2 . . . wordn* **; do** *commands* **; done**
> or
> **for** *var* **; do** *commands* **; done**

Notice the **;** character before the **do** and **done** commands. This is needed so that the **do** and **done** commands are separated from the previous commands.

The if Command

The **if** command is used to execute commands if a given condition is true. The basic syntax of the **if** command is:

> **if** *command1*
> **then**
> > *commands*
>
> **fi**

If *command1* returns a zero exit status, then the commands between **then** and **fi** are executed. Otherwise, the commands are skipped. For example, if **ANSWER** is set to **YES**, then the **print** command is executed.

```
if [[ $ANSWER = YES ]]
then
    print "Ok, the answer is $ANSWER"
fi
```

Here is a Korn shell script that uses the **if** command to check if a file exists, before trying to copy it.

```
$ cat fileck
FILE=$1

if [[ -f $FILE ]]
then
    print "Copying $FILE to PUBDIR"
    cp $FILE /local/pub
fi
```

We could add another **if** command to check the number of arguments. If there is less than one command-line argument, a usage message is printed and the script exits.

```
$ cat fileck
if (($# < 1))
then
    print "Usage: $0 file"
    exit 1
fi
FILE=$1
if [[ -f $FILE ]]
then
    print "Copying $FILE to PUBDIR"
    cp $FILE /local/pub
fi
```

The command-line argument check in **fileck** could have been written using the **&&** operator like this:

```
(($# < 1)) && {print "Usage:$0 file"; exit 1;}
```

This version is more compact, albeit less readable than the previous one using the **if** command.

Use this format if you want to give an **if** command on one line:

if *command1* **; then** *command2* **; fi**

The **;** characters are needed to separate **then** and **fi** from the previous commands.

Other if Syntax: else

This form of the **if** command is used to execute one set of commands if a condition is true, or another set of commands if the condition is not true.

> **if** *command1*
> **then**
>   *commands*
> **else**
>   *commands*
> **fi**

If *command1* returns a zero exit status, then the commands between **then** and **else** are executed. If *command1* returns a non-zero exit status, then commands between **else** and **fi** are executed. In this example, if **ANSWER** is **YES**, then the **print** command is executed.

Otherwise, it exits:

```
if [[ $ANSWER = YES ]]
then
    print "Ok, the answer is $ANSWER"
else
    exit 1
fi
```

We could add the **else** part to the **if** command in **fileck** to make sure the file existed before it was copied:

```
$ cat fileck
if (($# < 1))
then
    print "Usage: $0 file"
    exit 1
fi
FILE=$1

if [[ -f $FILE ]]
then
    print "Copying $FILE to PUBDIR"
    cp $FILE /local/pub
else
    print "$FILE non-existent"
    exit 2
fi
```

Here is some sample output:

```
$ fileck
Usage: fileck file
$ fileck nofile
nofile non-existent
$ fileck log.out
Copying log.out to PUBDIR
```

Notice that **exit 1** was used for a usage error, while **exit 2** was used for the non-existent file error. In Korn shell scripts, especially large ones, it's a good idea to use different exit codes for different types of error conditions. It can be helpful in debugging.

```
$ fileck; print $?
Usage: fileck file
1
$ fileck nofile; print $?
nofile  non-existent
2
$ fileck log.out; print $?
Copying log.out to PUBDIR
0
```

Other if Syntax: elif

This form of the **if** command is used to execute one set of commands if one condition is true, another set of commands if another condition is true, and so on, or else execute a set of commands if none of the conditions are true. The syntax for this **if** command is:

> **if** *command1*
> **then**
> > *commands*
>
> **elif** *command2*
> **then**
> > *commands*
>
> . . .
> **elif** *commandn*
> **then**
> > *commands*
>
> **else**
> > *commands*
>
> **fi**

If *command1* returns a zero exit status, or *command2* returns a zero exit status, or *commandn* returns a zero exit status, then execute the commands corresponding to the **if/elif** that returned a zero exit status. Otherwise, if all the **if/elif** commands return a non-zero exit status, execute the commands between **else** and **fi**. This **if** format is much easier to explain with an example. The following Korn shell script checks how many users are logged on, and prints the appropriate message:

```
$ cat whonu
USERS=$(who | wc -1)
if ((USERS == 1))
then
    print "There is 1 user logged on."
elif ((USERS == 2))
then
    print "There are 2 users logged on."
elif ((USERS == 3))
then
    print "There are 3 users logged on."
else
    print "More than 4 users are logged on."
fi
```

If **USERS** equals **1**, **2**, or **3**, then the corresponding **if/elif..then** clause is executed:

```
$ whonu
There are 3 users logged on.
```

Otherwise, the **else** clause is executed:

```
$ whonu
More than 4 users are logged on.
```

if/elif vs case

When there are more than a few conditions to check, the **case** statement should be considered instead of **if/elif**. Not only is it more readable, but less code is actually needed. The **whonu** script could be written using a **case** statement like this:

```
USERS=$(who | wc -1)
case $USERS in
    1 ) print "There is 1 user logged on" ;;
    2 ) print "There are 2 users logged on" ;;
    3 ) print "There are 3 users logged on" ;;
    * ) print "There are 4 or more users \
        logged on" ;;
esac
```

The **whonu** script had thirteen lines of code using **if/elif/else**, and only seven lines of code using a **case** statement.

The while Command

Here is another type of looping command. The syntax for the **while** command is:

> **while** *command1*
> **do**
> > *commands*
>
> **done**

where *command1* is executed, and if the exit status is zero, the *commands* between **do** and **done** are executed. *Command1* is executed again, and if the exit status is zero, the *commands* between **do** and **done** are also executed again. This continues until *command1* returns a non-zero exit status. The **listargs** script loops on the command-line arguments. For each loop, the positional parameter **$1** is displayed, then the positional parameters are shifted. This continues until the number of positional parameters is **0**.

```
$ cat listargs
while (($# != 0))
do
      print $1
      shift
done
```

In the first loop, $# equals **4**, so the value of **$1** is printed and the positional parameters are shifted left once. In the second loop, **$#** equals **3** and the loop commands are executed again. This continues until the fourth loop, where after the **print** command, **shift** sets **$#** to **0**. Back at the top of the loop on the fifth try, **$#** is now **0**, so the *commands* between **do** and **done** are skipped. Execution continues with commands following **done**.

```
$ listargs A B C D
A
B
C
D
```

The following **while** command loops until there is no **LOCKFILE**. Every 30 seconds, it wakes up to check if it's still there.

```
$ while [[ -f LOCKFILE ]]
> do
>     print "LOCKFILE still exists"
>     sleep 30
> done
LOCKFILE still exists
LOCKFILE still exists

. . .
```

You've heard the term "stuck in an endless loop". Well, here is one for you. This command will loop forever, since the **true** command always returns a zero exit status:

```
$ while true
> do
>   print  "Looping  forever..."
> done
Looping  forever...
Looping  forever...
Looping  forever...
. . .
```

To give the **while** command on one line, use this format:

while *command1* **; do** *commands* **; done**

Just like with **if** and **for** command on-line formats, the **;** characters are needed to separate **do** and **done** from the previous commands.

The until Command

The **until** command is another looping command. It's like the **while** command, except that instead of looping while the condition is true, it loops while the condition is false. So you can think of it as the opposite of the **while** command. The syntax for the **until** command is:

until *command1*
do
    commands
done

where *commands* are executed until *command1* returns a zero exit status. To demonstrate the differences between the **until** and **while** commands, let's rewrite the **listargs** script. In this version that uses the **until** command, $# is checked if it equals **0** before looping. This is in contrast to the **while** version that checked if $# was *not* equal to **0** before looping.

```
$ cat listargs
until (($# == 0))
do
      print $1
      shift
done
```

Here is sample output:

```
$ listargs A B
A
B
```

Just to prove that almost any **while** loop can be rewritten using **until**, let's take the second example from the **while** section and rewrite it. Now instead of looping while **LOCKFILE** exists, we loop until it is non-existent:

```
$ until [[ ! -f LOCKFILE ]]
> do
>    print "LOCKFILE still exists"
>    sleep 30
> done
LOCKFILE still exists
LOCKFILE still exists

. . .
```

Even the forever loop can be rewritten using **until**:

```
$ until false
> do
>    print "Looping forever..."
> done
Looping  forever...
Looping  forever...
Looping  forever...
 .  .  .
```

Nested Loops

There is another type of loop that is used to loop inside of another loop. In programming terms, this is called a *nested loop*. For example, in this script, the loops work together to count from 10 to 35 in increments of 5. The **for i in 1 2 3** is called the *outer loop*, and the **for j in 0 5** is called the *inner loop*.

```
$ cat nloop
for i in 1 2 3
do
     for j in 0 5
     do
         print  "$i$j"
     done
done
```

For each outer loop, the inner loop is executed twice. So, the first inner loop sets **j** to **0**, and the second inner loop sets **j** to **5**. This is repeated for each outer loop. The output explains this much better.

```
$ nloop
10
15
20
```

```
25
30
35
```

Breaking Out of Loops

You may want to exit from a loop before the loop condition is satisfied. This is where the **break** command comes in. It causes an exit from a loop-type command, but not from the entire script. Once you **break** from a loop, execution continues with the next command following the loop. For example, we could change the **listargs** script so that if a character argument was not given, the **while** loop would be terminated.

```
$ cat listargs
while (($# != 0))
do
      if [[ $1 = +([A-z]) ]]
      then
          print "$1: arg ok"
          shift
      else
          print "$1: Invalid argument!"
          break
      fi
done
print "Finished with args"
. . .
```

Here is sample output. Notice that the command following the **while** loop is executed after the **break**. If you wanted to terminate the entire script, **exit** would have to be used instead of **break**.

```
$ listargs A 1 B
A: arg ok
1: Invalid argument!
Finished with args
```

The **break** command can also be used to exit from a nested loop using this format:

> **break** *n*

where *n* specifies the *nth* enclosing loop to exit from. Here is a new version of the **nloop** script that breaks out of both loops if **i** equals **2** and **j** equals **0**:

```
$ cat nloop
for i in 1 2 3
do
     for j in 0 5
     do
        if ((i == 2 && j == 0))
        then
             break 2
        else
             print "$i$j"
        fi
     done
done
```

Now the output would be:

```
$ nloop
10
15
```

If **break** was used instead of **break 2**, then only the inner **for** loop would have been terminated, and execution would have continued with **i** set to **3** in the outer loop, and **j** set to **0** in the inner loop.

The continue Command

The **continue** command causes execution to continue at the top of the
current loop. It's like the **break** command, except instead of exiting
from the loop completely, only the remaining commands in the current
loop are skipped. Let's change the **listargs** script so that instead of
exiting on an invalid argument, it just prints out the error message, but
continues execution.

```
$ cat listargs
while (($# != 0))
do
      if [[ $1 = +([A-z]) ]]
      then
          print "$1: arg ok"
          shift
      else
          print "$1: Invalid argument!"
          shift
          continue
      fi
done
print "Finished with args"
. . .
```

Here is more sample output. Notice that this time, even though an
invalid argument was given, the next command-line argument was
processed.

```
$ listargs A 1 B
A: arg ok
1: Invalid argument!
B: arg ok
Finished with args
```

Like with the **break** command, an integer argument can be given to
the **continue** command to skip commands from nested loops.

The select Command

This is the last loop command we'll talk about. The **select** command is used to display a simple menu that contains numbered items, and a prompt message. The syntax for the **select** command is:

> **select** *variable* **in** *word1 word2 . . . wordn*
> **do**
> > *commands*
> **done**

where *word1* through *wordn* are displayed as numbered menu choices followed by a prompt (default **#?**). If the response is in the range **1** through *n*, then *variable* is set to the corresponding word, **REPLY** is set to the response, and the *commands* are executed. Execution continues until a **break**, **exit**, **return**, or EOF is encountered. Here is a simple **select** command that displays three numbered choices: **Choice-A**, **Choice-B**, and **Choice-C**.

```
$ cat stest
select  i  in  Choice-A  Choice-B  Choice-C
do
        print "You picked selection $REPLY: $i"
done
```

At the first prompt, selection **1** is entered, so **REPLY** is set to **1**, **i** is set to **Choice-A** and the value is printed. At the next prompt, selection **3** is entered, so **REPLY** is set to **3**, **i** is set to **Choice-C** and the value of **i** is displayed again.

```
$  stest
1)  Choice-A
2)  Choice-B
3)  Choice-C
#? 1
```

```
You picked selection 1: Choice-A
#? 3
You picked   selection  3:   Choice-C
```

Here the <RETURN> key is pressed, so the menu is just redisplayed:

```
#?   <RETURN>
1)   Choice-A
2)   Choice-B
3)   Choice-C
```

What if we enter an invalid choice?

```
1)   Choice-A
2)   Choice-B
3)   Choice-C
#?  5
You  picked  selection  5:
#?
```

The **print** command was still run, but because an invalid choice was given, **i** was not set to anything. Let's add an **if** command to check the value inside the loop.

```
$  cat  stest
select  i  in  Choice-A  Choice-B  Choice-C
do
    if  [[  $i  =  Choice-[A-C]  ]]
    then
        print  "You  picked  selection  $REPLY:  $i"
    else
        print  "$REPLY:  Invalid  choice!"
        continue
    fi
done
```

Now it works!

```
$ stest
1)  Choice-A
2)  Choice-B
3) Choice-C
#? 2
You picked selection 2: Choice-B
#? 5
5: Invalid choice!
#? 1
You picked selection 1: Choice-A
```

A different prompt can be used by setting the **PS3** variable like this:

```
$ typeset -x PS3="Enter selection>"
```

Now when **stest** is run again, the new message prompt is displayed:

```
$ stest
1)  Choice-A
2)  Choice-B
3)  Choice-C
Enter selection>3
You picked selection 3: Choice-C
```

The **select** and **case** commands are used in this Korn shell script to provide a simple menu interface to a few UNIX commands. Notice that the **LIST FILES** portion runs in a subshell so that the prompt (**PS3**) can be changed without having to reset it each time for the rest of the script.

```
$ cat smenu
PS3="Enter selection>"
select CMD in "CURRENT DIRECTORY NAME" \
"LIST FILES" MAIL DONE
do
    case $CMD in
        CURRENT* )
            pwd ;;
```

```
    LIST* )
        (   PS3="List which directory?"
        select DIR in HOME PUBDIR TOOLS \
        DONE
        do
            case $DIR in
                HOME  )  ls  $HOME  ;;
                PUBDIR)  ls  $PUBDIR ;;
                TOOLS )  ls  ~/tools  ;;
                DONE  )  break ;;
                *  )      print  "Bad  choice"
                          break ;;
            esac
        done  )  ;;
    MAIL  )
        mail ;;
    DONE  )
        break ;;
    * ) print  "Invalid  choice"
        break ;;
    esac
done
```

The first menu displays three numbered choices: **CURRENT DIRECTORY NAME, LIST FILES, MAIL,** and **DONE.** If you enter **1, pwd** is executed:

```
$  smenu
1)  CURRENT  DIRECTORY  NAME
2)  LIST  FILES
3)  MAIL
4)  DONE
Enter  selection>1
/home/anatole/tbin
```

If **2** is given, then another menu is displayed that gives you four numbered choices: **HOME, PUBDIR, TOOLS,** and **DONE.** Choices **1** through **3** cause contents of a directory to be listed, while choice **4** takes you back to the main menu.

```
1)  CURRENT  DIRECTORY  NAME
2)  LIST  FILES
3)  MAIL
4)  DONE
Enter  selection>2
1)  HOME
2)  PUBDIR
3)  TOOLS
4)  DONE
List  which  directory?1
NEWS     dialins     nohup.out   proc.doc
asp      mail           pc       tools
bin      newauto.bat             pers
List  which  directory?4
1)  CURRENT  DIRECTORY  NAME
2)  LIST  FILES
3)  MAIL
4)  DONE
Enter  selection>
```

If **3** is entered, **mail** is invoked, and if **4** is entered, we exit from the script:

```
Enter  selection>3
No  mail.
1)  CURRENT  DIRECTORY  NAME
2)  LIST  FILES
3)  MAIL
4)  DONE
Enter  selection>4
$
```

Other select Syntax

The **select** command can also be used without the list of *word* arguments:

> **select** *variable*
> **do**
> > *commands*
>
> **done**

It functions the same way as the previous **select** syntax, except that the positional parameters are displayed as numbered menu choices from 1 to *n*, instead of the words from the word list. It is equivalent to:

> **select** *variable* **in** "$@"
> **do**
> > *commands*
>
> **done**

The select Menu Format

The format of the **select** menu can be controlled by assigning values to the **LINES** and **COLUMNS** variables. The **LINES** variable specifies the number of lines to use for the menu. The menu choices are displayed vertically until about two-thirds of lines specified by **LINES** are filled. The **COLUMNS** variable specifies the menu width. This example displays how the **COLUMNS** and **LINES** variables affect a **select** menu. With the default setting, the **stest** menu is displayed like this:

```
$ stest
1)  Choice-A
2)  Choice-B
```

```
3) Choice-C
Enter selection>
```

If **LINES** is set to **2**, the menu choices are displayed on one line:

```
$ typeset -x LINES=2
$ stest
1) Choice-A          2) Choice-B      3) Choice-C
Enter  selection>
```

while if **COLUMNS** is set to **50**, the menu choices are displayed closer together on one line:

```
$ typeset -x COLUMNS=50
$ stest
1) Choice-A   2) Choice-B   3) Choice-C
Enter  selection>
```

If these variables are not explicitly set, the default used is **80** for **COLUMNS**, and **24** for **LINES**.

Comments

Comments are used in Korn shell scripts for debugging and documentation purposes. They provide a way to include text that is not executed. Good commenting makes it easier for you or someone else to read your scripts. Words beginning with # up to end of the current line are treated as comments and ignored. The **listargs** script could be commented like this:

```
$ cat listargs
#   listargs - List arguments
#   A Olczak ASP, Inc
```

```
# Loop on each argument
while (($# != 0))
do

    # Make sure argument is alphanumeric
    if [[ $1 = +([A-z]) ]]
    then
        print "$1: arg ok"
        shift
    else
        print "$1: Invalid argument!"
        shift
        continue
    fi
done
```

The # character can also be used to make your Korn shell scripts compatible with other shells. Any Korn shell script that begins with:

#!*interpreter*

is run by the given interpreter. So, for the C and Bourne shell users on your system, if you want your shell scripts to be run by the Korn shell (assuming it is installed in **/bin**), make sure they start with this:

```
#!/bin/ksh
```

Input/Output Commands

The Korn shell provides a number of input/output commands, which are covered in the following sections.

The print Command

You've already seen this command a hundred times since it was introduced in Chapter 3, but here it is again. This is a more formal definition of the command that describes the other things it can be used for. The **print** command displays *arguments* according to *options* with this format:

> **print** [*options*] *arguments*

Without options, special characters, or quotes, each argument is displayed separated with a space, and all the arguments are terminated with a newline:

```
$ print X     Y       Z
X Y Z
```

Notice that all the extra whitespace between the arguments was truncated. We could keep the whitespace by enclosing the arguments in quotes like this:

```
$ print "X     Y       Z "
X       Y       Z
```

Escape Characters

There are a number of special escape characters that allow you to format the **print** arguments. For example, to display arguments on separate lines, instead of using multiple **print** commands:

```
$ print X; print Y; print Z
X
Y
Z
```

the arguments could be separated with the newline escape character **\n**:

```
$  print  "X\nY\nZ"
X
Y
Z
```

The **print** arguments could be double-spaced like this:

```
$  print  "X\n\nY\n\nZ"
X

Y

Z
```

Make sure escape characters are enclosed in quotes. Otherwise they are not interpreted correctly. Here, without the quotes, **\n** is interpreted as an escaped '**n**', and not as the newline escape character:

```
$  print  X\nY\nZ
XnYnZ
```

The **** character can also be used to quote the escape characters:

```
$  print  X\\nY\\nZ
X
Y
Z
```

A tab can be displayed with the **\t** escape character:

```
$  print  "X\tY\tZ"
X    Y    Z
```

The **\c** escape character causes the trailing newline to be dropped from the output. It is often used to create prompts.

```
$ print "Enter choice: \c"
Enter choice: $
```

Notice that the command prompt was displayed following the argument, and not on the next line.

The \r escape character causes a carriage return without line feed to be displayed and can be used to format non-fixed length data. This command prints an **R** on the right side, then the \r escape character moves the cursor back to the beginning of the same line and prints an **L** on the left side followed by **TEXT**:

```
$ print '                R\rLTEXT'
LTEXT           R
$ print '                R\rL        TEXT'
L           TEXTR
```

Notice that the **L** and **R** characters are lined up, while **TEXT** is in a different position in both commands. In the Bourne shell, this is the easiest way to display non-fixed-length data in a fixed-length format. In the Korn shell, the same display could be created by using a fixed-length variable. First, variable **X** is set to ten-character wide, left-justified with a value of **TEXT**. Notice that {}'s must be given to delimit the variable name **X**:

```
$ typeset -L10  X=TEXT
$ print  "L${X}R"
LTEXT       R
```

To right-justify the value of **X**, the right-justify attribute is set:

```
$ typeset -R10  X
$ print  "L${X}R"
L       TEXTR
```

Table 8.5: print Escape Characters

\a	bell character
\b	backspace
\c	line without ending newline (remaining arguments ignored)
\f	formfeed
\n	newline
\r	return
\t	tab
\v	vertical tab
\\	backslash
\0x	8-bit character whose ASCII code is the 1-, 2-, or 3-digit octal number x

This **print** command displays a message and beeps:

```
$ print "Unexpected error!\a"
Unexpected error!<BEEP>
```

Using octal codes, the previous command could be given like this:

```
$ print "Unexpected error!\007"
Unexpected error!<BEEP>
```

print Options

The **print** command has a number of options that affect the way its arguments are interpreted. The – option is used if you want to **print** arguments that begin with a – character. In the next command, without the – argument, **–Z** is interpreted as an option and causes an error to be returned:

```
$ print -z
/bin/ksh: print: bad options(s)
$ print - -z
-z
```

The **–n** option is used when you don't want the trailing newline to be printed:

```
$ print -n "Enter choice:"
Enter choice:$
```

This is equivalent to:

```
$ print "Enter choice:\c"
Enter choice:$
```

The **–r** option causes the special escape characters to be ignored. Here, **\t** is printed without interpretation as the tab character:

```
$ print -r 'a\tb'
a\tb
```

The **–R** option is the same as **–r**, except that it also causes arguments beginning with – (except **–n**) to be interpreted as regular arguments and not as options.

```
$ print -R - '-a\tb'
- -a\tb
```

The **–s** option redirects the given arguments to the history file.

Table 8.6: print Options

–	treat everything following – as an argument, even if it begins with –
–n	do not add a ending newline to the output
–p	redirect the given arguments to a co-process
–r	ignore the \ escape conventions
–R	ignore the \ escape conventions; do not interpret –arguments as options (except **–n**)
–s	redirect the given arguments to the history file
–un	redirect arguments to file descriptor *n*. If the file descriptor is greater than **2**, it must first be opened with the **exec** command. If *n* is not specified, the default file descriptor is **1**.

```
$ print -s "This is a history entry"
$ history -2
165 This is a history entry
166 history -2
```

The **–u** option is used to redirect arguments to a specific file descriptor. Instead of displaying a message to standard error like this:

```
$ print "This is going to standard error >&2
This is going to standard error
```

the **print –u2** command can be used.

```
$ print -u2 "This is going to standard error"
This is going to standard error
```

The echo Command

The **echo** command displays its' arguments on standard output and is provided for compatibility with the Bourne shell. In the Korn shell, **echo** is an exported alias set to "**print –**".

The exec Command

The **exec** command is used to perform I/O redirection with file descriptors **0** through **9** using this format:

    exec *I/O-redirection-command*

The I/O redirection performed by the **exec** command stays in effect until specifically closed, changed, or if the script or shell terminates. We could use this idea so direct standard output to a file. First, let's start a subshell. You know that **1>std.out** directs standard output to **std.out**. So if we put the **exec** command in front of it, *all* subsequent standard output will be redirected.

```
$ ksh
$ exec 1>std.out
```

Now anything that goes to standard output is redirected to **std.out** until file descriptor 1 is specifically reset.

```
$ pwd
$ whoami
$ print "Where is this going?"
```

Notice that standard error is still attached to your terminal:

```
$ print -u2 "This is going to standard error"
This is going to standard error
```

Let's exit from the subshell, and take a look at the output file:

```
$ exit
$ cat std.out
/home/anatole/bin
anatole
Where is this going?
```

Here, file **rd.out** is opened as file descriptor 5 for reading and writing:

```
$ exec 5<>rd.out
```

Now the **print** command writes something to file descriptor 5:

```
$ print —u5 "This is going to fd 5"
```

and the **cat** command reads from it:

```
$ cat <&5
This is going to fd 5
```

To finish up, we use another **exec** to close file descriptor 5:

```
$ exec  5<&—
```

Any subsequent attempts to write to it or read from it would generate this error message:

```
$ print —u5 "Trying to write to fd 5 again"
/bin/ksh:   5: bad file unit number
```

Standard input can be taken from a file like this:

```
exec 0<file
```

Commands could be read in from file, and it would be almost as if you typed them at your terminal.

The **exec** command can also be used to replace the current program with a new one. For example, you know that if you wanted to run the C shell, you could invoke it as a subshell like this:

```
$ csh
{aspd:1}
```

But why have the extra parent shell process hanging around if you don't need it? In this case, the **exec** command could be used to *replace* the current shell with the C shell:

```
$ exec csh
{aspd:1}
```

Now if you exited from the C shell, you would be logged out.

Here is another application. Remember the **smenu** script from the **select** command section?   You could make a full-blown UNIX interface menu out of it by adding some more commands. If you wanted to set it up as a login shell, this would need to be added to a **.profile** file:

```
exec   smenu
```

and execution would be restricted to **smenu**.

The read Command

The **read** command is used to read input from a terminal or file. The basic format for the **read** command is:

read *variables*

where a line is read from standard input. Each word in the input is assigned to a corresponding variable, so the first variable gets the first word, the second variable the second word, and so on. Here, "**This is output**" is read in to the variables **X**, **Y**, and **Z**. The first word of the input is **This**, so it is assigned to the first variable **X**. The second word is **is**, so it is assigned to the second variable **Y**. The third word is **output**, so it is assigned to **Z**.

```
$ print "This is output" | read X Y Z
$ print $X
This
$ print $Y
is
$ print $Z
output
```

If there aren't enough variables for all the words in the input, the last variable gets all the remaining words. This command is the same as the last one, except that an extra string "**again**" is given.

```
$ print "This is output again " | read X Y Z
$ print $X
This
$ print $Y
is
```

Because there are four strings, but only three variables, **Z** gets the remaining unassigned words:

```
$ print $Z
output  again
```

If one variable argument is given to the **read** command, it gets assigned the entire line. Here, the variable **LINE** is set to the entire line:

```
$ print "This is output again" | read LINE
$ print $LINE
This is output again
```

The **kftp** script could be modified so that it prompted for a source file and target system. This is just a bare-bones script that demonstrates the use of the **read** command.

```
$ cat kftp

# Prompt for source file
print -n "Enter source file: "
read FILE

# Prompt for system name
print -n "Enter system name: "
read SYS

print "Copying $FILE to $SYS"

ftp <<- END
open $SYS
user anonymous
cd pub
put $FILE
quit
END
```

Here is some sample output:

```
$ kftp
Enter source file: rt.c
Enter remote system name: mhhd
Copying rt.c to mhhd
```

Reading Input from Files

Besides reading input from your terminal, the **read** command is also used to read input from a file. The **read** command by itself will only read one line of input, so you need a looping command with it. To read in the contents of a file, use this format:

> **exec 0<**_file_
> **while read** _variable_
> **do**
> > _commands_
>
> **done**

The **exec** command opens _file_ for standard input, and the **while** command causes input to be read a line at a time until there is no more input. If the **exec** open on _file_ fails, the script will exit with this error message:

> _script-name_: _file_: **cannot open**

Here is a stripped-down version of **kcat**. It is a simple version of the UNIX **cat** command. It displays the given file on standard output one line at a time.

```
$ cat kcat
exec  0<$1
while read LINE
do
    print $LINE
done
```

In terms of performance, it is about 3-4 times slower than the UNIX **cat** command, but it will do for demonstration purposes. Here is sample output:

```
$ kcat test.input
1: All work and no play makes Jack a dull boy.
2: All  work  and  no  play  makes  Jack  a  dull  boy.
3: All  work  and  no  play  makes  Jack  a  dull  boy.
. . .
```

The real version of the **kcat** command is listed in **Appendix D**.

Here is an alternate format that will also work for reading input from files:

> **cat** *file* **| while read** *variable*
> **do**
> > *commands*
> **done**

On the systems tested, the **exec** format for reading input from files was about 40-60 times faster than the last version above. It may be different on your system, but that's still a significant performance improvement.

The IFS Variable

The **read** command normally uses the **IFS** (Internal Field Separator) variable as the word separators. The default for **IFS** is space, tab, or newline character, in that order, but it can be set to something else. It is useful for when you want to read data that is not separated with whitespace. In this example, **IFS** is set to a comma:

```
$ IFS=,
```

then the **print** arguments are separated with the new word separator
for **read**:

```
$ print 'This,is,output' | read WORD1 WORD2 \
WORD3
$ print $WORD1 $WORD2 $WORD3
This is output
```

By setting **IFS** to **:**, the fields in the **/etc/passwd** file could be read into
separate variables.

```
$ cat ifs_test
IFS=:
exec 0</etc/passwd
while read -r NAME PASS UID GID COMM HOME \
SHELL
do
     print "Account name=      $NAME
Home directory=    $HOME
Login Shell=   $SHELL"
done
```

Here is sample output:

```
$ ifs_test
Account name=   root
Home directory= /
Login Shell=    /bin/ksh
Account name=   anatole
Home directory=    /home/anatole
Login Shell=    /bin/ksh
   . . .
```

More with read

Another format for the **read** command is:

> **read** *options* [*variables*]

where input is read and assigned to *variables* according to the given
options. The **−u** option is used to read input from a specific file
descriptor. If the file descriptor is greater than **2**, then it must first be
opened with the **exec** command. Let's look at the stripped-down
version of **kcat** again. It could be changed to prompt to continue
before displaying the next line like this:

```
$ cat kcat
exec  0<$1
while read LINE
do
    print $LINE
    print −n "Do you want to continue?"
    read ANSWER
    [[ $ANSWER = @([Nn])* ]] && exit 1
done
```

Here is the **test.input** file again:

```
$ cat test.input
1: All work and no play makes Jack a dull boy.
2: All work and no play makes Jack a dull boy.
3: All work and no play makes Jack a dull boy.
. . .
```

When the new version of **kcat** is run, the output looks strange. Can
you figure out the problem? The reason is that we redirected
standard input from **test.input**, but we are also expecting the input to
ANSWER from standard input. In the first loop, line 1 from
test.input is assigned to **LINE**. The next **read** command, which is

inside the loop, reads the next line into **ANSWER**. In the second loop, we're up to line 3, so it gets assigned to **LINE**, and so on.

```
$ kcat test.input
1: All work and no play makes Jack a dull boy.
Do you want to continue?3: All work and no
play
    makes Jack a dull boy.
    Do you want to continue?
    . . .
```

Instead of redirecting standard input (file descriptor **0**) from **test.input**, we could redirect it from another file descriptor and read it using the – **u** option. Then it wouldn't interfere with **read ANSWER** which is expecting input from standard input. Here is the new and improved version:

```
$ cat kcat
exec 4<$1
while read -u4 LINE
do
    print $LINE
    print -n "Do you want to continue?"
    read ANSWER
    [[ $ANSWER = @([Nn])* ]] && exit 1
done
```

Now it works.

```
$ kcat test.input
1: All work and no play makes Jack a dull boy.
Do you want to continue?<RETURN>
2: All work and no play makes Jack a dull boy.
Do you want to continue?<RETURN>
3: All work and no play makes Jack a dull boy.
Do you want to continue?n
$
```

The **–s** option saves a copy of the input in the history file. Here is an example:

```
$ print "This is a history entry" | read -s
HVAR
```

Just to make sure, let's look at both the history file

```
$ history -2
170 This is a history entry
171 history -2
```

and **HVAR**:

```
$ print $HVAR
This is a history entry
```

Reading Input Interactively

The **read** command allows input to be read interactively using this format:

read *name?prompt*

where *prompt* is displayed on standard error and the response is read into *name*. So instead of using two commands to display a prompt and read the input:

```
$ print -n "Enter anything: "
$ read ANSWER
```

The same thing can be done with one command.

```
$ read ANSWER?"Enter anything: "
Enter anything: ANYTHING
```

Table 8.7: read Options

−p	read input line from a co-process
−r	do not treat \ as the line continuation character
−s	save a copy of input line in the command history file
−un	read input line from file descriptor n. If the file descriptor is greater than **2**, it must first be opened with the **exec** command. If n is not specified, the default file descriptor is **0**.

Here is **ANSWER**:

```
$ print $ANSWER
ANYTHING
```

Let's change the **kftp** script (again) so that this format of the read command was used:

```
$ cat kftp

read SOURCE?"Enter source file:  "
read SYS?"Enter remote system name:  "

print "Copying $SOURCE to $SYS"

ftp <<- END
open $SYS
user anonymous
cd pub
put $FILE
quit
END
```

The REPLY Variable

If no variables are given to the **read** command, the input is automatically assigned to the **REPLY** variable. Here, **ANYTHING** is read into **REPLY**:

```
$ print ANYTHING | read
$ print $REPLY
ANYTHING
```

Miscellaneous Programming Features

The next sections cover some miscellaneous programming features.

The . Command

The . command reads in a complete file, then executes the commands in it as if they were typed in at the prompt. This is done in the current shell, so any variable, alias, or function settings stay in effect. It is typically used to read in and execute a profile, environment, alias, or functions file. Here the **.profile** file is read in and executed:

```
$ . .profile
```

The following example illustrates the difference between executing files as Korn shell scripts and reading/executing them using the . command. The **.test** file sets the variable **X**:

```
$ cat .test
X=ABC
```

When the **.test** file is executed as a Korn shell script, variable **X** is not defined in the current environment, because scripts are run in a subshell:

```
$ ksh .test
$ print $X

$
```

After the **.test** file is read in and executed using the **.** command, notice that the variable **X** is still defined:

```
$ . .test
$ print $X
ABC
```

The standard search path, **PATH**, is checked if the file is not in the current directory.

Functions

Functions are a form of commands like aliases, scripts, and programs. They differ from Korn shell scripts, in that they do not have to be read in from the disk each time they are referenced, so they execute faster. Functions differ from aliases, in that functions can take arguments. They provide a way to organize scripts into routines like in other high-level programming languages. Since functions can have local variables, recursion is possible. Functions are most efficient for commands with arguments that are invoked fairly often, and are defined with the following format:

function *name* {
    commands
}

To maintain compatibility with the Bourne shell, functions can also be declared with this format:

function-name() {
   commands
}

Here is a function called **md** that makes a directory and **cd**'s to it:

```
$ cat md
function md {
    (($# < 1)) && { print "$0: dir"; exit 1; }
    mkdir $1 && cd $1
    pwd
}
```

To be able to execute a function, it must first be read in. This is done with the **.** command:

```
$ . md
```

Now the **md** function can be invoked. Here, we try it with the **dtmp** directory:

```
$ md dtmp
/home/anatole/dtmp
```

Functions are executed in the current environment, so any variables and option settings are available to them.

Returning Function Exit Status

The **return** command is used to return from a function to the invoking Korn shell script and pass back an exit value. The syntax for the **return** command is:

return

or

return *n*

where *n* is a return value to pass back to the invoking Korn shell script or shell. If a return value is not given, the exit status of the last command is used. To exit from a function and the invoking Korn shell script, use the **exit** command from inside the function.

Scope & Availability

By default, functions are not available to subshells. This means that a regular function that was read in your working environment, **.profile** file, or environment file would not be available in a Korn shell script. To export a function, use the **typeset –fx** command:

typeset –fx *function-name*

To make a function available across separate invocations of the Korn shell, include the **typeset –fx** *function-name* command in the environment file.

Using Functions in Korn Shell Scripts

Functions are very useful in Korn shell scripts. Not only because you can organize scripts into routines, but it also provides a way to consolidate redundant sequences of commands. For example, instead printing out an error message and exiting each time an error condition is encountered, an all-purpose error function can be created. The arguments passed to it are the message to display and the exit code:

```
$ cat error
function error {
    print ${1:-"unexplained error encountered"}
    exit ${2:-1}
}
```

If function **error** is called without arguments, then you get the default error message "**unexplained error encountered**" and a default exit code if 1. Now on a non-existent file error, function **error** could be called like this:

```
error  "$FILE:non-existent  or  not  accessible"  3
```

It can save quite a bit of code, and it's easier to maintain. One more thing. Because functions need to be read in before they can be invoked, it's a good idea to put all function definitions at the top of Korn shell scripts.

Function Variables

All function variables, except those explicitly declared locally within the function with the **typeset** command, are inherited and shared by the calling Korn shell script. In this example, the **X**, **Y**, and **Z** variables are set within and outside of the function **f**:

```
$  cat  ftest
X=1
function  f  {
    Y=2
    typeset   Z=4
    print "In function f, X=$X, Y=$Y, Z=$Z"
    X=3
}
f
print  "Outside  function  f,   X=$X,  Y=$Y,  Z=$Z"
```

Notice that when executed, all the variable values are shared between the function and calling script, except for variable **Z**, because it is explicitly set to a local function variable using the **typeset** command. The value is not passed back to the calling Korn shell script:

```
$ ftest
In function f, X=1, Y=2, Z=4
Outside function f, X=3, Y=2, Z=
```

The current working directory, aliases, functions, traps, and open files from the invoking script or current environment are also shared with functions.

Displaying Current Functions

The list of currently available functions are displayed using the **typeset -f** command:

```
$ typeset -f
function _cd
{
    'cd' $1
    PS1="$PS0$PWD>    "
}
function md
{
    mkdir $1 && 'cd' $1
}
```

Auto-loading Functions

To improve performance, functions can be specified to autoload. This causes the function to be read in when invoked, instead of each time a Korn shell script is invoked, and is used with functions that are not invoked frequently. To define an autoloading function, use the **typeset -fu** *function-name* command. Here, **lsf** is made an autoloading function:

```
$ typeset -fu lsf
```

The **autoload** alias can also be used to define an autoloading function. On most systems, it is preset to **typeset –fu**.

FPATH

The **FPATH** variable contains a list of colon-separated directories to check when an autoloading function is invoked. It is analogous to **PATH** and **CDPATH**, except that the Korn shell checks for function files, instead of commands or directories. Each directory in **FPATH** is searched from left-to-right for a file whose name matches the name of the function. Once found, it is read in and executed in the current environment. With the following **FPATH** setting, if an autoloading function **lsf** was invoked, the Korn shell would check for a file called **lsf** in **/home/anatole/.fdir**, then **/etc/.functions**, and if existent, read and execute it:

```
$ print $FPATH
/home/anatole/.fdir:/etc/.functions
```

There is no default value for **FPATH**, so if not specifically set, this feature is not enabled.

Removing Function Definitions

Functions are removed by using the **unset –f** command. Here, the **rd** function is removed:

```
$ unset -f rd
```

and when invoked, it is now undefined:

```
$ rd
/bin/ksh: not found
```

Multiple function names can also be given to the **unset –f** command.

Traps

The **trap** command is used to execute commands when the specified signals are received.

> **trap** *commands signals*

Trap commands are useful in controlling side effects from Korn shell scripts. For example, if you have a script that creates a number of temporary files, and you hit the <BREAK> or <DELETE> key in the middle of execution, you may inadvertently leave the temporary files. By setting a **trap** command, the temporary files can be cleaned up on an error or interrupt.

The **trap_test** script creates some files, then removes them when an interrupt is received. Notice that the **trap** command is surrounded in single quotes. This is so that the **FILES** variable is evaluated when the signal is received, not when the **trap** is set.

```
$ cat trap_test
trap 'print "$0 interrupted - removing temp    \
files" ; rm —rf $FILES; exit 1' 1 2
FILES="a b c d e f"
touch $FILES
sleep 100
$ trap_test
Ctl-c
trap_test interrupted - removing temp files
```

If an invalid **trap** is set, an error is generated.

Ignoring Signals

The **trap** command can be used to ignore signals by specifying null as the command argument:

> **trap** "" *signals*

This could be used to make all or part of a Korn shell script uninterruptable using normal interrupt keys like **Ctl-c**. This **trap** command causes signals 2 and 3 to be ignored:

```
$ trap "" 2 3
```

The "" argument must be in this type of **trap** command, otherwise the trap is reset.

Resetting Traps

The **trap** command can also be used to reset traps to their default action by omitting the command argument:

> **trap** – *signals*
> or
> **trap** *signals*

Exit & Function Traps

A **trap** can be set to execute when a Korn shell script exits. This is done by using a **0** or **EXIT** as the signals argument to the **trap** command:

Table 8.8: Some Frequently-Used Signals

0	shell exit	**3**	quit
1	hangup	**15**	terminate
2	interrupt		

trap '*commands*' **0**
or
trap '*commands*' **EXIT**

This could be used to consolidate Korn shell script cleanup functions
into one place. The **trap_test** script contains a **trap** command that
causes a message to be printed out when the script finishes executing:

```
$ cat trap_test
trap 'print exit trap being executed' EXIT
print "This is just a test"
$ trap_test
This is just a test
exit trap being executed
```

If set within a function, the commands are executed when the function
returns to the invoking script. This feature is used to implement the C
shell **logout** function in **Appendix C**.

Debugging with trap

The **trap** command can be helpful in debugging Korn shell scripts.
The special signal arguments **DEBUG** and **ERR** are provided to
execute **trap** commands after each command or only when commands
in a script fail. This is discussed in the next section.

Trap Signal Precedence

If multiple traps are set, the order of precedence is:

- **DEBUG**
- **ERR**
- Signal Number
- **EXIT**

Debugging Korn Shell Scripts

The Korn shell provides a number of options that are useful in debugging scripts: **noexec**, **verbose**, and **xtrace**. The **noexec** option causes commands to be read without being executed. It is used to check for syntax errors in Korn shell scripts. The **verbose** option causes the input to be displayed as it is read. The **xtrace** option causes the commands in a script to be displayed as they are executed. This is the most useful, general debugging option.

Enabling Debug Options

These options are enabled in the same way other options are enabled. You can invoke the script with the option enabled:

```
$ ksh -option script
```

invoke a subshell with the option enabled:

```
$ ksh -option
$ script
```

set the option globally before invoking the script:

```
$ set -option
$ script
```

or set the option within the script.

```
$ cat  script
. . .
set  -option
. . .
```

Debugging Example

Here is a Korn shell script called **dbtest**. It sets variable **X** to **ABC**, then checks the value and prints a message. Notice that there is an unmatched double quote on line 2:

```
$ cat dbtest
X=ABC
if [ $X" = "foo" ]
then
    print "X is set to ABC"
fi
```

When run with the **noexec** option, the syntax error is flagged:

```
$ ksh -n dbtest
dbtest[2]: syntax  error  at  line  2:  `"'
unmatched
```

When an error is detected while executing a Korn shell script, the name of the script or function, the error message, and the line number enclosed in []'s are displayed. For functions, the line number relative to the beginning of the function is displayed. The **dbtest** script is fixed and run again with the **noexec** option:

```
$ ksh -n dbtest
$
```

Table 8.9: Korn Shell Debugging Options

set −e, set −o errexit
> execute **ERR** trap (if set) on non-zero exit status
> from any commands

set −n, set −o noexec
> read commands without executing them

set −v, set −o verbose
> display input lines as they are read

set −x, set −o xtrace
> display commands and arguments as they are
> executed

typeset −ft *function*
> display the commands and arguments from
> *function* as they are executed

No error is flagged this time, but also notice that no output is generated. This is because the **noexec** option causes the commands to be read, but not executed. Now, the **dbtest** script is run with the **xtrace** option:

```
$. ksh −x dbtest
+ alias −x echo=print −
+ alias −x vi=SHELL=/bin/sh vi
+ PS0=!:
+ PS1=!:/home/anatole/bin>
+ typeset −fx cd md
+ typeset −x EDITOR=vi
+ X=ABC
+ [ X = ABC ]
+ print X is set to ABC
```

```
X is set to ABC
```

Now there is a lot of output, most of which is execution trace output from processing of the environment file. The value of **PS4** is displayed in front of each line of execution trace. If not explicitly reset, the default is the + character. The line number can also be included in the debug prompt by including **LINENO** in the **PS4** setting.

```
$ typeset -x PS4='[$LINENO] '
```

Now the line number is displayed in brackets in the trace output:

```
$ ksh -x dbtest
[11] alias -x echo=print -
[12] alias -x vi=SHELL=/bin/sh vi
[13] PS0=!:
[14] PS1=!:/home/anatole/bin>
[15] typeset -fx cd md
[16] typeset -x EDITOR=vi
[1]  X=ABC
[2]  [ X = ABC ]
[4] print X is set to ABC
X is set to ABC
```

When the **dbtest** script is run without any debugging options, this is the output:

```
$ dbtest
X is set to ABC
```

Debugging with trap

The **trap** command can also be helpful in debugging Korn shell scripts. The syntax for this type of **trap** command is:

>   **trap** *commands* **DEBUG**
> or
>   **trap** *commands* **ERR**

If the **trap** command is set with **DEBUG**, then the trap commands are executed after each command in the script is executed. The following **trap** command causes **pwd** to be executed after each command if the variable **DB_MODE** is set to **yes**, otherwise a normal trap is executed.

```
if [[ $DB_MODE = yes ]]
then
    trap "pwd" DEBUG
else
    trap "rm -rf $TMPFILE; exit 1" 1 2 15
fi
```

If set with **ERR** and the **errexit** (**-e**) option is enabled, the trap is executed after commands that have a non-zero (unsuccessful) exit status. This **case** statement causes a different trap to be set, depending on the debug flag. If the debug flag is **0**, then a normal trap is set, which removes some temporary files on normal or abnormal termination. If the debug flag is **1**, then an **ERR** trap is set, which causes the line number to be displayed when an error occurs. If the debug flag is **2**, then a **DEBUG** trap is set, which causes the line number and current working directory to be displayed.

```
case $DB_FLAG in
    0 ) # Default trap - perform cleanup
        trap "rm -rf $FILES; exit 1" 0 1 2 15
;;

    1 ) # Execute trap for failed commands only
        set -o errexit
        trap 'print Error at $LINENO' ERR ;;

    2 ) # Execute trap for all commands
        trap 'print At $LINENO; pwd' DEBUG ;;

    * ) # Invalid debug flag
        print "Invalid debug flag" ; exit 1 ;;
esac
```

Parsing Command-line Arguments

Here is an alternative to using **case** to parse command-line arguments:
the **getopts** command. It works with the **OPTARG** and **OPTIND**
variables to parse command-line arguments using this format:

> **getopts** *optstring name args*
> or
> **getopts** *optstring name*

where *optstring* contains the list of legal options, *name* is the variable
that will contain the given option letter, and *args* is the list of
arguments to check. If not given, the positional parameters are
checked instead. If an option begins with a +, then + is prepended to
name. In all other cases, *name* is set to the option letter only.

There are some requirements on option format with the **getopts**
command. Options must begin with a + or –, and option arguments can
be separated from the options with or without whitespace. This

getopts command specifies that **a**, **b**, and **c** are valid options, and **OPT** will be set to the given option:

getopts abc OPT

A **:** after an option in *optstring* indicates that the option needs an argument, and **OPTARG** is set to the option argument. This **getopts** command specifies that the **a**, **b**, and **c** are valid options, and that options **a** and **c** have arguments:

getopts a:bc: OPT

If *optstring* begins with a **:**, then **OPTARG** is set to any invalid options given, and *name* is set to **?**. If an option argument is missing, *name* is set to ":". In the following Korn shell script, the **getopts** command is used in conjunction with the **case** command to process options and their arguments. The ":a:bc:" options string specifies that options **a** and **c** need arguments, and that invalid options are processed.

```
$ cat getopts_test
while getopts :a:bc: OPT
do
    case $OPT in
        a|+a ) print "$OPT received" ;;
        b|+b ) print "$OPT received" ;;
        c|+c ) print "$OPT received" ;;
        : )    print "$OPTARG needs arg" exit
;;
        \? )   print "$OPTARG:bad option"exit
;;
    esac
done
```

Here the **+b** and **−b** options are given:

```
$ getopts_test +b —b
+b received
b received
```

The **c** option needs an argument, so an error message is displayed:

```
$ getopts_test —c
c needs argument
```

Here, an invalid option is given:

```
$ getopts_test —x
x: unknown option
```

The **OPTIND** variable is set by the **getopts** command to the index of the next argument. It is initialized to **1** when a new function, Korn shell, or script is invoked.

More with Here Documents

The here document feature is also used in shareware software distribution. Multiple here documents are put into one file, and when executed, generate all the modules separately. Here is an example Korn shell archive file called **archive_test**:

```
$ cat archive_test
print "Extracting a"
cat >a <<—END
    This is file a.
END
print "Extracting b"
cat >b <<—END
    This is file b.
```

```
END
print "Extracting c"
cat >c <<-END
    This is file c.
END
```

When executed, it generates three files: **a**, **b**, and **c**.

```
$ ls
archive_test
$ archive_test
Extracting  a
Extracting  b
Extracting  c
```

This feature also allows you to edit a file from within a Korn shell script. The **htest** script edits the file **tmp** and inserts one line:

```
$ cat htest
ed - tmp <<EOF
a
This is a new line
.
w
q
EOF
```

After the **htest** Korn shell script is run, here is the result:

```
$ htest
$ cat tmp
This is a new line
```

The <<– operator is the same as <<, except that leading tab characters from each standard input line including the line with *word* are ignored. This is used to improve program readability by allowing the here document to be indented along with the rest of the code in Korn shell scripts.

The here document feature is also useful for generating form letters. The **hmail** script shows how to send a mail message to multiple users using this feature.

```
$ cat hmail
for i in terry larry mary
do
    mail $i <<-END
        $(date)
        Have a good holiday $i!
    END
done
```

Co-Processes

Co-processes are commands that are terminated with a **|&** character. They are executed in the background, but have their standard input and output attached to the current shell. The **print -p** command is used to write to the standard input of a co-process, while **read -p** is used to read from the standard output of a co-process. Here, the output of the **date** command is read into the **DATE** variable using the **read -p** command:

```
$ date |&
[2]  241
$ read -p DATE
$ print $DATE
Thu Jul 18 12:23:57 PST 1996
```

Co-processes can be used to edit a file from within a Korn shell script. In this example, we start with file **co.text**:

```
$ cat co.text
This is line 1
This is line 2
This is line 3
```

It is edited using a co-process, so the job number and process id are returned:

```
$ ed - co.text |&
[3]  244
```

The command (display line 3) is written to the co-process using **print - p**. The output of the **ed** command is then read into the **LINE** variable using **read LINE**:

```
$ print -p 3p
$ read -p LINE
$ print $LINE
This is line 3
```

The next commands delete line 2, then send the write and quit commands to **ed** via the co-process:

```
$ print -p 2d
$ print -p w
$ print -p q
[3]  + Done        ed - co.text |&
```

After editing from the co-process, **co.text** file looks like this:

```
$ cat co.text
This is line 1
This is line 3
```

Table 8.10: Co-Processes

command **|&**

        execute *command* in the background with the standard input and output attached to the shell

n<**&p**   redirect input from co-process to file descriptor *n*. If *n* is not specified, use standard input.

n>**&p**   redirect output of co-process to file descriptor *n*. If *n* is not specified, use standard output.

print –p write to the standard input of a co-process

read –p read from the standard output of a co-process

Chapter 9:
Miscellaneous
Commands

The following sections cover miscellaneous Korn shell commands.
Many of these are used in Korn shell scripts. The rest work with your
environment and system resources.

The : Command

The : command is the null command. If specified, arguments are
expanded. It is typically used as a no-op, to check if a variable is set,
or for endless loops. The : command here is used to check if **LBIN** is
set.

```
$ : ${LBIN:?}
LBIN: parameter null or not set
```

If given in a Korn shell script, it would cause it to exit with an error if
LBIN was not set.

This example counts the number of lines in the file **ftext**, then prints the total. The : command is used as a no-op, since we only want to print the total number of lines after the entire file has been read, not after each line.

```
$ integer NUM=0
$ exec 0<ftext && while read LINE && ((NUM+=1))
> do
>    :
> done; print $NUM
7
```

In the following Korn shell script, the : command is used to loop continuously until **fred** is logged on.

```
$ cat fred_test
while :
do
     FRED=$(who | grep fred)
     if [[ $FRED != "" ]]
     then
          print "Fred is here!"
          exit
     else
          sleep 30
     fi
done
```

The eval Command

The **eval** command reads and executes commands using the following format:

eval *commands*

It causes *commands* to be expanded twice. For simple commands, there is no difference in execution with or without **eval**:

```
$ eval print ~
/home/anatole
```

Here is a more complicated command that illustrates the use of **eval**. We want the contents of the **stext** file redirected when variable **X** is accessed.

```
$ cat stext
She sells seashells by the seashore.
```

First, variable **X** is set to "**<stext**":

```
$ X="<stext"
```

When the value of **X** is printed using simple variable expansion, it generates an error:

```
$ cat $X
<stext: No such file or directory
```

Using the **eval** command, **X** is first expanded to **<stext**, then the command **cat <stext** is executed. This causes the contents of **stext** to be displayed:

```
$ eval cat $X
She sells seashells by the seashore.
```

In this Korn shell script, the **eval** command is used to display the last command-line argument:

```
$ cat eval_test
print "Total command-line arguments is $#"
print "The last argument is $$#"
```

What you want is **$#** to be expanded first to the number of arguments, then **$n** to be expanded to the value of the last argument. Without the **eval** command, this is the output of **eval_test**:

```
$ eval_test a b c
Total command-line arguments is 3
The last argument is 581#
```

The output **581#** is generated because **$$** is first expanded to the process id. Using the **eval** command to expand the **print** command twice, we get the correct result.

```
$ cat eval_test
print "Total command-line arguments is $#"
print "The last argument is $(eval print \$$#)"
$ eval_test1 a b c
The number of command-line arguments is 3
The last argument is c
```

The \ is needed so that the **$** character is ignored on the first expansion. After the first expansion, the **$(eval print \$$#)** command becomes **$(print $3)**. This is then expanded to **c**.

The export Command

The **export** command sets and/or exports variables to the environment. It is equivalent to **typeset −x**, except when used within functions. Here, the **PATH** variable is set and exported:

```
$ export PATH=$PATH:/usr/5bin
```

Multiple variables can be given to the **export** command. In this example, the variables **A**, **B**, **C**, and **D** are set and/or exported:

```
$ export A B=1 C D=2
```

If no arguments are specified, the **export** command lists the names and values of exported variables:

```
$ export
EDITOR=vi
HOME=/home/anatole
LOGNAME=anatole
PATH=/usr/bin:/usr/ucb:/usr/etc:/usr/5bin:
PWD=/home/anatole/asp/pubs/ksh/v2
SHELL=/bin/ksh
TERM=sun
USER=anatole
```

The false Command

The **false** command returns a non-zero exit status. That's all. It is often used to generate infinite **until** loops. In some versions of the Korn shell, **false** is a preset alias **let 0**. In either case, it does the same thing.

The newgrp Command

The **newgrp** command changes the group id and is equivalent to "**exec /bin/newgrp** *group*". In this example, the group id is changed from **users** to **networks**:

```
$ id
uid=100(anatole)  gid=101(users)
$ newgrp networks
uid=100(anatole)  gid=12(networks)
```

Without arguments, **newgrp** resets the group-id to the default:

```
$ newgrp
uid=100(anatole)  gid=101(users)
```

The pwd Command

The **pwd** command prints the current working directory. It is a Korn shell built-in command and is equivalent to the **print −r − $PWD** command.

The readonly Command

The **readonly** command sets the value and/or **readonly** attribute of variables. It is equivalent to the **typeset −r** command, except that when used within a function, a local variable is not created. This command sets **X** to readonly and assigns it a value of **1**:

```
$ readonly X=1
```

This is equivalent to:

```
$ typeset −r X=1
```

Multiple variables can be given to the **readonly** command.

```
$ readonly X Y=1 Z=2
```

If no arguments are given, a list of readonly variables and their values is displayed:

```
$ readonly
Z=1
```

```
Y=1
Z=2
PPID=175
```

The set Command

Besides manipulating Korn shell options, the **set** command can be used to display a list of your local and exported variables.

```
$ set
EDITOR=vi
ENV=${HOME:-.}/.env
FCEDIT=/bin/ed
HOME=/home/anatole
LOGNAME=anatole
MAILCHECK=600
PATH=:/usr/bin:/usr/ucb:/usr/5bin
PPID=180
  . . .
```

It can also be used to "manually" reset positional parameters. For example:

```
$ set X Y Z
```

would set **$1** to **X**, **$2** to **Y**, **$3** to **Z**, and **$#** to **3**:

```
$ print $1 $2 $3 $#
X Y Z 3
```

The positional parameters **$@** and **$*** would be set **X Y Z**:

```
$ print $*
X Y Z
$ print $@
X Y Z
```

The $* and $@ parameters are basically the same, except for the way they are expanded when surrounded with double quotes. The positional parameters in $@ are interpreted as separate strings, while in the $*, they are interpreted as a single string. Using $@, the **wc** command counts three separate strings

```
$ print "$@" | wc -w
3
```

while with $*, only one string is counted:

```
$ print "$*" | wc -w
1
```

To manually set positional parameters that begin with the – character, use the **set –** command.

```
$ set - -X -Y -Z
$ print - $*
-X -Y -Z
```

All the positional parameters can be unset with the **set ––** command:

```
$ set A B C
$ print $*
A B C
$ set --
$ print $*

$
```

The time Command

The **time** command is a built-in command in the Korn shell and
functions the same as the UNIX **times** command. Here, the **ls**
command is timed. It indicates the amount of elapsed, user, and system
time spent executing the **ls** command:

```
$ time ls /usr/spool/uucppublic
mail

real    0m0.33s
user    0m0.05s
sys     0m0.18s
```

The times Command

The **times** command displays the amount of time the current Korn shell
and child processes. The first line shows the total user and system time
(in hundredths of a second) for the current Korn shell, while the second
line shows the totals for the child processes.

The true Command

The **true** command does one thing: return a zero exit status. It is often
used to generate infinite loops for argument-processing. In some
versions of the Korn shell, **true** is a preset alias ":". It also returns a
zero exit status.

The ulimit Command

The **ulimit** command manipulates system resource limits for current and child processes using the following format:

>**ulimit** [*options*]
>or
>**ulimit** [*options*] *n*

where *n* indicates to set a resource limit to *n* (except with the **-a** option). If *n* is not given, the specified resource limit is displayed. If no option is given, the default **-f** (file size limit) is used. Here, all the current resource limits are displayed:

```
$ ulimit -a
time(seconds)      unlimited
memory(kbytes)     unlimited
data(kbytes)       4294901761
stack(kbytes)      2048
file(blocks)       unlimited
coredump(blocks)   unlimited
```

This command sets the core dump size limit to 500 blocks:

```
$ ulimit -c 500
```

To disable generation of core dumps, the dump size should be set to 0 blocks:

```
$ ulimit -c 0
```

To display the current file size write limit, use **ulimit** without arguments:

```
$ ulimit
unlimited
```

Table 9.1: ulimit Options

−a	displays all the current resource limits
−c *n*	set the core dump size limit to *n* 512-byte blocks
−d *n*	set the data area size limit to *n* kilobytes
−f *n*	set the child process file write limit to *n* 512-byte blocks (default)
−m *n*	set the physical memory size limit to *n* kilobytes
−s *n*	set the stack area size limit to *n* kilobytes
−t *n*	set the process time limit to *n* seconds

Table 9.1 lists the **ulimit** options. If a size argument is not given, the current limit is displayed.

The **ulimit** command is system dependent. Some systems may have different resource limits, and some may not allow changing resource limits. Check your local system documentation for discrepancies.

The umask Command

The **umask** command sets the file-creation mask using this format:

umask *mask*

where *mask* is an octal number or symbolic value that correspond to the permissions to be disabled. Here, the write and execute permissions for group and others are removed:

```
$ umask 033
$ touch tmp
$ ls -l tmp
-rw-r--r--  1 root    9 Sep  2 11:18 tmp
```

This **umask** command adds write permission to the group:

```
$ umask 013
$ touch tmp1
$ ls -l tmp1
-rw-rw-r--  1 root  9 Sep  2 11:19 tmp1
```

To remove read permission for other using symbolic format:

```
$ umask o-r
$ touch tmp2
-rw-rw----  1 root  9 Sep  2 11:23 tmp2
```

With no arguments, **umask** displays the current value. This **umask** is set to remove write permission for group and others:

```
$ umask
022
```

The whence Command

The **whence** command is used to display information about a command, like if it is an alias, built-in Korn shell command, function, reserved Korn shell word, or just a regular UNIX command. The format for the **whence** command is:

whence *name*
or
whence −v *name*

where *name* is the command or whatever you want to get information about. Here, the **whence** command shows that **history** is set to **fc −l**:

```
$ whence history
fc −l
```

The **−v** option causes more information to be provided about the command. Now we see that **history** is an exported alias:

```
$ whence −v history
history is an exported alias for fc −l
```

and **until** is a keyword:

```
$ whence −v until
until is a keyword
```

For compatibility with the Bourne shell, a preset alias **type** is set to **whence −v**.

```
$ type md
md is an exported function
```

Appendix A: Sample .profile File

This section contains a sample **.profile** file. Notice that the
environment variables are set and exported with one **typeset** command.
This speeds up processing of the **.profile** file.

```
#
#    Sample .profile File
#
#    Anatole Olczak - ASP, Inc.
#

# Set/export environment variables
typeset -x CDPATH=:$HOME:/usr/spool \
    EDITOR=vi \
    ENV=${HOME:-.}/.env \
    HISTFILE=$HOME/.history \
    HISTSIZE=200 \
    HOME=/home/anatole \
    LOGNAME=anatole \
    MAILCHECK=300 \
```

```
        MAILPATH=~/inbox:/usr/spool/mail/$LOGNAME  \
        PAGER=$(whence more) \
        PATH=${PATH#:}:/usr/etc:$NEWS/bin:  \
        PS1='!:$PWD> ' \
        PS4='[$LINENO]+ ' \
        SHELL=/bin/ksh \
        TERM=sun \
        TMOUT=600 \
        USER=$LOGNAME


# Set global options
set -o noclobber -o markdirs +o bgnice

# Execute commands from the ~/.logout file on exit
trap '. ~/.logout' EXIT
```

Appendix B: Sample Environment File

This section contains a sample environment file. It sets the global functions, aliases, and prompt variable.

```
#
#    Sample env File
#
#    Anatole Olczak - ASP, Inc.
#

# Function md - make a directory and _cd to it
function md {
    mkdir $1 && _cd $1
}

# Set up the echo alias
alias -x echo='print -'
```

```
# Set temporary prompt variable to the command number
# followed by a colon
PS0='!:'

# Function _cd - changes directories, then sets the
# command prompt to: "command-number:pathname>"
function _cd {

    if (($# == 0))
    then
        'cd'
        PS1="$PS0$PWD> "
    fi

    if (($# == 1))
    then
        'cd' $1
        PS1="$PS0$PWD> "
    fi

    if (($# == 2))
    then
        'cd' $1 $2
        PS1="$PS0$PWD> "
    fi
}

# Alias the cd command to the _cd function
alias -x cd=_cd

# Export the _cd and md functions
typeset -fx _cd md
```

This section contains the source code listings for the C Shell directory management functions, and other miscellaneous C Shell commands.

Directory Functions

These Korn shell functions implement the C shell directory management commands: **dirs**, **popd**, and **pushd**. They can be put into a separate **cshfuncs** file and read in with the **.** command when necessary. Their basic functionality is:

dirs	display directory stack
popd	remove directory stack entry and **cd** to it
pushd	add directory stack entry and **cd** to it

The **dirs** function lists the current directory stack.

With no argument, the **popd** function removes the top entry (previous working directory) from the directory stack and changes directory to it. If a +*n* argument is given, then the *nth* directory stack entry (*nth* previous working directory) is removed.

With no argument, the **pushd** function switches the top two entries (current and previous working directory) and changes directory to the previous working directory. This is equivalent to "**cd –**". If a directory argument is given, **pushd** puts the directory on the top of the directory stack and changes directory to it. If a +*n* argument is given, **pushd** puts the *nth* directory stack entry (*nth* previous working directory) on the top of the stack and changes directory to it.

```
#
#    Sample C Shell Directory Management Functions
#
#    Anatole Olczak - ASP, Inc


# Function fcd - verify accessibility before changing
# to target directory
function fcd
{
    # Make sure directory exists
    if [[ ! -d $1 ]]
    then
        print "$1: No such file or directory"
        return 1
    else
        # Make sure directory is searchable
        if [[ ! -x $1 ]]
```

```
        then
                print "$1: Permission denied"
                return 1
        fi
    fi


    # Otherwise change directory to it
    cd $1
    return 0
}


# Function dirs - display directory stack
function dirs
{
    # Display current directory and directory stack
    print "$PWD ${DSTACK[*]}"
}


# Function pushd - add entry to directory stack
function pushd
{
    # Set stack depth (number of stack entries)
    integer DEPTH=${#DSTACK[*]}

    case $1 in
```

```
"" )# No argument - switch top 2 stack elements
    if (($(#DSTACK[*]} < 1))
    then
        print "$0: Only one stack entry."
        return 1
    else
        fcd ${DSTACK[0]} || return
        DSTACK[0]=$OLDPWD
        dirs
    fi
    ;;


+@([1-9])*([0-9])  )
    # Number argument 1-999* - move entry to top
    # of directory stack and cd to it
    integer ENTRY=${1#+}
    if (($(#DSTACK[*]} < $ENTRY))
    then
        print "$0: Directory stack not that deep"
        return 1
    else
        fcd ${DSTACK[ENTRY-1]} || return
        DSTACK[ENTRY-1]=$OLDPWD
        dirs
    fi
    ;;
* ) # Directory argument - verify argument
    # before changing directory and adjusting
```

```
        # rest of directory stack
        fcd $1 || return
        until ((DEPTH == 0))
        do
            DSTACK[DEPTH]=${DSTACK[DEPTH-1]}
            ((DEPTH-=1))
        done
        DSTACK[DEPTH]=$OLDPWD
        dirs
        ;;
    esac
}


# Function popd - remove entry from directory stack
function popd
{
    # Set stack depth (number of stack entries)
    integer i=0 DEPTH=${#DSTACK[*]} ENTRY=${1#+}
    case $1 in

    "" )
        # No argument - discard top stack entry
        if ((${#DSTACK[*]} < 1))
        then
            print "$0: Directory stack empty."
            return 1
        else
            fcd ${DSTACK[0]} || return
            while ((i < (DEPTH-1)))
```

```
        do
            DSTACK[i]=${DSTACK[i+1]}
            ((i+=1))
        done
        unset DSTACK[i]
        dirs
    fi
    ;;


+@([1-9])*([0-9]) )
    # Number argument 1-999* - discard nth
    # stack entry
    if (($(#DSTACK[*]} < ENTRY))
    then
        print "$0: Directory stack not that deep"
        return 1
    else
        while ((ENTRY < DEPTH))
        do
            DSTACK[ENTRY-1]=${DSTACK[ENTRY]}
            ((ENTRY+=1))
        done
        unset DSTACK[ENTRY-1]
        dirs
    fi
    ;;


# Invalid argument given
* ) print "$0: Invalid argument."
```

```
        return 1
        ;;

    esac
}
```

Miscellaneous Commands

The following sections contain Korn shell equivalents of some
miscellaneous C shell commands and functions.

The .logout File

In the C shell, commands in the **~/.logout** file are executed on
exit. If the following command is added to the **~/.profile** file,
then the same thing will happen in the Korn shell:

```
    trap '. ~/.logout' EXIT
```

The chdir Command

The C shell **chdir** command changes to the specified directory and can
be set to a Korn shell alias like this:

```
    alias chdir='cd'
```

The logout Command

The C shell **logout** command is equivalent to the **exit** command. It can be set to a Korn shell alias:

```
alias logout='exit 0'
```

The setenv Command

The C shell **setenv** command is used to set/display variables and can be invoked like this:

setenv   display a list of variables
setenv *variable*
              set *variable* to null
setenv *variable value*
              set *variable* to *value*, then export it

It can be set to a Korn shell function like this:

```
function setenv {
    set -o allexport
    typeset TMP="$1=$2"
    eval $(print ${1+$TMP})
    typeset -x $1
}
```

Appendix C: C Shell Functionality

The source Command

The C shell **source** reads and executes a file in the current environment. It can be aliased to the Korn shell . command:

```
alias source=.
```

Appendix D: Sample Korn Shell Scripts

*Display Files - **kcat***
*Interactive uucp - **kuucp***
*Basename - **kbasename***
*Dirname - **kdirname***
*Display Files with Line Numbers - **knl***
*Find Words - **match***
*Simple Calculator - **kcalc***
*Search for Patterns in Files - **kgrep***
*Calendar Program - **kcal***

This appendix contains listings for some Korn shell scripts.

Display Files - kcat

Here is a simple Korn shell version of the UNIX **cat** command. It is only 3-4 times slower than the UNIX version (on a 100-line file), because it uses the **exec** command for the file I/O.

```ksh
#!/bin/ksh
#
#   kcat - Korn shell version of cat
#
#   Anatole Olczak - ASP, Inc
#

# Check usage
if (($# < 1))
then
    print "Usage: $0 file ..."
    exit 1
fi

# Process each file
while (($# > 0))
do
    # Make sure file exists
    if [[ ! -f $1 ]]
    then
        print "$1: non-existent or not accessible"
    else
        # Open file for input
        exec 0<$1
        while read LINE
        do
            # Display output
            print $LINE
        done
    fi
```

```
    # Get next file argument
    shift
done
```

Interactive uucp - kuucp

Here is an interactive version of the **uucp** command. Instead of
looking for a system name in the uucp systems file using **grep**, the
remote system name is verified by using file I/O substitution and Korn
shell patterns.

```ksh
#!/bin/ksh
#
#   kuucp - Korn shell interactive uucp
#
#   Anatole Olczak - ASP, Inc
#


# Check usage
if (($# > 0))
then
    print "Usage: $0"
    exit 1
fi


# Set variables
PUBDIR=${PUBDIR:-/usr/spool/uucpublic}


# This sets UUSYS to the contents of the HDB-UUCP
# Systems file.  It may be different on your system.
UUSYS=$(</usr/lib/uucp/Systems)
```

```
# Get source file
read SOURCE?"Enter source file: "


# Check source file
if [[ ! -f $SOURCE ]]
then
    print "$SOURCE: non-existent or not accessible"
    exit 2
fi


# Get remote system name
read RSYS?"Enter remote system name: "


# Check remote system name.  It looks for a pattern
# match on the system name in the UUSYS file
#
# For the Bourne shell or older versions
# of Korn shell, this could be given as:
#   if [[ $(grep ^$RSYS $UUSYS) != "" ]]
if [[ $UUSYS != *$RSYS* ]]
then
    print "$RSYS: Invalid system name"
    exit 2
fi


print "Copying $SOURCE to $RSYS!$PUBDIR/$SOURCE"
uucp $SOURCE $RSYS!$PUBDIR/$SOURCE
```

Basename - kbasename

This is the Korn shell version of the UNIX **basename** command. It is
used to return the last part of a pathname. A suffix can also be given to
be stripped from the resulting base directory. The substring feature is
used to get the basename and strip off the suffix.

```ksh
#!/bin/ksh
#
#    kbasename - Korn shell basename
#
#    Anatole Olczak - ASP, Inc
#


# Check arguments
if (($# == 0 || $# > 2))
then
    print "Usage: $0 string [suffix]"
    exit 1
fi


# Get the basename
BASE=${1##*/}


# See if suffix arg was given
if (($# > 1))
then
    # Display basename without suffix
    print ${BASE%$2}
else
```

```
    # Display basename
    print $BASE
fi
```

Dirname - kdirname

Here is the Korn shell version of the UNIX **dirname** command. It returns a pathname minus the last directory. As in **kbasename**, the substring feature does all the work.

```
#!/bin/ksh
#
#    kdirname - Korn shell dirname
#
#    Anatole Olczak - ASP, Inc
#

# Check arguments
if (($# == 0 || $# > 1))
then
    print "Usage: $0 string"
    exit 1
fi

# Get the dirname
print ${1%/*}
```

Display Files with Line Numbers - knl

This is a simple Korn shell version of the UNIX **nl** command. It displays line-numbered output.

```
#!/bin/ksh
#
#   knl - Korn Shell line-numbering filter
#
#   A Olczak - ASP, Inc
#

# Initialize line number counter
integer LNUM=1

# Check usage
if (($# == 0))
then
    print "Usage: $0 file . . ."
    exit 1
fi

# Process each file
for FILE
do
    # Make sure file exists
    if [[ ! -f $FILE ]]
    then
        print "$FILE: non-existent or not readable"
        exit 1
    else
```

```
            # Open file for reading
            exec 0<$FILE

            # Read each line, print out with line number
            while read -r LINE
            do
                 print "$LNUM: $LINE"
                 ((LNUM+=1))
            done
     fi

     # Reset line number counter
     LNUM=1
done
```

Find Words - match

The **match** command uses Korn shell pattern-matching characters to find words in a dictionary. It can be used to help with crossword puzzles, or test your patterns.

```
#!/bin/ksh
#
#    match - Korn shell word-finder
#
#    Anatole Olczak - ASP, Inc
#
```

```
# Check usage
if (($# < 1 || $# > 2))
then
    print "Usage: $0 pattern [file]"
    exit 1
fi


# Check/set DICT to word dictionary
: ${DICT:=${2:-/usr/dict/words}}


# Open $DICT for input
exec 0<$DICT


# Read each word into WORD
while read WORD
do
    # This command didn't work on all systems.  If
    # it doesn't on yours, use this instead of
    # exec 0<$DICT:
    #   cat $DICT | while read WORD
    #
    # If WORD matches the given pattern,
    # print the match
    [[ $WORD = $1 ]] && print - $WORD
done
```

Simple Calculator - kcalc

This Korn shell script implements a simple **expr**-like command.
Arithmetic expressions are passed in as arguments, and the result is
displayed. Parentheses for grouping must be escaped.

```ksh
#!/bin/ksh
#
#   kcalc - Korn Shell calculator
#
#   Anatole Olczak - ASP, Inc
#

# Initialize expression
integer EXPR

# Check usage
if (($# == 0))
then
    print "$0: Must provide expression arguments."
    exit 1
fi

# Set/evaluate EXPR
((EXPR=$*))

# Print result
print $EXPR
```

Searching for Patterns in Files - kgrep

This is the Korn shell version of the UNIX **grep** command. The **–b** option is not supported, and the **–i** flag causes multi-character expressions to be matched in both all upper-case or all lower-case (**kgrep –i AbC test** matches **AbC**, **abc**, or **ABC** in **test**, but not **aBc** or other permutations). Here are the supported options:

–c	display the number of lines that contain the given pattern
–i	ignore case of letters during comparison (see above)
–l	display only names of files with matching lines once
–n	display the output with line numbers
–s	do not display error messages
–v	display all lines, except those that match the given expression

```ksh
#!/bin/ksh
#
#    kgrep - Korn Shell grep program
#
#    Anatole Olczak - ASP, Inc
#


# Declare default flags
CFLAG= IFLAG= LFLAG= NFLAG= SFLAG= VFLAG=
integer LNUM=0 COUNT=0 TOT_COUNT=0


# Disable file name generation
set -f
```

```
# Check usage
if (($# < 2))
then
    print "Usage: $0 [options] expression files"
    exit 1
fi

# Parse command-line options
while true
do
    case $1 in
        -b* ) print "b option not supported" ;;
        -c* ) CFLAG=1 ;;
        -i* ) IFLAG=1 ;;
        -l* ) LFLAG=1 ;;
        -n* ) NFLAG=1 ;;
        -s* ) SFLAG=1 ;;
        -v* ) VFLAG=1 ;;
        -* )  print "$0: unknown flag $1"
              exit 2 ;;
        * )   PATTERN=$1
              shift
              break ;;
    esac
    shift
done

# Set no-print flags
NOPRINT=$VFLAG$CFLAG$LFLAG
V_NOPRINT=$CFLAG$LFLAG
```

```
# Set upper/lower pattern
typeset -u UCPATTERN=$PATTERN
typeset -l LCPATTERN=$PATTERN


# Check for file arg
if (($# == 0))
then
    print "Must have file argument"
    exit 1
fi


# Process files
for FILE
do
    # Open file for standard input
    exec 0<$FILE

    # Read each line in file
    while read -r LINE
    do
        # Increment line number counter
        ((LNUM+=1))

        # Check each line for the pattern
        case $LINE in

            # See if PATTERN matches input
            *$PATTERN* )
                if [[ $VFLAG = "" ]]
                then
```

```
                        [[ $NOPRINT = "" ]] && print -r
"${NFLAG:+$LNUM:}$LINE"
                        ((COUNT+=1))
                fi ;;


            # For -i option: See if
            # upper/lowercase patterns match
            *$UCPATTERN* | *$LCPATTERN* )
                if [[ $IFLAG != "" ]]
                then
                    if [[ $VFLAG = "" ]]
                    then
                        [[ $NOPRINT = "" ]] && print
-r  "${NFLAG:+$LNUM:}$LINE"
                        ((COUNT+=1))
                    fi
                else
                    if [[ $VFLAG != "" ]]
                    then
                        [[ $V_NOPRINT = "" ]] &&
print -r  "${NFLAG:+$LNUM:}$LINE"
                        ((COUNT+=1))
                    fi
                fi ;;
            # For -v option: See if
            # pattern doesn't match
            !(*$PATTERN*)  )
                if [[ $VFLAG != "" ]]
                then
                    [[ $V_NOPRINT = "" ]] && print -r
"${NFLAG:+$LNUM:}$LINE"
```

```
                    ((COUNT+=1))
            fi ;;
    esac
done


# Process -l flag
# Display just the filename
# if there are matches in this file
if [[ $LFLAG != "" ]] && ((COUNT))
then
    print - $FILE
fi


# Increment the total match counter
# for when kgrep'ing multiple files
((TOT_COUNT+=COUNT))


# Reset the line number counter for the next file
LNUM=0


# Reset the match counter for the next file
COUNT=0
done


# Process -c flag
# Display the total number of matches found
[[ $CFLAG != "" ]] && print $TOT_COUNT


# Exit successfully
exit 0
```

Calendar Program - kcal

This is a Korn shell script that implements a menu-driven calendar
program. It supports addition, deletion, modification, and listing of
calendar entries. It also provides the ability to find the calendar entry
for the current day and list all calendar entries.

```ksh
#!/bin/ksh
#
#   kcal - Korn Shell calendar program
#
#   Anatole Olczak - ASP, Inc
#

# Process errors
function error {
    print ${1:-"unexplained error encountered"}
    exit ${2}
}

# Check arguments
if (($# > 0))
then
    error "Usage: $0" 1
fi

# Use environment variable setting or default
: ${CALFILE:=$HOME/.calfile}
```

```
# Create calendar file if non-existent; flag
# creation error
if [[ ! -f $CALFILE ]]
then
    print "Creating default $HOME/.calfile"
    > $HOME/.calfile || error "$HOME/.calfile: \
    cannot create" 1
fi

# Variable declaration/assignment
typeset DATE= LINE= ENTRY= REPLY="yes" \
PAGER=$(whence more) CLEAR=$(whence clear)

# Set trap to not allow interrupts
trap '$CLEAR; print "\aInterrupt ignored - use \
menu to quit.  Press <Return> to continue."; \
read TMP; $CLEAR' INT QUIT

# Set EXIT trap - perform cleanup
trap 'rm -rf /tmp/.FOUND$$ /tmp/.CHANGE$$ \
/tmp/.DEL$$' EXIT

# Check the date
function checkdate {
    while true
    do
        # Prompt for date
        read DATE?"Enter date in mmdd[yy] format
(default today):"
        case $DATE in
```

```
            # Default - use todays date
            "" ) DATE=$(date +%m-%d-%y)
                break ;;

            # Check the given date
            +([0-9]) )
                case ${#DATE} in
                    4|6)# Set month to first 2 chars
                        typeset -L2 MO=$DATE

                        # Check length for year;
                        # 4 = mmdd, 6 = mmddyy
                        if (($ {#DATE} == 6))
                        then
                            # Set TMP to get date
                            typeset -L4 TMP=$DATE

                            # Get day
                            typeset -R2 DA=$TMP

                            # Get year
                            typeset -R2 YR=$DATE
                        else
                            # Get day
                            typeset -R2 DA=$DATE

                            # Set to current year
                            YR=$(date +%y)
                            DATE=$DATE$YR
                        fi
```

```
                # Now check individual values
                # Day must be in range 01-31
                if ((DA < 01 || DA > 31))
                then
                     print "$DA: invalid day \
                     format - try again"
                     continue
                fi
                # Month must be 01-12
                if ((MO < 01 || MO > 12))
                then
                     print "$MO: invalid \
                     month format - try again"
                     continue
                fi

                # Set date format mm-dd-yy
                DATE=$MO-$DA-$YR
                break ;;

          * ) # Invalid format
                print "$DATE: invalid date \
                format - try again" ;;

          esac ;;

    # Invalid date given
    * ) print "$DATE: invalid format - try again" ;;

    esac
    done
}
```

```
# Add new calendar entry
function addentry {
    $CLEAR
    ENTRY="$DATE"

    # For existent entry, just add more data
    COUNT=$(grep -c "^$DATE" $CALFILE)
    if ((COUNT > 0))
    then
        changeentry
        return
    fi
    # Prompt for input
    print "Enter info for $DATE: (enter <Return> by
itself when finished)"
    while true
    do
        read LINE?"=>"
        if [[ -n $LINE ]]
        then
            ENTRY="$ENTRY,$LINE"
        else
            break
        fi
    done

    # Append to calendar file
    print $ENTRY>>$CALFILE
```

```
    # Sort the calendar file
    sort -o $CALFILE $CALFILE
}


function formatentry {
    $CLEAR

    typeset IFS="," \
    BORDER="**************************************" \
    BORDER1="*                                 *" \
    FILE=$1

    if [[ -s $FILE ]]
    then

        # Open calendar file for reading, and
        # format output
        (exec 0<$FILE
        while read -r ENTRY
        do
            print "$BORDER\n$BORDER1"
            set $ENTRY
            typeset -L35 LINE="DATE: $1"
            print "* $LINE*"
            shift
            print "$BORDER1"
            for i
            do
                LINE="$i"
                print "* $LINE*"
            done
```

```
            print "$BORDER1"
        done
        print "$BORDER"
        ) | $PAGER
    else
        print "No entries found."
    fi

    # Prompt to continue
    until [[ $REPLY = "" ]]
    do
        read REPLY?"Enter <Return> to continue..."
    done
}


# Find specific entry
function findentry {
    $CLEAR
    # Check for entry - put it in temp found file
    grep $DATE $CALFILE >/tmp/.FOUND$$

    # Format found entries
    formatentry /tmp/.FOUND$$
}


# Change an entry
function changeentry {

    # Find specific entry - put it in temp found file
    grep $DATE $CALFILE | tr ',' '\012'>/tmp/.FOUND$$
```

```
# Return if no entry was found
if [[ ! -s /tmp/.FOUND$$ ]]
then
     $CLEAR
     read TMP?"Entry for $DATE not found - press
<Return> to continue"
     return
fi

# Prompt again for change
while [[ $REPLY != "" ]]
do
     read REPLY?"Change/Add to entry for <$DATE>?"
     case $REPLY in

          [yY]* | "" )
               break ;;
          [nN]* ) print "Ok, aborting entry change"
               return ;;

          * ) print "Invalid reply - try again." ;;

     esac
done

# Edit the temporary found file
${EDITOR:-vi} /tmp/.FOUND$$
```

```
    # Remove the specified original entry
    grep -v $DATE $CALFILE > /tmp/.CHANGE$$

    # Put back new change in record format.
    # Add trailing \n
    (cat /tmp/.FOUND$$ | tr '\012' ',' ; print   ) \
    >>/tmp/.CHANGE$$

    # Put back new file
    cat /tmp/.CHANGE$$ > $CALFILE

    # Clean up tmp files
    rm -rf /tmp/.CHANGE$$ /tmp/.FOUND$$
}

# Remove specific entry
function delentry {

    # Look for entry
    grep $DATE $CALFILE >/tmp/.FOUND$$

    # Return if not found
    if [[ ! -s /tmp/.FOUND$$ ]]
    then
        $CLEAR
        read TMP?"Entry for $DATE not found - press
<Return> to continue"
        return
    fi
```

```
    # Prompt to delete
    while [[ $REPLY != "" ]]
    do
        read REPLY?"Delete entry for <$DATE>?"
        case $REPLY in

            [yY]* | "" ) break ;;

            [nN]* ) print "ok, aborting delete";
return ;;

            * ) print "Invalid reply - try again." ;;

        esac
    done
    # Merge changes - put them in temporary file
    grep -v $DATE $CALFILE > /tmp/.DEL$$

    # Put back new file
    cat /tmp/.DEL$$ > $CALFILE

    # Clean up tmp files
    rm -rf /tmp/.DEL$$ /tmp/.FOUND$$
}

# Set menu selection prompt
PS3="Enter selection or <Return> for default menu:"

# Display menu
while true
do
    $CLEAR
    select i in "Add calendar entry" "Delete calendar
entry" "Change calendar entry" "Find calendar entry"
"List all calendar entries" "List todays calendar
```

```
entry"  "Exit"
    do
        case $i in
                "Add calendar entry")
                    checkdate
                    addentry
                    $CLEAR ;;
                "Delete calendar entry")
                    checkdate
                    delentry
                    $CLEAR ;;
                "Change calendar entry")
                    checkdate
                    changeentry
                    $CLEAR ;;
                "Find calendar entry")

                    checkdate

                    findentry

                    $CLEAR ;;
                "List all calendar entries")

                    formatentry $CALFILE

                    $CLEAR ;;
                "List todays calendar entry")

                    DATE=$(date +%m-%d-%y)

                    findentry

                    $CLEAR ;;
                "Exit")

                    exit ;;
                * ) print "\aInvalid selection \c"

                    read TMP?"- press <Return> to
continue"

                    $CLEAR

                    continue ;;
```

```
        esac
    done
done
```

Example output:

```
$ kcal

1) Add calendar entry
2) Delete calendar entry
3) Change calendar entry
4) Find calendar entry
5) List all calendar entries
6) List todays calendar entry
7) Exit

Enter selection or <Return> for default menu:1
Enter date in mmdd[yy] format (default today):0912
Enter info for 09-12-96: (enter <Return> by itself
when finished)
=>Renata's birthday!
=>

Enter selection or <Return> for default menu:<Return>
1) Add calendar entry
2) Delete calendar entry
3) Change calendar entry
4) Find calendar entry
5) List all calendar entries
6) List todays calendar entry
7) Exit

Enter selection or <Return> for default menu:1
Enter date in mmdd[yy] format (default today):1225

Enter info for 12-25-96: (enter <Return> by itself
when finished)
=>Christmas
=>
```

```
Enter selection or <Return> for default menu:<Return>
1) Add calendar entry
2) Delete calendar entry
3) Change calendar entry
4) Find calendar entry
5) List all calendar entries
6) List todays calendar entry
7) Exit
Enter selection or <Return> for default menu:1
Enter date in mmdd[yy] format (default today):1021

Enter info for 10-21-96: (enter <Return> by itself
when finished)
=>Racquetball game at gym
=>1:00 PM
=>376-6313
=>

Enter selection or <Return> for default menu:<Return>
1) Add calendar entry
2) Delete calendar entry
3) Change calendar entry
4) Find calendar entry
5) List all calendar entries
6) List todays calendar entry
7) Exit

Enter selection or <Return> for default menu:5
**************************************
*                                    *
* DATE: 09-12-96                      *
*                                    *
* Renata's birthday!                  *
*                                    *
**************************************
*                                    *
```

```
* DATE: 10-21-96                      *
*                                     *
* Racquetball game at gym             *
* 1:00 PM                             *
* 370-6313                            *
*                                     *
***************************************
*                                     *
* DATE: 12-25-96                      *
*                                     *
* Christmas                           *
*                                     *
***************************************
Enter <Return> to continue...
Enter selection or <Return> for default menu:<Return>
1) Add calendar entry
2) Delete calendar entry
3) Change calendar entry
4) Find calendar entry
5) List all calendar entries
6) List todays calendar entry
7) Exit

Enter selection or <Return> for default menu:6
No entries found

Enter <Return> to continue...
Enter selection or <Return> for default menu:<Return>
1) Add calendar entry
2) Delete calendar entry
3) Change calendar entry
4) Find calendar entry
5) List all calendar entries
6) List todays calendar entry
7) Exit

Enter selection or <Return> for default menu:4
Enter date in mmdd[yy] format (default today):0912
```

```
******************************************
*                                        *
* DATE: 09-12-96                         *
*                                        *
* Renata's birthday!                     *
*                                        *
******************************************
Enter <Return> to continue...

Enter selection or <Return> for default menu:<Return>
1) Add calendar entry
2) Delete calendar entry
3) Change calendar entry
4) Find calendar entry
5) List all calendar entries
6) List todays calendar entry
7) Exit

Enter selection or <Return> for default menu:3
Enter date in mmdd[yy] format (default today):1021
Change/Add to entry for <10-21-96>?y
.  .  .
1:00 PM
376-6313
.  .  .
:wq
"/tmp/.FOUND313" 4 lines, 50 characters

Enter selection or <Return> for default menu:<Return>
1) Add calendar entry
2) Delete calendar entry
3) Change calendar entry
4) Find calendar entry
5) List all calendar entries
6) List todays calendar entry
7) Exit
```

```
Enter selection or <Return> for default menu:5

**************************************
*                                    *
* DATE: 09-12-96                     *
*                                    *
* Renata's birthday!                 *
*                                    *
**************************************
*                                    *
* DATE: 10-21-96                     *
*                                    *
* Racquetball game at gym            *
* 1:00 PM                            *
* 370-6313                           *
*                                    *
**************************************
*                                    *
* DATE: 12-25-96                     *
*                                    *
* Christmas                          *
*                                    *
**************************************
Enter <Return> to continue...
1) Add calendar entry
2) Delete calendar entry
3) Change calendar entry
4) Find calendar entry
5) List all calendar entries
6) List todays calendar entry
7) Exit

Enter selection or <Return> for default menu:2
Enter date in mmdd[yy] format (default today):1021
Delete entry for <10-21-96>?y
```

```
Enter <Return> to continue...

Enter selection or <Return> for default menu:<Return>
1) Add calendar entry
2) Delete calendar entry
3) Change calendar entry
4) Find calendar entry
5) List all calendar entries
6) List todays calendar entry
7) Exit

Enter selection or <Return> for default menu:7
```

Appendix E: Korn Shell Quick Reference

COMMAND EXECUTION

The primary prompt (**PS1** - default **$** or **#** for super-users) is displayed whenever the Korn shell is ready to read a command. The secondary prompt (**PS2** - default >) is displayed when the Korn shell needs more input.

Command Execution Format

command1 ; *command2*
> execute *command1* followed by *command2*

command &   execute *command* asynchronously in the background;
> do not wait for completion

command1 | *command2*
> pass the standard output of *command1* to standard input of *command2*

command1 && *command2*
> execute *command2* if *command1* returns zero (successful) exit status

command1 || *command2*
> execute *command2* if *command1* returns non-zero (unsuccessful) exit status

command |&   execute *command* asynchronously with its standard input and output attached to the parent shell; use **read –p/print –p** to manipulate the standard input/output

command \   continue *command* onto the next line

{ *command* ; } execute *command* in the current shell

(*command*)   execute *command* in a subshell

REDIRECTING INPUT/OUTPUT

The Korn shell provides a number of operators that can be used to manipulate command input/output, files, and co-processes.

I/O Redirection Operators

<file redirect standard input from *file*

>file redirect standard output to *file*. Create *file* if non-existent, else overwrite.

>>file append standard output to *file*. Create *file* if non-existent.

>|file redirect standard output to *file*. Create *file* if non-existent, else overwrite even if **noclobber** is set.

<>file open *file* for reading & writing as standard input

<&− close standard input

>&− close standard output

<&n redirect standard input from file descriptor *n*

>&n redirect standard output to file descriptor *n*

n<file redirect file descriptor *n* from *file*

n>file redirect file descriptor *n* to *file*

n>>file redirect file descriptor *n* to *file*. Create *file* if non-existent, else overwrite.

n>|file redirect file descriptor *n* to *file*. Create *file* if non-existent, else overwrite even if **noclobber** is set.

n<&m redirect file descriptor *n* from file descriptor *m*

n>&m redirect file descriptor *n* to file descriptor *m*

n<>file open *file* for reading & writing as file descriptor *n*

n<<word redirect to file descriptor *n* until *word* is read

n<<−word redirect to file descriptor *n* until *word* is read; ignore leading tabs

n<&− close file descriptor *n* for standard input

n>&− close file descriptor *n* for standard output

*n<&***p** redirect input from co-process to file descriptor *n*. If *n* is not specified, use standard input.

*n>&***p** redirect output of co-process to file descriptor *n*. If *n* is not specified, use standard output.

Appendix E: Korn Shell Quick Reference

FILENAME SUBSTITUTION

File name substitution is a feature which allows special characters and patterns to substituted with file names in the current directory, or arguments to the **case** and [[...]] commands.

Pattern-Matching Characters/Patterns

?	match any single character
*	match zero or more characters, including null
[abc]	match any characters between the brackets
[x−z]	match any characters in the range **x** to **z**
[a−c e−g]	match any characters in the range **a** to **c**, **e** to **g**
[!abc]	match any characters not between the brackets
[!x−z]	match any characters not in the range **x** to **z**
.	strings starting with '.' must be explicitly matched
?(*pattern-list*)	match zero or one occurrence of any *pattern*
*(*pattern-list*)	match zero or more occurrences of any *pattern*
+(*pattern-list*)	match one or more occurrence of any *pattern*
@(*pattern-list*)	match exactly one occurrence of any *pattern*
!(*pattern-list*)	match anything except any *pattern*
pattern-list	multiple patterns must be separated with a '|' character

VARIABLES

Like in other high-level progamming languages, variables are used by the Korn shell to store values. Variable names can begin with an alphabetic or underscore character, followed by one or more alphanumeric or underscore characters. Other variable names that contain only digits or special characters are reserved for special variables (called *parameters*) set directly by the Korn shell. Data types (called *attributes*) and one-dimensional arrays are also supported by the Korn shell.

Variable/Attribute Assignment Format

variable= declare *variable* and set it to null

typeset *variable=*
>	declare *variable* and set it to null. If used within a function, then a local variable is declared.

variable=value assign *value* to *variable*

typeset *variable=value*
>	assign *value* to *variable*. If used within a function, then a local variable is declared.

typeset *−attribute variable=value*
>	assign *attribute* and *value* to *variable*

typeset *−attribute variable*
>	assign *attribute* to *variable*

typeset *+attribute variable*
>	remove *attribute* from *variable* (except **readonly**)

Variable/Attribute Listing Format

typeset *−attribute*
>	display a list of variable names and their values that have attribute set

typeset *+attribute*
>	display a list of variable names that have attribute set

VARIABLE ATTRIBUTES

Variables can have one or more attributes that specify their internal representation, scope, or the way they are displayed.

Variable Attribute Assignment Format

typeset *−H variable*
>	Set UNIX to host-name file mapping for non-UNIX systems

typeset *−i variable*
>	Set *variable* to be integer type

typeset –i*n variable*

> Set *variable* to be integer type with base *n*

typeset –l *variable*

> Set *variable* to lower case

typeset –L *variable*

> Left justify *variable*; the field width is specified by the first assignment

typeset –L*n variable*

> Left justify *variable*; set field width to *n*

typeset –LZ*n variable*

> Left justify *variable*; set field width to *n* and strip leading zeros

typeset –r *variable*

> Set *variable* to be readonly (same as **readonly**)

typeset –R *variable*

> Right justify *variable*; the field width is specified by the first assignment

typeset –R*n variable*

> Right justify *variable*; set field width to *n*

typeset –RZ*n variable*

> Right justify *variable*; set field width to *n* and fill with leading zeros

typeset –t *variable*

> Set the user-defined attribute for *variable*. This has no meaning to the Korn shell.

typeset –u *variable*

> Set *variable* to upper case

typeset –x *variable*

> Automatically export variable to the environment (same as **export**)

typeset –Z *variable*

> Same as **typeset –RZ**

VARIABLE SUBSTITUTION

Variable values can be accessed and manipulated using variable expansion. Basic expansion is done by preceding the variable name with the $ character. Other types of expansion can be used to return portions or the length of variables, use default or alternate values, assign default or alternate values, and more.

Variable Expansion Format

${*variable*}   value of *variable*

${#*variable*}   length of *variable*

${*variable*:−*word*}

> value of *variable* if set and not null, else print *word*. If **:** is omitted, *variable* is only checked if it is set.

${*variable*:=*word*}

> value of *variable* if set and not null, else variable is set to *word*, then expanded. If **:** is omitted, *variable* is only checked if it is set.

${*variable*:?}   value of *variable* if set and not null, else print

> "**variable: parameter null or not set**". If **:** is omitted, *variable* is only checked if it is set.

${*variable*:?*word*}

> value of *variable* if set and not null, else print value of *word* and exit. If **:** is omitted, *variable* is only checked if it is set.

${*variable*:+*word*}

> value of *word* if *variable* is set and not null, else nothing is substituted. If **:** is omitted, *variable* is only checked if it is set.

${*variable*#*pattern*}

> value of *variable* without the smallest beginning portion that matches *pattern*

${*variable*##*pattern*}

> value of *variable* without the largest beginning portion that matches *pattern*

${*variable%pattern*}

> value of *variable* without the smallest ending portion that
> matches *pattern*

${*variable%%pattern*}

> value of *variable* without the largest ending portion that
> matches *pattern*

SPECIAL PARAMETERS

Some special parameters are automatically set by the Korn shell, and
usually cannot be directly set or modified.

Special Parameters

$#	number of positional parameters
$@	all positional parameters ("**$1**", "**$2**", ..., "**$***n**")
$*	all positional parameters ("**$1 $2 ... $***n**")
$?	exit status of the last command
$$	process id of the current shell
$–	current options in effect
$!	process id of last background command

SPECIAL VARIABLES

There are a number of variables provided by the Korn shell that allow
you to customize your working environment. Some are automatically
set by the Korn shell, some have a default value if not set, while others
have no value unless specifically set.

Special Variables

CDPATH search path for **cd** when not given a full pathname (no
default)

COLUMNS   window width for in-line edit mode and **select**
command lists (default **80**)

EDITOR pathname of the editor for in-line editing (default **/bin/ed**)

ENV   pathname of the environment file (no default)

ERRNO error number returned by most recently failed system call (system dependent)

FCEDIT default editor for the **fc** command

FPATH search path for auto-loaded functions
pathname of the history file

HISTFILE   pathname of the history file (default **$HOME/
.sh_history**)

HISTSIZE   number of commands to save in the command history file (default **128**)

HOME home directory

IFS internal field separator (default space, tab, newline)

LINES specifies column length for **select** lists

MAIL name of mail file

MAILCHECK
specifies how often to check for mail (default **600** seconds)

MAILPATH search path for mail files (no default)

OLDPWD previous working directory

OPTARG value of the last **getopts** option argument

OPTIND index of the last **getopts** option argument

PATH search path for commands (default **/bin:/usr/bin:**)

PPID process id of the parent shell

PS1 primary prompt string (default $, #)

PS2 secondary prompt string (default >)

PS3 **select** command prompt (default #?)

PS4 debug prompt string (default +)

RANDOM contains a random number

REPLY contains the input to the **read** command when no variables are given

SECONDS contains number of seconds since Korn shell invocation

SHELL pathname of shell

TERM specifies your terminal type (no default)

TMOUT Korn shell timeout variable (default **0**)

VISUAL pathname of the editor for in-line editing

ARRAY VARIABLES

One-dimensional arrays are supported by the Korn shell. On most systems, arrays can have a maximum of 512 elements. Array subscripts start at 0 and go up to 511. Any variable can become an array by simply referring to it with a subscript.

Array Variable Assignment Format

variable[0]=*value* *variable*[1]=*value* ... *variable*[*n*]=*value*
set −A *variable value0 value1 ... valuen*
typeset *variable*[0]=*value* *variable*[1]=*value* ... *variable*[*n*]=*value*
        assign values to array variable elements
set +A *variable value0 value1 ... valuen*
        reassign values to array variable elements
typeset *−attributes variable*[0]=*value variable*[1]=*value* ...
        variable[*n*]=*value*
        assign *attributes* and values to array variable elements
typeset *−attributes variable*
        assign *attributes* to array variable
typeset +*attributes variable*
        remove *attributes* from array variable (except **readonly**)

Array Variable Evaluation

${*array*}, $*array*
        array element zero
${*array*[*n*]}   array element *n*
${*array*[*]}, ${*array*[@]}
        all elements of an array
${#*array*[*]}, ${#*array*[@]}
        number of array elements
${#*array*[*n*]}   length of array element *n*

MISC SUBSTITUTION

$(*command*) replace with the standard output of *command*
$((*arithmetic-expression*))
              replace with the result of *arithmetic-expression*
$(<*file*)   replace with the contents of *file*
`command`   replace with the standard output of *command*
~   replace with **$HOME**
~*user*   replace with the home directory of *user*
~–   replace with **$OLDPWD** (previous directory)
~+   replace with **$PWD** (current directory)

QUOTING

Quotes are used when assigning values containing whitespace or special characters, to delimit variables, and to assign command output. They also improve readability by separating arguments from commands.

'...'   remove the special meaning of enclosed characters except '
"..."   remove the special meaning of enclosed characters except $,
              ', and \
\c   remove the special meaning of character *c*
`command`   replace with the standard output of *command*

IN-LINE EDITORS

In-line editing provides the ability to edit the current or previous commands before executing them. There are three in-line editing modes available: **emacs**, **gmacs**, and **vi**. The **emacs** and **gmacs** modes are basically the same, except for the way **Ctl-t** is handled. The in-line editing mode is specified by setting the **EDITOR** or **VISUAL** variables, or with the **set –o** command. The editing window width is specified by the **COLUMNS** variable. For lines longer than the window width, a mark is displayed to notify position. The marks >, <, and * specify that the line extends to the right, left, or both sides of the window.

Appendix E: Korn Shell Quick Reference

Vi Input Mode Commands

\#, \<Backspace>
        delete previous character
Ctl-d   terminate the Korn shell
Ctl-v   escape next character
Ctl-w   delete previous word
Ctl-x, **@** kill the entire line
\<Return> execute current line
\\   escape next *erase* or *kill* character

Vi Motion Edit Commands

$[n]$**h**, $[n]$\<Backspace>
        move left one character
$[n]$l, $[n]$\<Space>
        move forward one character
$[n]$**b**   move backward one word
$[n]$**B**   move backward one word; ignore punctuation
$[n]$**w**   move forward one word
$[n]$**W**   move forward one word; ignore punctuation
$[n]$**e**   move to end of next word
$[n]$**E**   move to end of next word; ignore punctuation
$[n]$**f**c move forward to character c
$[n]$**F**c move backward to character c
$[n]$**t**c move forward to character before character c
$[n]$**T**c move backward to character before character c
$[n]$;   repeat last **f**, **F**, **t**, or **T** command
$[n]$,   repeat last **f**, **F**, **t**, or **T** command, but in opposite direction
0   move cursor to start of line
^   move cursor to first non-blank character in line
$ move cursor to end of line

Korn Shell User and Programming Manual

Vi Search/Edit History Commands

[*n*]**G**	get last command (or command *n*)
[*n*]**j**, [*n*]**+**	get next command from history file
[*n*]**k**, [*n*]**−**	get previous command from history file
n	repeat last / or ? search
N	repeat last / or ? search, except in opposite direction
/*string*	search backward in history file for command that matches *string*
?*string*	search forward in history file for command that matches *string*

Vi Text Modification Commands

a	add text after current character
A	append text to end of current line
[*n*]**c**X, **c**[*n*]X	change current character up to cursor position defined by X
[*n*]**d**X, **d**[*n*]X	delete current character up to cursor position defined by X
[*n*]**y**X, **y**[*n*]X	copy current character up to cursor position defined by X into buffer
X	used to define ending cursor position for **c**, **d**, or **y** commands

    b   backwards to beginning of word
    e   cursor to end of current word
    w   cursor to beginning of next word
    W B E   same as **w b e**, but ignore punctuation
    0   before cursor to end of current line
    $ cursor to end of current line

C	change current character to end of line
D	delete current character through end of line
i	insert text left of the current character
I	insert text before beginning of line
[*n*]**p**	put previously yanked/deleted text after cursor

[*n*]**P**	put previously yanked/deleted text before cursor
[*n*]**r***c*	replace current character with *c*
R	replace text from cursor to <ESCAPE>
S	delete entire line and enter input mode
yy	copy current line into buffer
[*n*]x	delete current character
[*n*]X	delete previous character
[*n*]**.**	repeat last text modification command
[*n*]~	toggle case of current character
[*n*]_	append last word of previous **ksh** command
\	replace current word with filename that matches *word**. For unique matches, append a / to directories and " " (space) for files.

Vi Other Edit Commands

u	undo last text modification command
U	undo text modification commands on current line
[*n*]**v**	return output of **fc –e** command
Ctl-l	redisplay current line
Ctl-j	execute current line
Ctl-m	execute current line
#	insert a # (comment) at beginning of current line
=	list files that match current *word**
*	replace current word with files that match *word**
@_*c*	insert value of alias *c*

Emacs/Gmacs In-Line Editor Commands

Ctl-b	move left one character
Ctl-f	move right one character
Esc-b	move left one word
Esc-f	move right one word
Ctl-a	move to beginning of line
Ctl-e	move to end of line

Ctl-h	delete preceding character
Ctl-x	delete the entire line
Ctl-k	delete from cursor to end of line
Ctl-d	delete current character
Esc-d	delete current word
Ctl-w	delete from cursor to mark
Ctl-y	undo last delete (w/**Esc-p**)
Ctl-p	get previous command from history file
Ctl-n	get next command from history file
Ctl-o	execute current command line and get next command line
Ctl-r_string_	search backward in history file for command that contains _string_
Ctl-c	change current character to upper case
Esc-c	change current word to upper case
Esc-l	change current character to lower case
Esc-p	save to buffer from cursor to mark
Esc-<SPACE>, Ctl-@	mark current location
Ctl-l	redisplay current line
Ctl-]_c_	move cursor forward to character _c_
Ctl-xCtl-x	interchange the cursor and mark
erase	delete previous character
Esc-Ctl-h	delete previous word
Esc-h	delete previous word
Ctl-t	transpose current and next character (**emacs**)
Ctl-t	transpose two previous characters (**gmacs**)
Ctl-j	execute current line
Ctl-m	execute current line
Esc-<	get oldest command line
Esc->	get previous command line
Esc-_n_	define numeric parameter _n_ for next command (command can be **Ctl-c, Ctl-d, Ctl-k, Ctl-n, Ctl-p, Ctl-r, Esc-., Ctl-]**_c_, **Esc-_, Esc-b, Esc-c, Esc-d, Esc-f, Esc-h, Esc-l, Esc-Ctl-h**)

Esc-*c*	insert value of alias *_c* (*c* cannot be **b, c, d, f, h, l,** or **p**)
Esc-., Esc-_	insert last word of previous command
Esc-Esc	replace current word with filename that matches *word**. For unique matches, append a / to directories and " " (space) for files
Esc-=	list files that match current *word**
Ctl-u	multiply parameter of next command by 4
****	escape next character
Ctl-v	display version of shell
Esc-#	insert a # (comment) at beginning of current line

JOB CONTROL

Job control is a process manipulation feature found in the Korn shell. It allows programs to be stopped and restarted, moved between the foreground and background, their processing status to be displayed, and more. To enable job control, the **monitor** option must be enabled. By default, this is enabled on systems that support the job control feature. When a program is run in the background, a job number and process id are returned.

Job Control Commands

bg	put current stopped job in the background
bg *%n*	put stopped job *n* in the background
fg	move current background job into the foreground
fg *%n*	move background job *n* into the foreground
jobs	display status of all jobs
jobs –l	display status of all jobs along with process ids
jobs –p	display process ids of all jobs
kill –l	list all valid signal names
kill [*–signal*] *%n*	
	send specified signal to job *n* (default 9)
set –m, set –o monitor	
	enable job control
stty [*–*]**tostop**	allow/prevent background jobs from generating output

wait   wait for all background jobs to complete
wait *%n* wait for background job *n* to complete
Ctl-z   stop the current job

Job Name Format

%n   job *n*
%+, *%%* current job
%−   previous job
%string   job whose name begins with *string*
%?string job that matches part or all of *string*

ARITHMETIC

Integer arithmetic is performed with the **let** and **((...))** commands. All of the operators from the C programming language (except ++, −−, and ?:) are supported by the Korn shell. The format for arithmetic constants is:

> *number*
>
> or
>
> *base#number*

where *base* is a decimal number between **2** and **36** that specifies the arithmetic base. If not specified, the default is base **10**. The arithmetic base can also be set with the **typeset −i** command.

Arithmetic Commands

let *"arithmetic-expression"*
((*arithmetic-expression***))**
            evaluate arithmetic expression
integer *variable*
            declare an integer variable
integer *variable=integer-value*
            declare an integer variable and set it to a value

integer *variable="arithmetic-assignment-expression"*

        declare an integer variable and assign it the value of the *arithmetic-assignment-expression*

typeset –i*n variable[=value]*

        declare a base *n* integer variable, and optionally assign it a value

Arithmetic Operators

–	unary minus
!	logical negation
~	bitwise negation
*, /, %	multiplication, division, remainder (modulo)
+, –	addition, subtraction
<<, >>	left shift, right shift
<=, <	less than or equal to, less than
>=, >	greater than or equal to, greater than
==, !=	equal to, not equal to
&	bitwise AND
^	bitwise exclusive OR
|	bitwise OR
&&	logical AND
||	logical OR
=	assignment
*=, /=, %=	multiply assign, divide assign, modulo assign
+=, –=	increment, decrement
<<=, >>=	left shift assign, right shift assign
&=, ^=, |=	bitwise AND assign, bitwise exclusive OR assign, bitwise OR assign
(...)	grouping (used to override precedence rules)

OPTIONS

The Korn shell has a number of options that specify your environment
and control execution. They can be enabled/disabled with the **set**
command or on the **ksh** command line.

Enabling/Disabling Options

ksh [–/+*options*]

        enable/disable specified options

set [–/+*options*]

        enable/disable specified options

List of Options

–a	automatically export variables that are defined
–b	execute all background jobs at a lower priority
–c *cmds*	read and execute *cmds* (w/**ksh** only)
–e	execute **ERR** trap (if set) on non-zero exit status from any commands
–f	disable file name expansion
–h	make commands tracked aliases when first encountered
–i	execute in interactive mode (w/**ksh** only)
–k	put variable assignment arguments in environment
–m	enable job control (system dependent)
–n	read commands without executing them

–o allexport

        automatically export variables that are defined

–o bgnice execute all background jobs at a lower priority

–o emacs use emacs-style editor for in-line editing

–o errexit execute **ERR** trap (if set) on non-zero exit status from any commands

–o gmacs use gmacs-style editor for in-line editing

–o ignoreeof

        do not exit on end of file (default **Ctl-d**); use **exit**

−o keyword
> put variable assignment arguments in environment

−o markdirs
> display trailing / on directory names resulting from file
> name substitution

−o monitor
> enable job control (system dependent)

−o noclobber
> prevent I/O redirection from truncating existing files

−o noexec read commands without executing them

−o noglob disable file name expansion

−o nolog do not save function definitions in history file

−o nounset
> return error on substitution of unset variables

−o privileged
> disable processing of **$HOME/.profile**, and use **/etc/**
> **suid_profile** instead of **ENV** file

−o trackall
> make commands tracked aliases when first encountered

−o verbose display input lines as they are read

−o vi use vi-style editor for in-line editing

−o viraw process each character as it is typed in vi mode

−o xtrace display commands and arguments as executed

−p disable processing of **$HOME/.profile**, and use **/etc/**
> **suid_profile** instead of **ENV** file

−r run a restricted shell (w/**ksh** only)

−s read commands from standard input

−t exit after reading and executing one command

−u return error on substitution of unset variables

−v display input lines as they are read

−x display commands and arguments as executed

− disable −v and −x flags; don't process remaining flags

ALIASES

Aliases are command macros and are used as shorthand for other commands, especially frequently-used ones.

Alias Commands

alias   display a list of aliases and their values

alias *name*   display the value for alias *name*

alias *name='value'*
          create an alias *name* set to *value*

alias –t   display a list of tracked aliases

alias –t *name='value'*
          create a tracked alias *name* set to *value*

alias –x   display a list of exported aliases

alias –x *name='value'*
          create an exported alias *name* set to *value*

unalias *name*   remove the alias name

Some Preset Aliases

Alias	Value	Definition
autoload	**typeset –fu**	define an autoloading function
echo	**print –**	display arguments
functions	**typeset –f**	display list of functions
hash	**alias –t –**	display list of tracked aliases
history	**fc –l**	list commands from history file
integer	**typeset –i**	declare integer variable
r	**fc –e –**	re-execute previous command
stop	**kill –STOP**	suspend job
type	**whence –v**	display information about
	commands	

CONDITIONAL EXPRESSIONS

The [[...]] command is used to evaluate conditional expressions with file attributes, strings, and integers. The basic format is:

[[*expression*]]

where *expression* is the condition you are evaluating. There must be whitespace after the opening brackets, and before the closing brackets. Whitespace must also separate the expression arguments and operators. If the expression evaluates to true, then a zero exit status is returned, otherwise the expression evaluates to false and a non-zero exit status is returned.

[[...]] String Operators

−n *string*	true if length of *string* is not zero
−o *option*	true if *option* is set
−z *string*	true if length of *string* is zero
string1 = *string2*	true if *string1* is equal to *string2*
string1 != *string2*	true if *string1* is not equal to *string2*
string = *pattern*	true if *string* matches *pattern*
string != *pattern*	true if *string* does not match *pattern*
string1 < *string2*	true if *string1* is less than *string2*
string1 > *string2*	true if *string1* is greater than *string2*

[[...]] File Operators

−a *file*	true if *file* exists
−b *file*	true if *file* exists and is a block special file
−c *file*	true if *file* exists and is a character special file
−d *file*	true if *file* exists and is a directory
−f *file*	true if *file* exists is a regular file
−g *file*	true if *file* exists and its setgid bit is set
−G *file*	true if *file* exists and its group id matches the current effective group id
−k *file*	true if *file* exists and its sticky bit is set

−L *file*   true if *file* exists and is a symbolic link

−O *file*   true if *file* exists and is owned by the effective user id

−p *file*   true if *file* exists and is a fifo special file or a pipe

−r *file*   true if *file* exists and is readable

−s *file*   true if *file* exists and its size is greater than zero

−S *file*   true if *file* exists and is a socket

−t *n*   true if file descriptor *n* is open and associated with a terminal device

−u *file*   true if *file* exists and its set user-id bit is set

−w *file*   true if *file* exists and is writable

−x *file*   true if *file* exists and is executable. If *file* is a directory, then true indicates that the directory is readable.

file1 **−ef** *file2*
> true if *file1* and *file2* exist and refer to same file

file1 **−nt** *file2*
> true if *file1* exists and is newer than *file2*

file1 **−ot** *file2*
> true if *file1* exists and is older than *file2*

[[...]] Integer Operators

exp1 **−eq** *exp2* true if *exp1* is equal to *exp2*

exp1 **−ne** *exp2* true if *exp1* is not equal to *exp2*

exp1 **−le** *exp2* true if *exp1* is less than or equal to *exp2*

exp1 **−lt** *exp2* true if *exp1* is less than *exp2*

exp1 **−ge** *exp2* true if *exp1* is greater than or equal to *exp2*

exp1 **−gt** *exp2* true if *exp1* is greater than *exp2*

Other [[...]] Operators

!*expression*   true if *expression* is false

(*expression***)**   true if *expression* is true; used to group expressions

[[*expression1* **&&** *expression2* **]]**
> true if both *expression1* and *expression2* are true

[[*expression1* || *expression2*]]

> true either *expression1* or *expression2* are true

CONTROL COMMANDS

case *value* **in**

   pattern1) *commands1* **;;**

   pattern2) *commands2* **;;**

   . . .

   patternn) *commandsn* **;;**

esac

Execute *commands* associated with the *pattern* that matches *value*.

for *variable* **in** *word1 word2 . . . wordn*
do

   commands

done

Execute *commands* once for each *word*, setting *variable* to successive *words* each time.

for *variable*
do

   commands

done

Execute *commands* once for each positional parameter, setting *variable* to successive positional parameters each time.

if *command1*
then

   commands

fi

Execute *commands* if *command1* returns a zero exit status.

if *command1*
then
> *commands2*

else
> *commands3*

fi

Execute *commands2* if *commands1* returns a zero exit status, otherwise execute *commands3*.

if *command1*
then
> *commands*

elif *command2*
then
> *commands*

. . .

elif *commandn*
then
> *commands*

else
> *commands*

fi

If *command1* returns a zero exit status, or *command2* returns a zero exit status, or *commandn* returns a zero exit status, then execute the *commands* corresponding to the **if/elif** that returned a zero exit status. Otherwise, if all the **if/elif** commands return a non-zero exit status, execute the commands between **else** and **fi**.

select *variable* **in** *word1 word2 . . . wordn*
do
> *commands*

done

Display a menu of numbered choices *word1* through *wordn* followed by a prompt (**#?** or **$PS3**). Execute *commands* for each menu selection, setting *variable* to each selection and **REPLY** to the response until a **break**, **exit**, or EOF is encountered.

select *variable*
do
>   *commands*

done

Display a menu of numbered choices for each positional parameter followed by a prompt (**#?** or **$PS3**). Execute *commands* for each menu selection, setting *variable* to each selection and **REPLY** to the response until a **break**, **exit**, or EOF is encountered.

until *command1*
do
>   *commands*

done

Execute *commands* until *command1* returns a zero exit status

while *command1*
do
>   *commands*

done

Execute *commands* while *command1* returns a zero exit status.

COMMANDS

:   null command; returns zero exit status

. *file*   read and execute commands in *file*

break   exit from current enclosing **for**, **select**, **until**, or **while** loop

break *n*   exit from *nth* enclosing **for**, **select**, **until**, or **while** loop

cd *dir*   change directory to *dir*(default **$HOME**)

cd *dir1 dir2*

>   change to directory where *dir1* in current pathname is substituted with *dir2*

cd –   change directory to previous directory

echo *args* display arguments

eval *cmds* read and execute commands

exec *I/O-redirection-command*

>   perform I/O redirection on file descriptors

exec *command*

       replace current process with *command*

exit   exit from current program with exit status of the last command. If given at command prompt, terminate the login shell.

exit *n*   exit from current program with exit status *n*

export display list of exported variables

export *var=val* set *var* to *value* and export

export *vars*

       Appendix E: Korn Shell Quick Referenceexport *vars*

false   return non-zero exit status

fc −l[*options*] [*range*]

       display *range* commands from history file according to *options*. If no *range* argument given, display last 16 commands.Options can be:

     −n   do not display command numbers

     −r   reverse order (latest commands first)

     and *range* can be:

     n1 [*n2*] display list from command *n1* to command *n2*. If *n2* not specified, display all commands from current command back to command *n1*.

     −*count* display last *count* commands

     string display all previous commands back to command that matches *string*

fc [*options*] [*range*]

       edit and re-execute range commands from history file according to *options*. If no *range* argument given, edit and re-execute last command. Options can be:

     −e *editor* use specified editor (default **FCEDIT** or **/bin/ed**)

     −r   reverse order (latest commands first)

     and *range* can be:

     n1 n2 edit command *n1* to command *n2*

     n   edit command *n*

     −*n*   edit previous *nth* command

string   use all the previous commands back to the command that matches *string*

fc −e − [*old=new*] [*command*]

edit and re-execute *command* where *old=new* specified to replace string *old* with *new* before executing. If no *command* argument is given, use last command. The *command* can be given as:

n   edit and re-execute command number *n*

−*n*   edit and re-execute last *nth* command

string edit and re-execute most previous command that matches *string*

getopts *optsring name arguments*

parse *arguments*, using *optstring* as list of valid options; save option letter in *name*

getopts *optsring name*

parse positional parameters, using *optstring* as list of valid options; save option letter in *name*

newgrp   change group-id to default group-id

newgrp *gid*

change group id to *gid*

pwd   display pathname of current directory

readonly display a list of readonly variables

readonly *var*

set *var* to be readonly

readonly *var=value*

set *var* to *value* and make it readonly

set   display list of current variables and their values

set −o   display current option settings

set *args* set positional parameters

set *−args* set positional parameters that begin with −

set −s   sort positional parameters

set − −   unset positional parameters

shift   shift positional parameters once left

shift *n*   shift positional parameters *n* times left

Korn Shell User and Programming Manual

test *expression*

evaluate *expression*

time *command* display elapsed, user, and system time spent executing
command

times display total user and system time for current Korn shell and
its child processes

trap *commands signals*

execute *commands* when *signals* are received

trap "" *signals* ignore *signals*

trap *signals*, **trap** *−signals*

reset traps to their default values

trap *commands* **0**, **trap** *commands* **EXIT**

execute *commands* on exit

trap display a list of current traps

trap *commands* **DEBUG**

execute *commands* after each command is executed

trap *commands* **ERR**

if **errexit** (**−e**) option enabled, execute *commands* after
commands that have a non-zero exit status

true return a non-zero exit status

typeset display a list of current variables and their values

ulimit [*options*] *n*

set a resource limit to *n*. If *n* is not given, the specified
resource limit is displayed. If no *option* given, file size limit
(**−f**) is displayed.

−a displays all current resource limits

−c *n* set core dump size limit to *n* 512-byte blocks

−d *n* set data area size limit to *n* kilobytes

−f *n* set child process file write limit to *n* 512-byte blocks
(default)

−m *n* set physical memory size limit to *n* kilobytes

−s *n* set stack area size limit to *n* kilobytes

−t *n* set process time limit to *n* seconds

umask display current file creation mask value

umask *mask*   set default file creation mask to *mask*

unset *var* remove definition of *var*

whence *name*   display information about *name*

whence −v *name*

        display more information about *name*

FUNCTIONS

Functions are a form of commands like aliases, and scripts. They differ from Korn shell scripts, in that they do not have to read in from the disk each time they are referenced, so they execute faster. They also provide a way to organize scripts into routines, like in other high-level programming languages. Since functions can have local variables, recursion is possible. Functions are defined with the following format:

      function *name* { *commands* **;** }

Local function variables are declared with the **typeset** command within the function.

Function Commands

return   return from a function

return *n*   return from a function; pass back return value of *n*

typeset −f

        display a list of functions and their definitions

typeset +f

        display a list of function names only

typeset −fu

        display a list of autoloading functions

typeset −fu *name*

        make function name autoloading

typeset −fx

        display a list of exported functions

typeset −fx *name*

        export function *name*

typeset –ft *name*
> display function commands and arguments as they are
> executed

unset –f *name*
> remove function *name*

THE PRINT COMMAND

print [*options*] *arguments*
> display *arguments* according to *options*

print Options

–	treat everything following – as an argument, even if it begins with –
–n	do not add a ending newline to output
–p	redirect the given arguments to a co-process
–r	ignore \ escape conventions
–R	ignore \ escape conventions; do not interpret – arguments as options (except **–n**)
–s	redirect given arguments to history file
–u*n*	redirect arguments to file descriptor *n*.If file descriptor is greater than **2**, it must first be opened with **exec**. If *n* is not specified, default file descriptor is **1** (standard output).

print Escape Characters

\a	Bell character
\b	Backspace
\c	Line without ending newline
\f	Formfeed
\n	Newline
\r	Return
\t	Tab
\v	Vertical tab
****	Backslash
\0*x*	8-bit character whose ASCII code is the 1-, 2-, or 3-digit octal number x

Appendix E: Korn Shell Quick Reference

THE READ COMMAND

read [*options*] *variables*
> read input into *variables* according to *options*

read *name?prompt*
> display *prompt* and read the response into *name*

read Options

–p   read input line from a co-process
–r   do not treat \ as line continuation character
–s   save a copy of input line in command history file
–u*n*   read input line from file descriptor *n*.If file descriptor is greater than **2**, it must first be opened with **exec**. If *n* is not specified, default file descriptor is 0.

MISC

anything following a # to the end of the current line is treated as a comment and ignored
#!*interpreter*   if the first line of a script starts with this, then the script is run by the specified interpreter
rsh   running under the restricted shell is equivalent to **ksh**, except that the following is not allowed:
  • changing directories
  • setting value of **ENV**, **PATH**, or **SHELL**
  • specifying path or command names containing /
  • redirecting command output command with >, >|, <>, or >>

DEBUGGING KORN SHELL SCRIPTS

The Korn shell provides a number of options that are useful in debugging scripts: **noexec (–n)**, **verbose (–v)**, and **xtrace (–x)**. The **noexec (–n)** option causes commands to be read without being executed and is used to check for syntax errors. The **verbose (–v)** option causes the input to displayed as it is read. The **xtrace (–x)** option causes commands in Korn shell scripts to be displayed as they are executed. This is the most useful, general debugging option. For example, **tscript** could be run in trace mode if invoked "**ksh –x tscript**".

FILES

$HOME/.profile
> contains local environment settings, such as the search path, execution options, local variables, aliases, and more. At login time, it is read in and executed after the **/etc/profile** file.

$HOME/.sh_history
> contains previously executed commands

$ENV   contains the name of the file that has aliases, function, options, variables, and other environment settings that are to be available to subshells

/etc/profile
> contains the system-wide environment settings, such as a basic search path, a default **TERM** variable, the system **umask** value, and more (system dependent). If existent, it is read in and executed at login time before the **$HOME/.profile** file.

/etc/suid_profile
> contains local and system environment settings for privileged mode (system dependent)

EXAMPLE COMMANDS

```
# Execute multiple commands on one line
    $ pwd ; ls tmp ; print "Hello world"
# Run the find command in the background
    $ find . —name tmp.out —print &
# Connect the output of who to grep
    $ who | grep fred
# Talk to fred if he is logged on
    $ { who | grep fred ; } && talk fred
```

Send **ls** output to **ls.out**, even if **noclobber** is set
```
$ ls >| ls.out
```
Append output of **ls** to **ls.out**
```
$ ls >> ls.out
```
Send **invite.txt** to **dick**, **jane**, and **spot**
```
$ mail dick jane spot < invite.txt
```
List file names that begin with **z**
```
$ ls z*
```
List two, three, and four character file names
```
$ ls ?? ??? ????
```
List file names that begin with **a**, **b**, or **c**
```
$ ls [a-c]*
```
List file names that do not end with **.c**
```
$ ls *[!.c]
```
List file names that contain any number of consecutive **x**'s
```
$ ls *(x)
```
List file names that contain only numbers
```
$ ls +([0-9])
```
List file names tha do not end in **.c**, **.Z**, or **.o**
```
$ ls !(*.c|*.Z|*.o)
```
Set **NU** to the number of users that are logged on
```
$ NU=$(who | wc -1)
```
Set **HOSTS** to the contents of the **/etc/hosts** file
```
$ HOSTS=$(</etc/hosts)
```
Set **TOTAL** to the sum of **4 + 3**
```
$ TOTAL=$((4+3))
```
Change directory to **jane**'s home directory
```
$ cd ~jane
```
Set the right-justify attribute on variable **SUM** and set it to **70**
```
$ typeset -R SUM=70
```
Set and export the variable **LBIN**
```
$ typeset -x LBIN=/usr/lbin
```
Set the field width of **SUM** to **5**
```
$ typeset -R5 SUM
```
Remove the lowercase attribute from **MSYS**
```
$ typeset +l MSYS
```

Unset variable **LBIN**
```
$ unset LBIN
```
Display the length of variable **FNAME**
```
$ print ${#FNAME}
```
Set **SYS** to the hostname if not set, then display its value
```
$ print ${SYS:=$(hostname)}
```
Display an error message if **XBIN** is not set
```
$ : ${XBIN:?}
```
Display the base directory in **LBIN**
```
$ print ${LBIN##*/}
```
Set array variable **MONTHS** to the first four month names
```
$ set -A MONTHS jan feb mar apr
```
Display element 3 of the **XBUF** array variable
```
$ print ${XBUF[3]}
```
Display the length of the **TMP** array element 2
```
$ print ${#TMP[2]}
```
Display **$HOME set to /home/anatole**
```
$ print '$HOME set to' $HOME
```
Display the value of **$ENV**
```
$ print $ENV
```
Display the last five commands from the history file
```
$ history -5
```
Retrieve last **print** command in vi edit mode
```
$ set -o vi; <ESCAPE>/^print<RETURN>
```
Bring background job 3 into the foreground
```
$ fg %3
```
Display all information about current jobs
```
$ jobs -l
```
Terminate job 5
```
$ kill %5
```
Increment variable **X**
```
$ integer X; ((X+=1))
```
Set variable **X** to **5** in base **2**
```
$ typeset -i2 X=5
```
Set variable **X** to **20** modulo **5**
```
$ ((X=20%5))
```

```
# Set Y to 5*4 if X equals 3
    $ ((X==3 && (Y=5*4)))
# Terminate the Korn shell if no input given in 30 minutes
    $ TMOUT=1800
# Automatically export variables when defined
    $ set -o allexport
# Set diagnostic mode
    $ set -x
# Create an alias for the ls command
    $ alias l='ls -FAc | ${PAGER:-/bin/pg}'
# Create a tracked alias for the cp -r command
    $ alias -t "cp -r"
# Put the command number and current directory in the prompt
    $ typeset -x PS1="!:$PWD> "
# Check if variable X is set to a number
    $ [[$X=+([0-9])]] && print "$X is num"
# Check if X is set to null
    $ [[-z $X]] && print "X set to null"
# Check if FILE1 is newer than FILE2
    $ [[ $FILE1 -nt $FILE2 ]]
# Check if VAR is set to ABC
    $ [[ $VAR = ABC ]]
# Check if the bgnice option is set
    $ [[-o bgnice]] && print "bgnice set"
# Check if TMP is a readable directory
    $ [[ -d $TMP && -x $TMP ]]
# Check the number of arguments
    $(($#==0)) && {print "Need arg"; exit 1;}
# Display an error message, then beep
    $ print "Unexpected error!\a"
# Display a message on standard error
    $ print -u2 "This is going to stderr"
# Write a message to the command history file
    $ print -s "su attempted on $(date)"
# Take standard input from FILE
    $ exec 0<FILE
```

Open file descriptor **5** for reading and writing
```
$ exec <> 5
```
Display a prompt and read the reply into **ANSWER**
```
$ read ANSWER?"Enter response: "
```
Create a function **md** that creates a directory and **cd**'s to it
```
$ function md {mkdir $1 && cd $1 ; pwd}
```
Set a trap to ignore signals **2** and **3**
```
$ trap "" 2 3
```
Run **dbtest** in **noexec** mode
```
$ ksh -n dbtest
```
Set a trap to execute **pwd** after each command
```
$ trap "pwd" DEBUG
```
Set **X** to **1** and make it readonly
```
$ readonly X=1
```
Set **VAR** to **1** and export it
```
$ export VAR=1
```
Set the positional parametersto **A B C**
```
$ set A B C
```
Set the file size creation limit to 1000 blocks
```
$ ulimit 1000
```
Disable core dumps
```
$ ulimit -c 0
```
Add group write permission to the file creation mask
```
$ umask 013
```
Return information about the **true** command
```
$ whence -v true
```

NAME

ksh, **rsh** - Korn shell, a standard/restricted command and programming language

SYNOPSIS

ksh [+/–**aefhikmnoprstuvx**] [+/–**o** *option*] ... [–**c** *string*] [*arg*]
rsh [+/–**aefhikmnoprstuvx**] [+/–**o** *option*] ... [–**c** *string*] [*arg*]

DESCRIPTION

Ksh is a command and programming language that executes commands read from a terminal or a file. **Rsh** is a restricted version of the standard command interpreter **ksh**; it is used to set up login names and execution environments whose capabilities are more controlled than those of the standard Korn shell. See **Invocation** below for the meaning of arguments to the shell.

Definitions.

A metacharacter is one of the following characters:

    ; & ( ) | < > new-line space tab

A blank is a tab or a space. An identifier is a sequence of letters, digits, or underscores starting with a letter or underscore.

Identifiers are used as names for functions and named parameters. A word is a sequence of characters separated by one or more non-quoted metacharacters. A command is a sequence of characters in the syntax of the shell language. The Korn shell reads each command and carries out the desired action either directly or by invoking separate utilities. A special command is a command that is carried out by the shell without creating a separate process. Except for documented side effects, most special commands can be implemented as separate utilities.

Commands.

A simple-command is a sequence of blank separated words which may be preceded by a parameter assignment list. (See **Environment** below). The first word specifies the name of the command to be executed. Except as specified below, the remaining words are passed as arguments to the invoked command. The command name is passed as argument 0 (see **exec(2)**). The value of a simple-command is its' exit status if it terminates normally, or (octal) 200+ status if it terminates abnormally (see **signal(2)** for a list of status values).

A pipeline is a sequence of one or more commands separated by |. The standard output of each command but the last is connected by a **pipe(2)** to the standard input of the next command. Each command is run as a separate process; the shell waits for the last command to terminate. The exit status of a pipeline is the exit status of the last command.

A list is a sequence of one or more pipelines separated by ;, **&**, **&&**, or ||, and optionally terminated by ;, **&**, or |**&**. Of these five symbols, ;, **&**, and |**&** have equal precedence, which is lower than that of **&&** and ||. The symbols **&&** and || also have equal precedence. A semicolon (;) causes sequential execution of the preceding pipeline; an ampersand (**&**) causes asynchronous execution of the preceding pipeline (i.e., the shell does not wait for that pipeline to finish). The symbol **|&** causes asynchronous execution of the preceding command or pipeline with a two-way pipe established to the parent shell. The standard input and output of the spawned command can be written to and read from by the parent shell using the **–p** option of the special commands **read** and **print** described later. The symbol **&&** (**||**) causes the list following it to be executed only if the preceding pipeline returns a zero (non-zero) value. An arbitrary number of new-lines may appear in a list, instead of a semicolon, to delimit a command.

A command is either a simple-command or one of the following. Unless otherwise stated, the value returned by a command is that of the last simple-command executed in the command.

for *identifier* [**in** *word* ...] ; **do** *list* ; **done**
> Each time a **for** command is executed, *identifier* is set to the next *word* taken from the in *word* list. If **in** *word* ... is omitted, then the **for** command executes the **do** *list* once for each positional parameter that is set (see **Parameter Substitution** below). Execution ends when there are no more words in the list.

select *identifier* [**in** *word* ...] ; **do** *list* ; **done**
> A **select** command prints on standard error (file descriptor 2), the set of *words*, each preceded by a number. If **in** *word* ... is omitted, then the positional parameters are used instead (see **Parameter Substitution** below). The **PS3** prompt is printed and a line is read from the standard input. If this line consists of the number of one of the listed *words*, then the value of the parameter identifier is set to the *word* corresponding to this number. If this line is empty the selection list is printed again. Otherwise the value of the parameter identifier is set to null. The contents of the line

read from standard input is saved in the parameter **REPLY**. The list is executed for each selection until a **break** or end-of-file is encountered.

case *word* **in** [[(]*pattern* [| *pattern*] ...) *list* **;;** ... **esac**
A **case** command executes the *list* associated with the first *pattern* that matches *word*. The form of the patterns is the same as that used for file-name generation (see **File Name Generation** below).

if *list* **; then** *list* **elif** *list* **; then** *list* ... **; else** *list* **; fi**
The *list* following **if** is executed and, if it returns a zero exit status, the *list* following the first **then** is executed. Otherwise, the *list* following **elif** is executed and, if its value is zero, the *list* following the next **then** is executed. Failing that, the **else** list is executed. If no **else** *list* or **then** *list* is executed, then the **if** command returns a zero exit status.

while *list* **; do** *list* **; done**
until *list* **; do** *list* **; done**
A **while** command repeatedly executes the **while** *list* and, if the exit status of the last command in the list is zero, executes the do *list*; otherwise the loop terminates. If no commands in the **do** *list* are executed, then the **while** command returns a zero exit status; **until** may be used in place of **while** to negate the loop termination test.

(*list*)
Execute *list* in a separate environment. Note, that if two adjacent open parentheses are needed for nesting, a space must be inserted to avoid arithmetic evaluation as described below.

{list;}

> *list* is simply executed. Note that unlike the metacharacters (and), { and } are reserved words and must at the beginning of a line or after a **;** in order to be recognized.

[[*expression* **]]**

> Evaluates *expression* and returns a zero exit status when expression is true. See **Conditional Expressions** below, for a description of *expression*.

function *identifier* *{list;}*
identifier () *{list;}*

> Define a **function** which is referenced by *identifier*. The body of the **function** is the *list* of commands between { and }. (See **Functions** below).

time *pipeline*

> The *pipeline* is executed and the elapsed time as well as the user and system time are printed on standard error.

The following reserved words are only recognized as the first word of a command and when not quoted:

if then else elif fi case esac for while until do done { } function select time [[ ]]

Comments.

> A word beginning with **#** causes that word and all the following characters up to a new-line to be ignored.

Aliasing.

The first word of each command is replaced by the text of an alias if an alias for this word has been defined. The first character of an alias name can be any non-special printable character, but the rest of the characters must be the same as for a valid identifier. The replacement string can contain any valid shell script including the metacharacters listed above. The first word of each command in the replaced text, other than any that are in the process of being replaced, will be tested for aliases. If the last character of the alias value is a blank then the word following the alias will also be checked for alias substitution. Aliases can be used to redefine special builtin commands but cannot be used to redefine the reserved words listed above. Aliases can be created, listed, and exported with the **alias** command and can be removed with the **unalias** command. Exported aliases remain in effect for scripts invoked by name, but must be reinitialized for separate invocations of the Korn shell (See **Invocation** below).

Aliasing is performed when scripts are read, not while they are executed. Therefore, for an alias to take effect the **alias** definition command has to be executed before the command which references the alias is read. Aliases are frequently used as a short hand for full path names. An option to the aliasing facility allows the value of the alias to be automatically set to the full pathname of the corresponding command. These aliases are called tracked aliases. The value of a tracked alias is defined the first time the corresponding command is looked up and becomes undefined each time the **PATH** variable is reset. These aliases remain tracked so that the next subsequent reference will redefine the value. Several tracked aliases are compiled into the Korn shell. The **−h** option of the **set** command makes each referenced command name into a tracked alias. The following exported aliases are compiled into the Korn shell but can be unset or redefined:

```
autoload='typeset –fu'
functions='typeset –f'
hash='alias  –t'
history='fc –l'
integer='typeset –i'
nohup='nohup '
r='fc –e '
type='whence –v'
```

Tilde Substitution.

After alias substitution is performed, each word is checked to see
if it begins with an unquoted ~. If it does, then the word up to a /
is checked to see if it matches a user name in the   **/etc/passwd**
file. If a match is found, the ~ and the matched login name is
replaced by the login directory of the matched user. This is called
a tilde substitution. If no match is found, the original text is left
unchanged. A ~ by itself, or in front of a /, is replaced by the
value of the **HOME** parameter. A ~ followed by a + or – is
replaced by **$PWD** and **$OLDPWD** respectively. In addition,
tilde substitution is attempted when the value of a variable
assignment parameter begins with a ~.

Command Substitution.

The standard output from a command enclosed in parenthesis
preceded by a dollar sign (**$()**) or a pair of grave accents (``` `` ```) may
be used as part or all of a word; trailing new-lines are removed.
In the second (archaic) form, the string between the quotes is
processed for special quoting characters before the command is
executed. (See **Quoting** below). The command substitution **$(cat
file)** can be replaced by the equivalent but faster **$(<file)**.
Command substitution of most special commands that do not
perform input/output redirection are carried out without creating a
separate process.

An arithmetic expression enclosed in double parenthesis preceded by a dollar sign (**$((...))**) is replaced by the value of the arithmetic expression within the double parenthesis.

Process Substitution.

This feature is only available on versions of the UNIX operating system that support the **/dev/fd** directory for naming open files. Each command argument of the form <(*list*) or >(*list*) will run process list asynchronously connected to some file in **/dev/fd**. The name of this file will become the argument to the command. If the form with > is selected then writing on this file will provide input for list. If < is used, then the file passed as an argument will contain the output of the list process. For example,

paste <(cut –f *file1*) **<(cut –f3** *file2*) **| tee >(***process1*) **>(***process2*)

cuts fields 1 and 3 from the files *file1* and *file2* respectively, pastes the results together, and sends it to the processes *process1* and *process2*, as well as putting it onto the standard output. Note that the file, which is passed as an argument to the command, is a UNIX system **pipe(2)** so programs that expect to **lseek(2)** on the file will not work.

Parameter Substitution.

A **parameter** is an identifier, one or more digits, or any of the characters *, @, #, ?, –, $, and !. A named parameter (a parameter denoted by an identifier) has a value and zero or more attributes. Named parameters can be assigned values and attributes by using the **typeset** special command. The attributes supported by the shell are described later with the **typeset** special command. Exported parameters pass values and attributes to the environment.

The Korn shell supports a one-dimensional array facility. An element of an array parameter is referenced by a subscript. A subscript is denoted by a [, followed by an arithmetic expression (see **Arithmetic evaluation** below) followed by a]. To assign values to an array, use **set –A** *name value* . . .. The value of all subscripts must be in the range of 0 through 1023. Arrays need not be declared. Any reference to a named parameter with a valid subscript is legal and an array will be created if necessary. Referencing an array without a subscript is equivalent to referencing the element zero.

The value of a named parameter may also be assigned by writing:

name=value [*name=value*] . . .

If the integer attribute, **–i**, is set for *name* the *value* is subject to arithmetic evaluation as described below.

Positional parameters, parameters denoted by a number, may be assigned values with the **set** special command. Parameter **$0** is set from argument zero when the Korn shell is invoked. The character $ is used to introduce substitutable parameters.

${*parameter*}
> The shell reads all the characters from **${** to the matching **}** as part of the same word even if it contains braces or metacharacters. The value, if any, of the parameter is substituted. The braces are required when parameter is followed by a letter, digit, or underscore that is not to be interpreted as part of its name or when a named parameter is subscripted. If *parameter* is one or more digits then it is a positional parameter. A positional parameter of more than one digit must be enclosed in braces. If *parameter* is * or @, then all the positional parameters, starting with $, are

substituted (separated by a field separator character). If an array identifier with subscript * or @ is used, then the value for each of the elements is substituted (separated by a field separator character).

${#*parameter*}

>   If *parameter* is * or #, the number of positional parameters is substituted. Otherwise, the length of the value of the parameter is substituted.

${#*identifier*[*]}

>   The number of elements in the array *identifier* is substituted.

${*parameter*:–*word*}

>   If *parameter* is set and is non-null then substitute its value; otherwise substitute *word* .

${*parameter*:=*word*}

>   If *parameter* is not set or is null then set it to *word*; the value of the parameter is then substituted. Positional parameters may not be assigned to in this way.

${*parameter*:?*word*}

>   If *parameter* is set and is non-null then substitute its' value; otherwise, print *word* and exit from the shell. If *word* is omitted then a standard message is printed.

${*parameter*:+*word*}

>   If *parameter* is set and is non-null then substitute *word*; otherwise substitute nothing.

${*parameter*#*pattern*}
${*parameter*##*pattern*}

>   If the *pattern* matches the beginning of the value of *parameter*, then the value of this substitution is the value of the *parameter* with the matched portion deleted; otherwise

the value of this parameter is substituted. In the first form the smallest matching *pattern* is deleted and in the second form the largest matching *pattern* is deleted.

${*parameter%pattern*}
${*parameter%%pattern*}

If the *pattern* matches the end of the value of *parameter*, then the value of this substitution is the value of the *parameter* with the matched part deleted; otherwise substitute the value of *parameter*. In the first form the smallest matching *pattern* is deleted and in the second form the largest matching *pattern* is deleted.

In the above, word is not evaluated unless it is to be used as the substituted string, so that, in the following example, **pwd** is executed only if **d** is not set or is null:

echo ${d:–$(pwd)}

If the colon (**:**) is omitted from the above expressions, then the Korn shell only checks whether parameter is set or not.

The following parameters are automatically set by the shell:

#	The number of positional parameters in decimal.
–	Flags supplied to the Korn shell on invocation or by the **set** command.
?	The decimal value returned by the last executed command.
$	The process number of this Korn shell. Initially, the value is an absolute pathname of the Korn shell or script being executed as passed in the environment. Subsequently it is assigned the last argument of the previous command. This parameter is not set for commands which are asynchronous. This parameter is

also used to hold the name of the matching **MAIL** file
when checking for mail.

! The process number of the last background command
invoked.

ERRNO

The value of **errno** as set by the most recently failed
system call. This value is system dependent and is
intended for debugging purposes.

LINENO

The line number of the current line within the script or
function being executed.

OLDPWD

The previous working directory set by the **cd**
command.

OPTARG

The value of the last option argument processed by the
getopts special command.

OPTIND

The index of the last option argument processed by the
getopts special command.

PPID

The process number of the parent of the Korn shell.

PWD

The present working directory set by the **cd** command.

RANDOM

Each time this parameter is referenced, a random
integer, uniformly distributed between 0 and 32767, is
generated. The sequence of random numbers can be
initialized by assigning a numeric value to **RANDOM**.

REPLY

This parameter is set by the **select** statement and by the
read special command when no arguments are
supplied.

SECONDS

Each time this parameter is referenced, the number of seconds since Korn shell invocation is returned. If this parameter is assigned a value, then the value returned upon reference will be the value that was assigned plus the number of seconds since the assignment.

The following parameters are used by the Korn shell:

CDPATH

The search path for the **cd** command.

COLUMNS

If this variable is set, the value is used to define the width of the edit window for the Korn shell edit modes and for printing **select** lists.

EDITOR

If the value of this variable ends in **emacs**, **gmacs**, or **vi** and the **VISUAL** variable is not set, then the corresponding option (see **Special Command set** below) will be turned on.

ENV

If this parameter is set, then parameter substitution is performed on the value to generate the pathname of the script that will be executed when the Korn shell is invoked. (See **Invocation** below.) This file is typically used for alias and function definitions.

FCEDIT

The default editor name for the **fc** command.

FPATH

The search path for function definitions. This path is searched when a function with the **–u** attribute is referenced and when a command is not found. If an executable file is found, then it is read and executed in the current environment.

IFS Internal field separators, normally space, tab, and new-line that is used to separate command words which result from command or parameter substitution and for separating words with the special command read. The first character of the **IFS** parameter is used to separate arguments for the "$" substitution (See **Quoting** below).

HISTFILE

If this parameter is set when the Korn shell is invoked, then the value is the pathname of the file that will be used to store the command history. (See **Command re-entry** below.)

HISTSIZE

If this parameter is set when the Korn shell is invoked, then the number of previously entered commands that are accessible by this Korn shell will be greater than or equal to this number. The default is 128.

HOME

The default argument (home directory) for the **cd** command.

LINES

If this variable is set, the value is used to determine the column length for printing **select** lists. Select lists will print vertically until about two-thirds of **LINES** lines are filled.

MAIL

If this parameter is set to the name of a mail file and the **MAILPATH** parameter is not set, then the Korn shell informs the user of arrival of mail in the specified file.

MAILCHECK

This variable specifies how often (in seconds) the Korn shell will check for changes in the modification time of any of the files specified by the **MAILPATH** or **MAIL** parameters. The default value is 600 seconds. When the time has elapsed the Korn shell will check before issuing the next prompt.

MAILPATH

A colon (:) separated list of file names. If this parameter is set then the Korn shell informs the user of any modifications to the specified files that have occurred within the last **MAILCHECK** seconds. Each file name can be followed by a ? and a message that will be printed. The message will undergo parameter substitution with the parameter, $ defined as the name of the file that has changed. The default message is **you have mail in** $.

PATH

The search path for commands (see **Execution** below). The user may not change **PATH** if executing under **rsh** (except in **.profile**).

PS1 The value of this parameter is expanded for parameter substitution to define the primary prompt string which by default is "$ ". The ! character in the primary prompt string is replaced by the command number (see **Command Re-entry** below).

PS2 Secondary prompt string, by default >.

PS3 Selection prompt string used within a **select** loop, by default #?.

PS4 The value of this parameter is expanded for parameter substitution and precedes each line of an execution trace. If omitted, the execution trace prompt is "+".

SHELL

The pathname of the shell is kept in the environment. At invocation, if the basename of this variable matches the pattern **rsh**, then the shell becomes restricted.

TMOUT

If set to a value greater than zero, the Korn shell will terminate if a command is not entered within the prescribed number of seconds after issuing the **PS1**

> prompt. (Note that the Korn shell can be compiled
> with a maximum bound for this value which cannot be
> exceeded.)
>
> **VISUAL**
>> If the value of this variable ends in **emacs**, **gmacs**, or **vi**
>> then the corresponding option (see **Special Command
>> set** below) will be turned on.
>
> The Korn shell gives default values to **PATH**, **PS1**, **PS2**,
> **MAILCHECK**, **TMOUT** and **IFS**, while **HOME**, **SHELL**,
> **ENV**, and **MAIL** are not set at all by the Korn shell (although
> **HOME** is set by **login** ( )). On some systems **MAIL** and **SHELL**
> are also set by **login** ( )).

Blank Interpretation.
> After parameter and command substitution, the results of
> substitutions are scanned for the field separator characters (those
> found in **IFS**) and split into distinct arguments where such
> characters are found. Explicit null arguments ("" or ") are
> retained. Implicit null arguments (those resulting from
> parameters that have no values) are removed.

File Name Generation.
> Following substitution, each command word is scanned for the
> characters *, ?, and [unless the **–f** option has been **set**. If one of
> these characters appears then the word is regarded as a pattern.
> The word is replaced with lexicographically sorted file names that
> match the pattern. If no file name is found that matches the
> pattern, then the word is left unchanged. When a pattern is used
> for file name generation, the character . at the start of a file name
> or immediately following a /, as well as the character / itself, must
> be matched explicitly. In other instances of pattern matching the /
> and . are not treated specially.

* Matches any string, including the null string.
? Matches any single character.
[. . .] Matches any one of the enclosed characters. A pair of
characters separated by – matches any character
lexically between the pair, inclusive. If the first
character following the opening "[" is a "! " then any
character not enclosed is matched. A – can be included
in the character set by putting it as the
first or last character.

A *pattern-list* is a list of one or more patterns separated by each
other with a |. Composite patterns can be formed with one or
more of the following:
?(*pattern-list*)
Optionally matches any one of the given patterns.
*(*pattern-list*)
Matches zero or more occurrences of the given patterns.
+(*pattern-list*)
Matches one or more occurrences of the given patterns.
@(*pattern-list*)
Matches exactly one of the given patterns.
!(*pattern-list*)
Matches anything, except one of the given patterns.

Quoting.

Each of the metacharacters listed above (See **Definitions** above)
has a special meaning to the Korn shell and causes termination of
a word unless quoted. A character may be quoted (i.e., made to
stand for itself) by preceding it with a \. The pair \new-line is
ignored. All characters enclosed between a pair of single quote
marks ("), are quoted. A single quote cannot appear within single
quotes. Inside double quote marks (""), parameter and command
substitution occurs and \ quotes the characters \, `, " , and $. The
meaning of $* and $@ is identical when not quoted or when used

as a parameter assignment value or as a file name. However, when used as a command argument, "$*" is equivalent to "$1*d*$2*d*..." , where *d* is the first character of the **IFS** parameter, whereas "$@" is equivalent to "$1" "$2" .... Inside grave quote marks (``) \ quotes the characters \, `, and $. If the grave quotes occur within double quotes then \ also quotes the character ".

The special meaning of reserved words or aliases can be removed by quoting any character of the reserved word. The recognition of function names or special command names listed below cannot be altered by quoting them.

Arithmetic Evaluation.

An ability to perform integer arithmetic is provided with the special command **let**. Evaluations are performed using long arithmetic. Constants are of the form [*base*#]*n* where *base* is a decimal number between two and thirty-six representing the arithmetic base and *n* is a number in that base. If *base* is omitted then base 10 is used.

An arithmetic expression uses the same syntax, precedence, and associativity of expression of the C language. All the integral operators, other than + +,−−, and ?: are supported. Named parameters can be referenced by name within an arithmetic expression without using the parameter substitution syntax. When a named parameter is referenced, its' value is evaluated as an arithmetic expression.

An internal integer representation of a named parameter can be specified with the **−i** option of the **typeset** special command. Arithmetic evaluation is performed on the value of each assignment to a named parameter with the **−i** attribute. If you do not specify an arithmetic base, the first assignment to the parameter determines the arithmetic base. This base is used when parameter substitution occurs.

Since many of the arithmetic operators require quoting, an alternative form of the **let** command is provided. For any command which begins with a ((, all the characters until a matching)) are treated as a quoted expression. More precisely, ((. . .)) is equivalent to let "...".

Prompting.

When used interactively, the Korn shell prompts with the value of **PS1** before reading a command. If at any time a new-line is typed and further input is needed to complete a command, then the secondary prompt (i.e., the value of **PS2**) is issued.

Conditional Expressions.

A conditional expression is used with the [[compound command to test attributes of files and to compare strings. Word splitting and file name generation are not performed on the words between [[and]]. Each expression can be constructed from one or more of the following unary or binary expressions:

–a *file*   True, if *file* exists.
–b *file*   True, if *file* exists and is a block special file.
–c *file*   True, if *file* exists and is a character special file.
–d *file*   True, if *file* exists and is a directory.
–f *file*   True, if *file* exists and is an ordinary file.
–g *file*   True, if *file* exists and is has its' **setgid** bit set.
–k *file*   True, if *file* exists and is has its' sticky bit set.
–n *string* True, if length of *string* is non-zero.
–o *option* True, if option named *option* is on.
–p *file*   True, if *file* exists and is a fifo special file or a pipe.
–r *file*   True, if *file* exists and is readable by current process.
–s *file*   True, if *file* exists and has size greater than zero.
–t *fildes* True, if file descriptor number *fildes* is open and associated with a terminal device.
–u *file*   True, if *file* exists and is has its' **setuid** bit set.

–w *file*   True, if *file* exists and is writable by current process.

–x *file*   True, if *file* exists and is executable by current process. If *file* exists and is a directory, then the current process has permission to search in the directory.

–z *string*   True, if length of string is zero.

–L *file*   True, if *file* exists and is a symbolic link.

–O *file*   True, if *file* exists and is owned by the effective user id of this process.

–G *file*   True, if *file* exists and its' group matches the effective group id of this process.

–S *file*   True, if *file* exists and is a socket.

file1 **–nt** *file2*
> True, if *file1* exists and is newer than *file2*.

file1 **–ot** *file2*
> True, if *file1* exists and is older than *file2*.

file1 **–ef** *file2*
> True, if *file1* and *file2* exist and refer to the same file.

string = *pattern*
> True, if *string* matches *pattern*.

string != *pattern*
> True, if *string* does not match *pattern*.

string1 < *string2*
> True, if *string1* comes before *string2* based on ASCII value of their characters.

string1 > *string2*
> True, if *string1* comes after *string2* based on ASCII value of their characters.

exp1 **–eq** *exp2*
> True, if *exp1* is equal to *exp2*.

exp1 **–ne** *exp2*
> True, if *exp1* is not equal to *exp2*.

exp1 **–lt** *exp2*
> True, if *exp1* is less than *exp2*.

exp1 **–gt** *exp2*
> True, if *exp1* is greater than *exp2*.

exp1 **–le** *exp2*

> True, if *exp1* is less than or equal to *exp2*.

exp1 **–ge** *exp2*

> True, if *exp1* is greater than or equal to *exp2*.

In each of the above expressions, if *file* is of the form **/dev/fd/***n*, where *n* is an integer, then the test applied to the open file whose descriptor number is *n*.

A compound expression can be constructed from these primitives by using any of the following, listed in decreasing order of precedence.

(*expression*)

> True, if *expression* is true. Used to group expressions.

! *expression*

> True if *expression* is false.

expression1 && *expression2*

> True, if *expression1* and *expression2* are both true.

expression1 || *expression2*

> True, if either *expression1* or *expression2* is true.

Input/Output.

Before a command is executed, its input and output may be redirected using a special notation interpreted by the Korn shell. The following may appear anywhere in a simple-command or may precede or follow a command and are not passed on to the invoked command. Command and parameter substitution occurs before *word* or *digit* is used except as noted below. File name generation occurs only if the pattern matches a single file and blank interpretation is not performed.

<*word* Use file *word* as standard input (file descriptor 0).

>*word*   Use file *word* as standard output (file descriptor 1). If the file does not exist then it is created. If the file exists, and the **noclobber** option is on, this causes an error; otherwise, it is truncated to zero length.

>|*word*   Same as >, except that it overrides the **noclobber** option.

>>*word*   Use file *word* as standard output. If the file exists then output is appended to it (by first seeking to the end-of-file); otherwise, the file is created.

<>*word*   Open file *word* for reading and writing as standard input.

<<[–]*word*

The Korn shell input is read up to a line that is the same as *word*, or to an end-of-file. No parameter substitution, command substitution or file name generation is performed on *word*. The resulting document, called a *here-document*, becomes the standard input. If any character of *word* is quoted, then no interpretation is placed upon the characters of the document; otherwise, parameter and command substitution occurs, \new-line is ignored, and \ must be used to quote the characters \, $, `, and the first character of word. If – is appended to <<, then all leading tabs are stripped from *word* and from the document.

<&*digit*   The standard input is duplicated from file descriptor *digit* (see **dup(2)**). Similarly for the standard output using >& *digit*.

<&–   The standard input is closed. Similarly for the standard output using >&–.

<&p   The input from the co-process is moved to standard input.

>&p   The output to the co-process is moved to standard output.

If one of the above is preceded by a *digit*, then the file descriptor number referred to is that specified by the digit (instead of the default **0** or **1**). For example:
      ... 2>&1

means file descriptor 2 is to be opened for writing as a duplicate of file descriptor 1.

The order in which redirections are specified is significant. The Korn shell evaluates each redirection in terms of the file descriptor/file association at the time of evaluation. For example:

   ... 1 >*fname* **2>&1**

first associates file descriptor 1 with file *fname*. It then associates file descriptor 2 with the file associated with file descriptor 1 (i.e. *fname*). If the order of redirections were reversed, file descriptor 2 would be associated with the terminal (assuming file descriptor 1 had been) and then file descriptor 1 would be associated with file *fname*.

If a command is followed by & and job control is not active, then the default standard input for the command is the empty file **/dev/null**. Otherwise, the environment for the execution of a command contains the file descriptors of the invoking shell as modified by input/output specifications.

Environment.

The environment (see **environ(7)**) is a list of name-value pairs that is passed to an executed program in the same way as a normal argument list. The names must be identifiers and the values are character strings. The Korn shell interacts with the environment in several ways. On invocation, it scans the environment and creates a parameter for each name found, giving it the corresponding value and marking it **export**. Executed commands inherit the environment. If the user modifies the values of these parameters or creates new ones, using the **export** or **typeset −x** commands they become part of the environment. The environment seen by any executed command is thus composed of any name-value pairs originally inherited by the shell, whose values may be modified by the current Korn shell, plus any additions which must be noted in **export** or **typeset −x** commands.

The environment for any simple-command or function may be augmented by prefixing it with one or more parameter assignments. A parameter assignment argument is a word of the form *identifier=value*. Thus:

TERM=450 *cmd args*
and

(export TERM; TERM=450; *cmd args***)**

are equivalent (as far as the above execution of *cmd* is concerned).

If the **−k** flag is set, all parameter assignment arguments are placed in the environment, even if they occur after the command name. The following first prints **a=b c** and then **c**:

> **echo a=b c**
> **set –k**
> **echo a=b c**

This feature is intended for use with scripts written for early versions of the Korn shell and its use in new scripts is strongly discouraged. It is likely to disappear someday.

Functions.

The **function** reserved word, described in the **Commands** section above, is used to define Korn shell functions. Korn shell functions are read in and stored internally. Alias names are resolved when the function is read. Functions are executed like commands with the arguments passed as positional parameters. (See **Execution** below).

Functions execute in the same process as the caller and share all files and present working directory with the caller. Traps caught by the caller are reset to their default action inside the function. A trap condition that is not caught or ignored by the function causes the function to terminate and the condition to be passed on to the caller. A trap on **EXIT** set inside a function is executed after the function completes in the environment of the caller. Ordinarily, variables are shared between the calling program and the function. However, the **typeset** special command used within a function defines local variables whose scope includes the current function and all functions it calls.

The special command **return** is used to return from function calls. Errors within functions return control to the caller.

Function identifiers can be listed with the **–f** or **+f** option of the **typeset** special command. The text of functions will also be listed with **–f**. Function can be undefined with the **–f** option of the **unset** special command.

Ordinarily, functions are unset when the shell executes a shell script. The **–xf** option of the **typeset** command allows a function to be exported to scripts that are executed without a separate invocation of the Korn shell. Functions that need to be defined across separate invocations of the shell should be specified in the **ENV** file with the **–xf** option of **typeset**.

Jobs.

If the **monitor** option of the **set** command is turned on, an interactive Korn shell associates a job with each pipeline. It keeps a table of current jobs, printed by the **jobs** command, and assigns them small integer numbers. When a job is started asynchronously with &, the Korn shell prints a line which looks like:

[1] 1234

indicating that the job which was started asynchronously was job number 1 and had one (top-level) process, whose process id was 1234.

This paragraph and the next require features that are not in all versions of the UNIX operating system and may not apply. If you are running a job and wish to do something else you may hit the key **^Z** (control-Z) which sends a **STOP** signal to the current job. The Korn shell will then normally indicate that the job has been 'Stopped', and print another prompt. You can then manipulate the state of this job, putting it in the background with the **bg** command, or run some other commands and then eventually bring the job back into the foreground with the foreground command **fg**. A **^Z** takes effect immediately and is like an interrupt in that pending output and unread input are discarded when it is typed.

A job being run in the background will stop if it tries to read from the terminal. Background jobs are normally allowed to produce output, but this can be disabled by giving the command "**stty tostop**". If you set this **tty** option, then background jobs will stop when they try to produce output like they do when they try to read input.

There are several ways to refer to jobs in the Korn shell. A job can be referred to by the process id of any process of the job or by one of the following:

%number
        The job with the given number.
%string   Any job whose command line begins with *string*.
%?string Any job whose command line contains *string*.
%%   Current job.
%+   Equivalent to *%%*.
%−   Previous job.

This Korn shell learns immediately whenever a process changes state. It normally informs you whenever a job becomes blocked so that no further progress is possible, but only just before it prints a prompt. This is done so that it does not otherwise disturb your work.

When the **monitor** mode is on, each background job that completes triggers any trap set for **CHLD**.

When you try to leave the Korn shell while jobs are running or stopped, you will be warned that **"You have stopped(running) jobs."**. You may use the **jobs** command to see what they are. If you do this or immediately try to exit again, the Korn shell will not warn you a second time, and the stopped jobs will be terminated.

Signals.

The **INT** and **QUIT** signals for an invoked command are ignored if the command is followed by & and job **monitor** option is not active. Otherwise, signals have the values inherited by the Korn shell from its parent (but see also the **trap** command below).

Execution.

Each time a command is executed, the above substitutions are carried out. If the command name matches one of the **Special Commands** listed below, it is executed within the current Korn shell process. Next, the command name is checked to see if it matches one of the user defined functions. If it does, the positional parameters are saved and then reset to the arguments of the function call. When the function completes or issues a **return**, the positional parameter list is restored and any trap set on **EXIT** within the function is executed. The value of a function is the value of the last command executed. A function is also executed in the current shell process. If a command name is not a special command or a user defined function, a process is created and an attempt is made to execute the command via **exec(2)**.

The Korn shell parameter **PATH** defines the search path for the directory containing the command. Alternative directory names are separated by a colon (**:**). The default path is **/bin:/usr/bin:** (specifying **/bin**, **/usr/bin**, and the current directory in that order). The current directory can be specified by two or more adjacent colons, or by a colon at the beginning or end of the path list. If the command name contains a **/** then the search path is not used. Otherwise, each directory in the path is searched for an executable file. If the file has execute permission but is not a directory or an **a.out** file, it is assumed to be a file containing Korn shell commands. A sub-shell is spawned to read it. All non-exported aliases, functions, and named parameters are removed in this case.

If the Korn shell command file doesn't have read permission, or if the setuid and/or setgid bits are set on the file, then the Korn shell executes an agent whose job it is to set up the permissions and execute the Korn shell with the Korn shell command file passed down as an open file. A parenthesized command is executed in a sub-shell without removing non-exported quantities.

Command Re-entry.

The text of the last **HISTSIZE** (default 128) commands entered from a terminal device is saved in a history file. The file **$HOME/.sh_history** is used if the **HISTFILE** variable is not set or is not writable. A Korn shell can access the commands of all interactive shells which use the same named **HISTFILE**. The special command **fc** is used to list or edit a portion of this file. The portion of the file to be edited or listed can be selected by number or by giving the first character or characters of the command. A single command or range of commands can be specified. If you do not specify an editor program as an argument to **fc** then the value of the parameter **FCEDIT** is used. If **FCEDIT** is not defined then **/bin/ed** is used.

The edited command(s) is printed and re-executed upon leaving the editor. The editor name − is used to skip the editing phase and to re-execute the command. In this case a substitution parameter of the form *old=new* can be used to modify the command before execution. For example, if **r** is aliased to 'fc −e −' then typing 'r **bad=good c**' will re-execute the most recent command which starts with the letter **c**, replacing the first occurrence of the string **bad** with the **good**.

In-line Editing Options

Normally, each command line entered from a terminal device is simply typed followed by a newline (**Return** or **Linefeed**). If either the **emacs**, **gmacs**, or **vi** option is active, the user can edit the command line. To be in either of these edit modes set the corresponding option. An editing option is automatically selected each time the **VISUAL** or **EDITOR** variable is assigned a value ending in either of these option names.

The editing features require that the user's terminal accept **Return** as carriage return without line feed and that a space must overwrite the current character on the screen. ADM terminal users should set the "space - advance" switch to "space". Hewlett-Packard series 2621 terminal users should set the straps to "**bcGHxZ etX**".

The editing modes implement a concept where the user is looking through a window at the current line. The window width is the value of **COLUMNS** if it is defined, otherwise 80. If the line is longer than the window width minus two, a mark is displayed at the end of the window to notify the user. As the cursor moves and reaches the window boundaries the window will be centered about the cursor. The mark is a > (<,*) if the line extends on the right (left, both) side(s) of the window.

The search commands in each edit mode provide access to the history file. Only strings are matched, not patterns, although a leading in the string restricts the match to begin at the first character in the line.

Emacs Editing Mode

This mode is entered by enabling either the **emacs** or **gmacs** option. The only difference between these two modes is the way they handle **^T**. To edit, the user moves the cursor to the point needing correction and then inserts or deletes characters or words as needed. All the editing commands are control characters or escape sequences. The notation for control characters is caret (^) followed by the character. For example, **^F** is the notation for **Control F**. This is entered by depressing **f** while holding down the **Ctrl** (control) key. The **Shift** key is not depressed. (The notation **^?** indicates the **Delete** key.)

The notation for escape sequences is **M-** followed by a character. For example, **M-f** (pronounced **Meta f**) is entered by depressing **Escape** (ascii 33) followed by **f**. (**M-F** would be the notation for **Escape** followed by **Shift** (capital) **F**.)

All edit commands operate from any place on the line (not just at the beginning). Neither the **Return** nor the **Linefeed** key is entered after edit commands except when noted.

^F	Move cursor forward (right) one character.
M-f	Move cursor forward one word. (The emacs editor's idea of a word is a string of characters consisting of only letters, digits and underscores.)
^B	Move cursor backward (left) one character.
M-b	Move cursor backward one word.
^A	Move cursor to start of line.
^E	Move cursor to end of line.
b^]*char*	Move cursor forward to character *char* on current line.
M-^]*char*	Move cursor back to character *char* on current line.
^X^X	Interchange the cursor and mark.
erase	Delete previous character. (User defined erase character as defined by the **stty** command, usually **^H** or **#**.)
^D	Delete current character.
M-d	Delete current word.
M-^H	(Meta-backspace) Delete previous word.
M-h	Delete previous word.
M-^?	(Meta-Delete) Delete previous word (if your interrupt character is (**Delete**, the default) then this command will not work).

^T	Transpose current character with next character in emacs mode. Transpose two previous characters in gmacs mode.
^C	Capitalize current character.
M-c	Capitalize current word.
M-l	Change the current word to lower case.
^K	Delete from the cursor to the end of the line. If preceded by a numerical parameter whose value is less than the current cursor position, then delete from given position up to the cursor. If preceded by a numerical parameter whose value is greater than the current cursor position, then delete from cursor up to given cursor position.
^W	Kill from the cursor to the mark.
M-p	Push the region from the cursor to the mark on the stack.
kill	(User defined kill character as defined by the **stty** command, usually **^G** or **@**.) Kill the entire current line. If two kill characters are entered in succession, all kill characters from then on cause a line feed (useful when using paper terminals).
^Y	Restore last item removed from line. (Yank item back to the line.)
^L	Line feed and print current line.
^@	(Null character) Set mark.
M-*space*	(Meta space) Set mark.
^J	(New line) Execute the current line.
^M	(Return) Execute the current line.
eof	End-of-file character, normally **^D**, is processed as an End-of-file only if the current line is null.
^P	Fetch previous command. Each time **^P** is entered the previous command back in time is accessed. Moves back one line when not on the first line of a multi-line command.

M-<   Fetch the least recent (oldest) history line.

M->   Fetch the most recent (youngest) history line.

^N   Fetch next command line. Each time **^N** is entered the next command line forward in time is accessed.

^R_string_   Reverse search history for a previous command line containing string. If a parameter of zero is given, the search is forward. String is terminated by a **Return** or **Newline**. If string is preceded by a ^, the matched line must begin with string. If string is omitted, then the next command line containing the most recent string is accessed. In this case a parameter of zero reverses the direction of the search.

^O   Operate - Execute the current line and fetch the next line relative to current line from the history file.

M-_digits_   (**Escape**) Define numeric parameter, the _digits_ are taken as a parameter to the next command. The commands that accept a parameter are **^F**, **^B**, _erase_, **^C**, **^D**, **^K**, **^R**, **^P**, **^N**, **M-.**, **M-^]**, **M-_**, **M-b**, **M-c**, **M-d**, **M-f**, **M-h**, **M-l** and **M-^H**.

M- _letter_   Soft-key - Your alias list is searched for an alias by the name _letter_ and if an alias of this name is defined, its value will be inserted on the input queue. The letter must not be one of the above meta-functions.

M-] _letter_

    Soft-key - Your alias list is searched for an alias by the name letter and if an alias of this name is defined, its value will be inserted on the input queue. The can be used to program functions keys on many terminals.

M-.   The last word of the previous command is inserted on the line. If preceded by a numeric parameter, the value of this parameter determines which word to insert rather than the last word.

M-_   Same as **M-.**.

M-*   Attempt file name generation on the current word. An asterisk is appended if the word doesn't match any file or contain any special pattern characters.

M-*Esc*   File name completion. Replaces the current word with the longest common prefix of all filenames matching the current word with an asterisk appended. If the match is unique, a / is appended if the file is a directory and a space is appended if the file is not a directory.

M-=   List files matching current word pattern if an asterisk were appended.

^U   Multiply parameter of next command by **4**.

**   Escape next character. Editing characters, the user's *erase*, *kill* and *interrupt* (normally **^?) characters may be entered in a command line or in a search string if preceded by a \\. The \\ removes the next character's editing features (if any).

^V   Display version of the Korn shell.

M-#   Insert a # at the beginning of the line and execute it. This causes a comment to be inserted in the history file.

Vi Editing Mode

There are two typing modes. Initially, when you enter a *command* you are in the *input* mode. To edit, the user enters control mode by typing **Escape** (033) and moves the cursor to the point needing correction and then inserts or deletes characters or words as needed. Most control commands accept an optional repeat count prior to the command.

When in **vi** mode on most systems, canonical processing is initially enabled and the command will be echoed again if the speed is 1200 baud or greater and it contains any control characters or less than one second has elapsed since the prompt was printed. The **Escape** character terminates canonical processing for the remainder of the command and the user can then modify the command line. This scheme has the advantages of canonical processing with the type-ahead echoing of raw mode.

If the option **viraw** is also set, the terminal will always have canonical processing disabled. This mode is implicit for systems that do not support two alternate end of line delimiters, and may be helpful for certain terminals.

Input Edit Commands

By default the editor is in *input* mode.

erase   (User defined erase character as defined by the **stty** command, usually ^H or **#**.) Delete previous character.

^W   Delete the previous blank separated word.

^D   Terminate the shell.

^V   Escape next character. Editing characters, the user's *erase* or *kill* characters may be entered in a command line or in a search string if preceded by a **^V**. The **^V** removes the next character's editing features (if any).

\   Escape the next *erase* or *kill* character.

Motion Edit Commands

These commands will move the cursor.

[*count*]**l**   Cursor forward (right) one character.

[*count*]**w**   Cursor forward one alpha-numeric word.

[count]**W**   Cursor to the beginning of the next word that follows a blank.

[*count*]**e**   Cursor to end of word.

[*count*]**E**   Cursor to end of the current blank delimited word.

[*count*]**h**   Cursor backward (left) one character.

[*count*]**b**   Cursor backward one word.

[*count*]**B**   Cursor to preceding blank separated word.

[*count*]**l**   Cursor to column 1 count.

[*count*]**f** *c*
        Find the next character *c* in the current line.

[*count*]**F** *c*
        Find the previous character *c* in the current line.

[*count*]**t** *c*
        Equivalent to **f** followed by **h**.

[*count*]**T** *c*
> Equivalent to **F** followed by **l**.

[*count*]**;** Repeats count times, the last single character find command, **f**, **F**, **t**, or **T**.

[*count*]**,** Reverses the last single character find command count times.

0 Cursor to start of line.

^ Cursor to first non-blank character in line.

$ Cursor to end of line.

Search Edit Commands

These commands access your command history.

[*count*] **k** Fetch previous command. Each time **k** is entered the previous command back in time is accessed.

[*count*]**–** Equivalent to **k**.

[*count*]**j** Fetch next command. Each time **j** is entered the next command forward in time is accessed.

[*count*]**+** Equivalent to **j**.

[*count*]**G** The command number *count* is fetched. The default is the least recent history command.

/string Search backward through history for a previous command containing *string*. String is terminated by a **Return** or **Newline**. If *string* is preceded by a ^, the matched line must begin with *string*. If *string* is null the previous string will be used.

? *string* Same as **/** except that search will be in the forward direction.

n Search for next match of the last pattern to **/** or **?** commands.

N Search for next match of the last pattern to **/** or **?**, but in reverse direction. Search history for the string entered by the previous **/** command.

Text Modification Edit Commands

These commands will modify the line.

a   Enter input mode and enter text after the current
             character.

A   Append text to the end of the line. Equivalent to **$a**.

[*count*]**c***motion*
c[*count*]*motion*
             Delete current character through the character that
             motion would move the cursor to and enter input mode.
             If *motion* is **c**, the entire line will be deleted and input
             mode entered.

C   Delete the current character through the end of line and
             enter input mode **c$**. Equivalent to **c$**.

S   Equivalent to **cc**.

D   Delete the current character through the end of line.
             Equivalent to **d$**.

[*count*]**d***motion*
d[*count*]*motion*
             Delete current character through the character that
             motion would move to. If *motion* is **d**, the entire line
             will be deleted.

i   Enter input mode and insert text before the current
             character.

I   Insert text before the beginning of the line. Equivalent
             to **i**.

[*count*]**P** Place the previous text modification before the cursor.

[*count*]**p** Place the previous text modification after the cursor.

R   Enter input mode and replace characters on the screen
             with characters you type overlay fashion.

[*count*]**r***c* Replace the count character(s) starting at the current
             cursor position with *c*, and advance the cursor.

[*count*]**x** Delete current character.

[*count*]**X** Delete preceding character.

[*count*]**.** Repeat the previous text modification command.

[*count*]**~** Invert the case of the count character(s) starting at the
             current cursor position and advance the cursor.

[*count*]_   Causes the *count* word of the previous command to be appended and input mode entered. The last word is used if *count* is omitted. Causes an * to be appended to the current word and file name generation attempted. If no match is found, it rings the bell. Otherwise, the word is replaced by the matching pattern and input mode is entered.

\   Filename completion. Replaces the current word with the longest common prefix of all filenames matching the current word with an asterisk appended. If the match is unique, a / is appended if the file is a directory and a space is appended if the file is not a directory.

Other Edit Commands

Miscellaneous commands.

[*count*]**y***motion*

y[*count*]*motion*

   Yank current character through character that motion would move the cursor to and puts them into the delete buffer. The text and cursor are unchanged.

Y   Yanks from current position to end of line. Equivalent to **y$**.

u   Undo the last text modifying command.

U   Undo all the text modifying commands performed on the line.

[*count*]**v**   Returns the command **fc –e ${VISUAL:– ${EDITOR:–vi}}** *count* in the input buffer. If *count* is omitted, then the current line is used.

^L   Line feed and print current line. Has effect only in control mode.

^J   (New line) Execute the current line, regardless of mode.

^M   (Return) Execute current line, regardless of mode.

Sends the line after inserting a **#** in front of the line. If

line already commented, then remove the # character.
Useful for causing the current line to be inserted in the
history without being executed.

=   List the file names that match the current word if an
asterisk were appended it.

@letter   Your alias list is searched for an alias *letter* and if
defined, its value is inserted on the input queue.

%   find the matching (), { }

Special Commands.

The following simple-commands are executed in the Korn shell
process. Input/Output redirection is permitted. Unless otherwise
indicated, the output is written on file descriptor **1** and the exit
status, when there is no syntax error, is zero. Commands that are
preceded by one or two **!** marks are treated specially in the
following ways:

1. Parameter assignment lists preceding the command remain in
effect when the command completes.

2. I/O redirections are processed after parameter assignments.

3. Errors cause Korn shell scripts that contain them to abort.

4. Words, following a command preceded by **!!**, that are in the
format of a parameter assignment, are expanded with the same
rules as a parameter assignment. This means that tilde
substitution is performed after the = sign and word splitting and
file name generation are not performed.

!: [*arg* ...]

The command only expands parameters.

!!. *file* [*arg* ...]

Read the complete *file* then execute the commands. The
commands are executed in the current shell environment.
The search path specified by **PATH** is used to find the
directory containing *file*. If any arguments *arg* are given,
they become the positional parameters. Otherwise the

positional parameters are unchanged. The exit status is the
exit status of the last command executed.

alias [**–tx**] [*name*[=*value*]] ...

Alias with no arguments prints the list of aliases in the form
name=value on standard output. An alias is defined for each
name whose *value* is given. A trailing space in *value* causes
the next word to be checked for alias substitution. The **–t**
flag is used to set and list tracked aliases. The value of a
tracked alias is the full pathname corresponding to the given
name. The value becomes undefined when the value of
PATH is reset but the aliases remained tracked. Without the
–t flag, for each name in the argument list for which no
value is given, the name and value of the alias is printed.
The **–x** flag is used to set or print exported aliases. An
exported alias is defined for Korn shell scripts invoked by
name.

bg [*%job* ...]

This command is only on systems that support job control.
Puts each specified *job* into the background. The current job
is put in the background if *job* is not specified. See **Jobs** for
a description of the format of *job*.

break [*n*]

Exit from the enclosing **for while until** or **select** loop, if any.
If *n* is specified then break *n* levels.

!cd [*arg*]
!cd *old new*

This command can be in either of two forms. In the first
form it changes the current directory to *arg*. If *arg* is – the
directory is changed to the previous directory. The Korn
shell parameter **HOME** is the default *arg*. The parameter
PWD is set to the current directory. The Korn shell
parameter **CDPATH** defines the search path for the directory

containing *arg*. Alternative directory names are separated by a colon (**:**). The default path is <null> (specifying the current directory). Note that the current directory is specified by a null path name, which can appear immediately after the equal sign or between the colon delimiters anywhere else in the path list. If *arg* begins with a **/** then the search path is not used. Otherwise, each directory in the path is searched for *arg*.

The second form of **cd** substitutes the string *new* for the string *old* in the current directory name, **PWD** and tries to change to this new directory. The **cd** command may not be executed by **rsh**.

continue [*n*]

Resume the next iteration of the enclosing **for while until** or **select** loop. If *n* is specified then resume at the *nth* enclosing loop.

echo *arg* ...

See **echo(1)** for usage and description.

‼eval [*arg* ...]

The arguments are read as input to the Korn shell and the resulting command(s) executed.

‼exec [*arg* ...]

If *arg* is given, the command specified by the arguments is executed in place of this Korn shell without creating a new process. Input/output arguments may appear and affect the current process. If no arguments are given the effect of this command is to modify file descriptors as prescribed by the input/output redirection list. In this case, any file descriptor numbers greater than 2 that are opened with this mechanism are closed when invoking another program.

exit [*n*]

> Causes the Korn shell to exit with the exit status specified by *n*. If *n* is omitted, then the exit status is that of the last command executed. An end-of-file will also cause the Korn shell to exit except for a Korn shell which has the **ignoreeof** option (see **set** below) turned on.

!!export [*name*=[*value*]] ...

> The given names are marked for automatic export to the environment of subsequently-executed commands.

!!fc [**-e** *ename*] [**-nlr**] [*first* [*last*]]
!!fc -e - [*old*=*new*] [*command*]

> In the first form, a range of commands from *first* to *last* is selected from the last **HISTSIZE** commands that were typed at the terminal. The arguments *first* and *last* may be specified as a number or as a string. A string is used to locate the most recent command starting with the given string. A negative number is used as an offset to the current command number. If the flag **-l**, is selected, the commands are listed on standard output. Otherwise, the editor program *ename* is invoked on a file containing these keyboard commands. If *ename* is not supplied, then the value of the parameter **FCEDIT** (default   **/bin/ed**) is used as the editor. When editing is complete, the edited command(s) is executed. If *last* is not specified then it will be set to *first*. If *first* is not specified the default is the previous command for editing and **16** for listing. The flag **-r** reverses the order of the commands and the flag **-n** suppresses command numbers when listing. In the second form the command is re-executed after the substitution *old*=*new* is performed.

fg [*job...*]

> This command is only on systems that support job control. Each job specified is brought to the foreground. Otherwise,

the current job is brought into the foreground. See **Jobs** for
a description of the format of job.

getopts *optstring name* [*arg...*]

Checks *arg* for legal options. If *arg* is omitted, the
positional parameters are used. An option argument begins
with a + or a –. An option not beginning with + or – or the
argument – – ends the options. *optstring* contains the letters
that **getopts** recognizes. If a letter is followed by a **:**, that
option is expected to have an argument. The options can be
separated from the argument by blanks. **getopts** places the
next option letter it finds inside variable *name* each time it is
invoked with a + prepended when *arg* begins with a +. The
index of the next *arg* is stored in **OPTIND**. The *option*
argument, if any, gets stored in **OPTARG**. A leading **:** in
optstring causes **getopts** to store the letter of an invalid
option in **OPTARG**, and to set name to **?** for an unknown
option and to **:** when a required option is missing.
Otherwise, **getopts** prints an error message. The exit status
is non-zero when there are no more options.

jobs [–**lnp**] [*job...*]

Lists information about each given job; or all active jobs if
job is omitted. The –**l** flag lists process ids in addition to the
normal information. The –**n** flag only displays jobs that
have stopped or exited since last notified. The –**p** flag
causes only the process group to be listed. See **Jobs** for a
description of the format of *job*.

kill [–*sig*] *job ...*
kill –**l**

Sends either the **TERM** (terminate) signal or the specified
signal to the specified jobs or processes. Signals are either
given by number or by names (as given in **/usr/include/**
signal.h, stripped of the prefix **SIG**). If the signal being sent

is **TERM** (terminate) or **HUP** (hangup), then the job or
process will be sent a **CONT** (continue) signal if it is
stopped. The argument *job* can the process id of a process
that is not a member of one of the active jobs. See **Jobs** for
a description of the format of *job*. In the second form, **kill –
l**, the signal numbers and names are listed.

let *arg* ...

Each *arg* is a separate arithmetic expression to be evaluated.
See **Arithmetic Evaluation** above, for a description of
arithmetic expression evaluation. The exit status is **0** if the
value of the last expression is non-zero, and **1** otherwise.

‼newgrp [arg ...]

Equivalent to **exec /bin/newgrp** *arg* ....

print [**–Rnprsu** [*n*]] [*arg* ...]

The Korn shell output mechanism. With no flags or with
flag **–** or **––** the arguments are printed on standard output as
described by **echo(1)**. In raw mode, **–R** or **–r**, the escape
conventions of **echo** are ignored. The **–R** option will print
all subsequent arguments and options other than **–n**. The **–p**
option causes the arguments to be written onto the pipe of
the process spawned with **|&** instead of standard output. The
–s option causes the arguments to be written onto the history
file instead of standard output. The **–u** flag can be used to
specify a one digit file descriptor unit number *n* on which the
output will be placed. The default is **1**. If the flag **–n** is
used, no new-line is added to the output.

pwd

Equivalent to **print –r – $PWD**

read [**–prsu**[**n**]] [*name?prompt*] [*name ...*]

The Korn shell input mechanism. One line is read and is broken up into fields using the characters in **IFS** as separators. In raw mode, **–r**, a \ at the end of a line does not signify line continuation. The first field is assigned to the first name, the second field to the second name, etc., with leftover fields assigned to the last name. The **–p** option causes the input line to be taken from the input pipe of a process spawned by the Korn shell using |&. If the **–s** flag is present, the input will be saved as a command in the history file. The flag **–u** can be used to specify a one digit file descriptor unit to read from. The file descriptor can be opened with the **exec** special command. The default value of is **0**. If *name* is omitted then **REPLY** is used as the default name. The exit status is **0** unless an end-of-file is encountered. An end-of-file with the **–p** option causes cleanup for this process so that another can be spawned. If the first argument contains a ?, the remainder of this word is used as a prompt on standard error when the shell is interactive. The exit status is **0** unless an end-of-file is encountered.

!!readonly [*name*[*=value*]]...

The given names are marked **readonly** and these names cannot be changed by subsequent assignment.

!!return [*n*]

Causes a Korn shell function to return to the invoking script with the return status specified by *n*. If *n* is omitted, then the return status is that of the last command executed. If **return** is invoked while not in a function or a **.** (dot) script, then it is the same as an **exit**.

set [+/–**aefhkmnopstuvx**] [+/–**o** *option*] ... [+/–**A** *name*] [*arg*]

The flags for this command have meaning as follows:

–A Array assignment. Unset the variable *name* and assign values sequentially from the list arg. If **+A** is used, the variable name is not **unset** first.

–a All subsequent parameters that are defined are automatically exported.

–e If a command has a non-zero exit status, execute the **ERR** trap, if set, and exit. This mode is disabled while reading profiles.

–f Disables file name generation.

–h Each command becomes a tracked alias when first encountered.

–k All parameter assignment arguments are placed in the environment for a command, not just those that precede the command name.

–m Background jobs will run in a separate process group and a line will print upon completion. The exit status of background jobs is reported in a completion message. On systems with job control, this flag is turned on automatically for interactive shells.

–n Read commands and check them for syntax errors, but do not execute them. Ignored for interactive Korn shells.

–o The following argument can be one of the following option names:

allexport	Same as **–a**.
errexit	Same as **–e**.
bgnice	All background jobs are run at a lower priority. This is the default mode.
emacs	Puts you in an emacs style in-line editor for command entry.
gmacs	Puts you in a gmacs style in-line editor for command entry.

ignoreeof	do not exit on end-of-file. The **exit** command must be used.
keyword	Same as **–k**.
markdirs	All directory names resulting from file name generation have a trailing **/** appended.
monitor	Same as **–m**.
noclobber	Prevents redirection from truncating existing files. Require >| to truncate a file when turned on.
noexec	Same as **–n**.
noglob	Same as **–f**.
nolog	Do not save function definitions in history file.
nounset	Same as **–u**.
privileged	Same as **–p**.
verbose	Same as **–v**.
trackall	Same as **–h**.
vi	Puts you in insert mode of a vi style in-line editor until you hit escape character (033). This puts you in move mode. A return sends the line.
viraw	Each character is processed as it is typed in **vi** mode.
xtrace	Same as **–x**.

If no option name is supplied then the current option settings are printed.

–p Disables processing of the **$HOME/.profile** file and uses the file **/etc/suidprofile** instead of the **ENV** file. This mode is on whenever the effective uid (gid) is not equal to the real uid (gid). Turning this off causes the effective uid and gid to be set to the real uid and gid.

–s Sort the positional parameters lexicographically.

–t Exit after reading and executing one command.

–u   Treat unset parameters as an error when substituting.

–v   Print Korn shell input lines as they are read.

–x   Print commands and their arguments as they are executed.

–   Turns off **–x** and **–v** flags and stops examining arguments for flags.

– –   Do not change any of the flags; useful in setting **$1** to a value beginning with **–**. If no arguments follow this flag then the positional parameters are unset.

Using + rather – than causes these flags to be turned off. These flags can also be used upon invocation of the Korn shell. The current set of flags may be found in **$–**. Unless **– A** is specified, the remaining arguments are positional parameters and are assigned, in order, to **$1**, **$2** .... If no arguments are given then the names and values of all named parameters are printed on the standard output. If the only argument is +, the names of all named parameters are printed.

!shift [*n*]

The positional parameters from **$*n*+1** ... are renamed **$1** ..., default *n* is **1**. The parameter *n* can be any arithmetic expression that evaluates to a non-negative number less than or equal to **$#**.

times

Print the accumulated user and system times for the Korn shell and for processes run from the Korn shell.

trap [*arg*] [*sig*] ...

arg is a command to be read and executed when the Korn shell receives signal(s) *sig*. (Note that *arg* is scanned once when the **trap** is set and once when the trap is taken.) Each *sig* can be given as a number or as the name of the signal.

Trap commands are executed in order of signal number. Any attempt to set a trap on a signal that was ignored on entry to the current shell is ineffective. If *arg* is omitted or is –, then all trap(s) sig are reset to their original values. If *arg* is the null string then this signal is ignored by the Korn shell and by the commands it invokes. If *sig* is **ERR** then *arg* will be executed whenever a command has a non-zero exit status. If *sig* is **DEBUG** then *arg* will be executed after each command. If *sig* is **0** or **EXIT** and the trap statement is executed inside the body of a function, then the command *arg* is executed after the function completes. If *sig* is **0** or **EXIT** for a trap set outside any function then the command *arg* is executed on exit from the shell. The **trap** command with no arguments prints a list of commands associated with each signal number.

!!**typeset** [+/–**HLRZfilrtux** [*n*]] [*name*[=*value*]] ...

Sets attributes and values for Korn shell parameters. When invoked inside a function, a new instance of the parameter name is created. The parameter value and type are restored when the function completes. The following list of attributes may be specified:

–**H** This flag provides UNIX system to host-name file mapping on non-UNIX system machines.

–**L** Left justify and remove leading blanks from value. If *n* is non-zero it defines the width of the field, otherwise it is determined by the width of the value of first assignment. When the parameter is assigned to, it is filled on the right with blanks or truncated, if necessary, to fit into the field. Leading zeros are removed if the –**Z** flag is also set. The –**R** flag is turned off.

–**R** Right justify and fill with leading blanks. If *n* is non-zero it defines the width of the field, otherwise it is determined by the width of the value of first assignment. The field is left filled with blanks or truncated from the end if the parameter is reassigned. The **–L** flag is turned off.

–Z Right justify and fill with leading zeros if the first non-blank character is a digit and the flag has not been set. If *n* is non-zero, it defines the width of the field, otherwise it is determined by the width of the value of first assignment.

–f The names refer to function names rather than parameter names. No assignments can be made and the only other valid flags are **–t**, **–u** an **–x**. The flag **–t** turns on execution tracing for this function. The flag **–u** causes this function to be marked undefined. The **FPATH** variable will be searched to find the function definition when the function is referenced. The flag **–x** allows the function definition to remain in effect across Korn shell scripts invoked by name.

–i Parameter is an integer. This makes arithmetic faster. If *n* is non-zero it defines the output arithmetic base, otherwise the first assignment determines the output base.

–l All upper-case characters converted to lower-case. The upper-case flag, **–u** is turned off.

–r The given names are marked **readonly** and cannot be changed by subsequent assignment.

–t Tags the named parameters. Tags are user definable and have no special meaning to the Korn shell.

–u All lower-case characters are converted to upper-case characters. The lower-case flag (**–l**) is turned off.

–x The given name are marked for automatic export to the environment of subsequently-executed commands.

Using + rather than – causes these flags to be turned off. If no *name* arguments are given but flags are specified, a list of names (and optionally the values) of the parameters which have these flags set is printed. (Using + rather than − keeps the values from being printed.) If no name and flags are given, the names and attributes of all parameters are printed.

ulimit [−acdfmnpstvw] [*limit*]

Set or display a resource limit. The available resources limits listed below. Many systems to not contain one or more of these limits. The limit for a specified resource is set when *limit* is specifed. The value of limit can be a number in the unit specifed below with each resource, or the value unlimited. The current resource limit is printed when *limit* is omitted. When more that one resource is specifed, then the limit name and unit is printed before the value.

−a   Lists all of the current resource limits.

−c   The number of 512-byte blocks on the size of core dumps.

−d   The number of K-bytes on the size of the data area.

−f   The number of 512-byte blocks on files written by child processes (files of any size may be read).

−m The number of K-bytes on the size of physical memory.

−n   The number of file descriptors.

−p   The number of 512-byte blocks for pipe buffering.

−s   The number of K-bytes on the size of the stack area.

−t   The number of seconds to be used by each process.

−v   The number of K-bytes for virtual memory.

−w The number of K-bytes for the swap area.

If no option is given, −**f** is assumed.

umask [*mask*]

The user file-creation mask is set to *mask* (see **umask(2)**). *mask* can either be an octal number or a symbolic value as described in **chmod(1)**. If a symbolic value is given, the new **umask** value is the complement of the result of applying mask to the complement of the previous **umask** value. If *mask* is omitted, the current value of the mask is printed.

unalias *name* ...

> The parameters given by the list of *names* are removed from the alias list.

unset [**–f**] *name* ...

> The parameters given by the list of *names* are unassigned, i.e., their values and attributes are erased. Readonly variables cannot be unset. If the flag, **–f**, is set, then the names refer to function names. Unsetting **ERRNO, LINENO, MAILCHECK, OPTARG, OPTIND, RANDOM, SECONDS,** and **TMOUT** causes removal of their special meaning even if they are subsequently assigned to.

wait [*job*]

> Wait for the specified job and report its termination status. If *job* is not given then all currently active child processes are waited for. The exit status from this command is that of the process waited for. See **Jobs** for a description of the format of *job*.

whence [**–pv**] *name* ...

> For each *name*, indicate how it would be interpreted if used as a command name. The flag, **–v**, produces a more verbose report. The flag, **–p**, does a path search for *name* even if *name* is an alias, a function, or a reserved word.

Invocation.

If the Korn shell is invoked by **exec(2)** and the first character of argument zero (**$0**) is –, then the Korn shell is assumed to be a login shell and commands are read from **/etc/profile** and then from either **.profile** in the current directory or **$HOME/ .profile**, if either file exists. Next, commands are read from the file named by performing parameter substitution on the value of the environment parameter **ENV** if the file exists. If the **–s** flag is not present and *arg* is, then a path search is performed on the first *arg* to determine the name of the script to execute. The script *arg* must have read permission and any **setuid** and **getgid** settings will be ignored. Commands are then read as described below; the following flags are interpreted by the Korn shell when it is invoked:

–c *string*
> If the **–c** flag is present then commands are read from *string*.

–s If the **–s** flag is present or if no arguments remain then commands are read from the standard input. Korn shell output, except for the output of the special commands listed above, is written to file descriptor **2**.

–i If the **–i** flag is present or if the Korn shell input and output are attached to a terminal (as told by **ioctl(2)**) then this Korn shell is interactive. In this case **TERM** is ignored (so that **kill 0** does not kill an interactive Korn shell) and **INTR** is caught and ignored (so that **wait** is interruptible). In all cases, **QUIT** is ignored by the Korn shell.

–r If the **–r** flag is present, the Korn shell is a restricted Korn shell.

The remaining flags and arguments are described under the **set** command above.

Rsh Only.

Rsh is used to set up login names and execution environments whose capabilities are more controlled than those of the standard Korn shell. The actions of **rsh** are identical to those of **ksh**, except that the following are disallowed:
> changing directory (see **cd(1)**), setting the value of **SHELL**, **ENV**, or **PATH**, specifying path or command names containing /, redirecting output (>, >|, <>, and >>).

The restrictions above are enforced after **.profile** and the **ENV** files are interpreted.

When a command to be executed is found to be a Korn shell procedure, **rsh** invokes **ksh** to execute it. Thus, it is possible to provide to the end-user Korn shell procedures that have access to the full power of the standard Korn shell, while imposing a limited menu of commands; this scheme assumes that the end-user does not have write and execute permissions in the same directory.

The net effect of these rules is that the writer of the **.profile** has complete control over user actions, by performing guaranteed setup actions and leaving the user in an appropriate directory (probably not the login directory).

The system administrator often sets up a directory of commands (i.e., **/usr/rbin**) that can be safely invoked by **rsh**. Some systems also provide a restricted editor **red** .

EXIT STATUS

Errors detected by the Korn shell, such as syntax errors, cause the Korn shell to return a non-zero exit status. Otherwise, the Korn shell returns the exit status of the last command executed (see also the **exit** command above). If the Korn shell is being used non-interactively then execution of the Korn shell file is abandoned. Run time errors detected by the Korn shell are reported by printing the command or function name and the error condition. If the line number that the error occurred on is greater than one, then the line number is also printed in square brackets ([]) after the command or function name.

FILES
> **/etc/passwd**
> **/etc/profile**
> **/etc/suid_profile**
> **$HOME/.profile**
> **/dev/null**

CAVEATS
> If a command which is a tracked alias is executed, and then a command with the same name is installed in a directory in the search path before the directory where the original command was found, the Korn shell will continue to **exec** the original command. Use the **–t** option of the **alias** command to correct this situation.
>
> Some very old shell scripts contain a ^ as a synonym for the pipe character.
>
> Using the **fc** built-in command within a compound command will cause the whole command to disappear from the history file.
>
> The built-in command **.** *file* reads the whole *file* before any commands are executed. Therefore, **alias** and **unalias** commands in the file will not apply to any functions defined in the file.
>
> Traps are not processed while a job is waiting for a foreground process. Thus, a trap on **CHLD** won't be executed until the forground job terminates.

Index

! file name substitution, 29
! logical negation, 106
! [[...]] negation, 157, 159
! command-number in prompt, 136
!(*pattern*) file name substitution,
    34-35, 343
!= not equal to operator, 112
"..." quoting, 70-72
comment character, 188
super-user prompt, 125, 135
#!*interpreter*, 189
#? **select** command prompt, 125
$ variable value, 53
$ default prompt, 125, 135-136
$! process ID, 55, 338
$# positional parameters, 144, 238,
    338
$$ current process id, 52-53, 337
$(...) command substitution, 36,
    333
$((...)) arithmetic operation
    substitution, 38
$(<...) file input substitution, 36
$* positional parameters, 144, 166,
    187, 237
$- current options, 53, 337
$? exit value, 51, 53, 337
$@ positional parameters, 144,
    166, 237

$0 variable, 144
$*n* variable, 144
${*variable*}, 54, 62, 335
${#*variable*}, 54, 62, 336
${*variable*:–*word*}, 55, 62, 336
${*variable*:=*word*}, 55, 62, 336
${*variable*:?*word*}, 57, 62, 336
${*variable*:+*word*}, 59, 62, 336
${*variable*#*pattern*}, 60, 62, 336
${*variable*##*pattern*}, 60, 62, 336
${*variable*%*pattern*}, 61, 62, 336
${*variable*%%*pattern*}, 61, 62,
    336
${*array*[*n*]}, 63-65
${*array*[*]}, 63-65, 336
${*array*[@]}, 63-65
${#*array*[*n*]}, 65
% modulo operator, 101, 108
% job name prefix, 97
%= modulo-assign operator, 108
& background jobs, 9, 14, 328
& bitwise AND operator, 101, 112
&& logical AND operator, 113, 158
&& conditional execution, 10, 14,
    328
&= bitwise AND assign operator,
    101, 112
'...' quoting, 69-70, 135
() subshells, 114, 159

(...) precedence override, 114, 159

((...)) command, 102

    vs **let**, 102

    with integer expressions, 156

* file name substitution, 25, 30

* multiplication operator, 107

* edit window overflow, 84

*(*pattern*) file name substitution, 30, 343

*= multiplication-assign operator, 107

\+ addition operator, 108

\+ debug prompt string, 125, 221

\+ file name substitution, 33

\+(*pattern*) file name substitution, 33, 35, 343

\+= increment operator, 101

\- unary minus, 101, 106

\- minus operator, 101, 108

\-= decrement operator, 101, 108

. command, 208-209, 257

. character-matching, 25

.logout file, 255

.profile file, 6, 78, 89, 124

    logging in, 117

    reading in, 208

    restricted shell, 139

    sample, 245-246

.sh_history file, 74, 125

/ division operator, 100

/= division-assign operator, 101, 107

/bin/csh (see C shell)

/bin/ksh (see Korn shell)

/bin/sh (see Bourne shell)

/bin/ed, 76, 78, 125

/dev/fd, 160-161

/dev/null, 25

/etc/profile file, 117, 122, 124, 130

/etc/suid_profile file, 140

: command, 133, 231-232

: current directory in **PATH**, 120-121

: **getopts** option argument, 223

; command terminator, 8, 12, 14, 168, 169, 176, 328

;; **case** command terminator, 161

<, <= less than, less than or equal to operator, 101, 110

< edit window overflow, 84

< redirect operator, 17-18, 347

<< left shift operator, 101, 109

<<, <<- redirect operator, 22-23, 229-230, 348

<<= left shift assign operator, 101, 109

<&- redirect operator, 19, 348

<> redirect operator, 19, 139, 348

= assignment operator, 101, 109

= string equal to operator, 150-152

== arithmetic equal to operator, 101, 111

> secondary prompt, 8, 18-21, 125, 135

> redirect operator, 15, 19, 139, 348

> edit window overflow, 86

>, >= greater than, greater than or equal to operator, 101, 111

>> redirect operator, 16, 19, 139, 348

>> right shift operator, 101, 110

>>= right shift assign operator, 101, 110

>&– redirect operator, 16, 19, 22, 51, 348

>| redirect operator, 18-19, 127, 139, 331

? file name substitution, 25, 34

? **getopts** options argument, 223

?(*pattern*) file name substitution, 32, 35, 343

@ file name substitution, 33

@(*pattern*) file name substitution, 33, 35, 343

^ bitwise exclusive OR operator, 101, 112

^= bitwise exclusive OR assign operator, 101, 112

_ variable, 123

`...` command substitution, 37, 50, 72

\ continuation character, 8, 14

\ escape character, 72, 193

   \a bell character, 193

   \b backspace character, 193

   \c line without newline character, 193

   \f formfeed, 193

   \n newline character, 193

   \r return character, 193

   \t tab character, 193

   \v vertical tab character, 193

   \0*x* octal character *x*, 193

   ignoring 195

[...] command (see [[...]] command)

[] file name substitution, 28

[[...]] command, 149-160, 345-347

   compound expressions, 157-159

   file attribute expressions, 151-153

   general description, 149

   integer expressions, 156

   operators, 151, 154, 156, 159

   string expressions, 150

      with patterns, 150-151

   vs **test** and [...], 160

{...} grouping commands, 12, 15

| bitwise OR operator, 101

| pipe, 9, 15, 328

   exit status, 52

|& co-process, 15, 227-230, 328

|= bitwise OR assign operator, 101

|| logical OR operator, 101, 114

|| conditional execution, 10, 15, 328-329

~ bitwise negation, 101, 106

~ tilde substitution, 39, 333

~+, current working directory, 39, 333

~–, previous working directory, 39, 333

alias command, 130-135, 138, 332, 366

aliases, 3, 130-135, 332

   defining, 130, 132

   displaying current, 130

   displaying exported, 134

   exporting, 138

   general description, 130

   ignoring, 70, 135

   preset, 134

   removing, 135

   tracked aliases, 133, 135

   value ending in space, 130

allexport (**–a**) option, 129, 138, 144, 372
appending to file, 16, 19
Apple Computer, 3
archive files, 225-226
arguments (see command-line arguments)
arithmetic, 38, 99-115, 344-345
  base, 104
  constants, 104-105
  operators, 101, 105-116
    comparing to C, 99
    comparison, 152
    expression 102-103
    precedence, 101
  performance, 102
  random numbers, 115-116
  variables, 102
arrays, 41, 63-67
  assignments and declarations, 63-64, 334-335
  attributes, 66-67
  elements, 63
  expansion, 64-65
  general description, 63
  reassigning, 67
  subscripts, 63
ASP, Inc.,
  email address, xv, xvi
assignments,
  aliases, 130
  functions, 209
  parameters, 144-147
  variable, 42-48
    array, 102
    integer, 102
attributes, variable, 43-48, 375-376

autoload alias, 134, 333
auto-loading functions, 213

back quotes, 37, 50
background commands, 90-91
background jobs (see job control)
backslash escape character, 72, 193
backspace character, 193
bell character, 193
bg command, 91, 93, 96, 364
bgnice (**–b**) option, 129, 372
bitwise arithmetic operators, 107, 112, 116
Bourne shell
  command substitution
    compatibility, 37, 50
  compared to Korn shell, 1-2, 41, 192
  function compatibility, 209
  script compatibility, 190
break command, 179-181, 182, 366
breaking out of loops, 179

C shell,
  compared to Korn shell, 1-2, 41
  directory functions, 249-254
  job control, 89
  script compatibility, 189
  tilde substitution, 38
case command, 160-163, 330
  specifying patterns with, 25, 162
  vs **if** command, 174
  with **getopts** command, 223-225

with **select** command, 184

cat command, 202, 259
cd command, 40, 118-120
CDPATH variable, 120, 125, 339
changing the login shell, 4-5
chdir alias, 255
checking,
    command-line arguments,
        155-156, 169
    file descriptors, 160-161
chmod command, 142
clobbering files, 127
COLUMNS variable, 78, 83-84,
    125, 187-188, 339, 356
command aliasing (see aliases)
command execution,
    background, 90-91
    conditional, 10
    exit status, 10, 52, 148, 171
    pipes, 9
    suspending, 90 timing 239,
        331
command history, 74-76, 355-364
command history file, 74-76, 79
    defining, 74, 125, 245
    displaying, 74-76
    editing, 76
    size, 74, 125, 245
command input substitution (see
    command substitution)
command-line options, 130
command-line arguments
    checking, 156-157, 169
    parsing with **getopts**, 223-225
    setting, 237-238
    shifting, 146, 238

command prompt, 125, 136, 246
command re-entry (see editing
    commands)
command substitution, 36-38, 50,
    333
    arithmetic operations, 38
    Bourne shell compatibility,
        37, 50
    directing file input, 37, 50
    general description, 36
commands, 7-15, 328
    background, 90-91
    continuing, 8, 15
    co-processes, 15, 227-230
    editing, 73-96, 355-364
    exit status, 10-11, 52, 148,
        171
    expanding, 232-234
    format, 15
    grouping, 12, 330-331
    multiple, 8, 12
    separating, 8, 12, 15, 168-
        169, 175
    substituting (see command
        substitution)
    timing 238, 331
comments, 188, 331
compound commands, 8, 12
compound expressions (see
    expressions)
conditional expressions (see
    expressions)
constants, arithmetic, 104
continuation character, 8, 15
continue command, 195, 352
continuing commands, 8, 15

control commands, 161-187, 328-
331
co-processes, 15, 227-228
   reading from, 227
   writing to, 227
creating,
   aliases, 130-131
      exported, 138
   co-processes, 229-230
   functions, 209
   menus, 182-187
   prompts, 135
   traps, 215
   variables, 41-67
      integer, 45, 103-105
      exported, 138, 144, 234-
235
csh (see C shell)
Ctl-Z, 96, 352
current shell, 12, 15, 208-209

data types, 41
debug prompt string, 125, 221, 246
DEBUG signal, 217, 222
debugging korn shell scripts, 3,
218-222
   debug prompt, 125, 221, 246
   options, 218-219
   with exit status, 172
   with **trap**, 218, 222
directory functions, C shell, 249-
257
dirs function, 249-255
displaying,
   aliases, 131
      exported, 129

command-line arguments,
126, 166
file creation mask, 241-242
functions, 213
history file, 74-76
jobs, 92, 96
menus, 182-187
options, 128
resource limits, 240
signals, 96
traps, 374-375
variables, 237
   attributes, 49
   exported, 234
do, done keywords (see **for, until,**
while commands)
double quotes, 70-72

echo alias, 42, 134, 196, 367
editing commands, 73-96, 355-364
   command history file, 74-76
   enabling, 78
   in-line editors, 78-84
   displaying long command
      lines, 84
editor, in-line, 78-84, 355-364
EDITOR variable, 5, 78, 125, 245,
339
elif keyword (see **if** command)
else keyword (see **if** command)
emacs option, 78, 124, 130, 372
endless loops, 176, 178, 231
environment file, 118, 138-139,
247-248
ENV variable, 5, 118, 125, 139,
245, 339

environment, 117-139, 350-351
    file, 118, 138-139, 212, 247
    variables, 118-125, 338-342
errexit (**–e**) option, 219, 222, 223
ERR signal, 217, 222-223
ERRNO variable, 53, 55, 338
esac keyword (see **case** command)
escape characters, **print**, 190-199
eval command, 232-234, 367
evaluating expressions,
    arithmetic, 102-104
    compound, 157-159
    file attribute, 151-155
    string, 150-151
exec command, 200, 196-197, 367
    general description, 196
    performance, 202, 259
    reading input from files, 201-
        202, 204-212
    replacing current program,
        197
    with file descriptors 19-21,
        196-197
executing commands (see command
    execution)
executing Korn shell scripts, 141,
    208
exit command, 148-149, 256, 368
    exiting the shell, 149
    from functions, 211
    from **select** command, 182
    general description, 148
    leaving stopped jobs, 98
exit status 10-11, 148, 171, 380
    from pipes, 52
EXIT signal, 217-217
export command, 47, 234, 368

exporting,
    aliases, 138
    auto-exporting, 47-48
    functions, 138, 211
    variables, 138, 234, 237
expr command, 99
    evaluating arithmetic
        expressions, 102, 268
expressions, 38, 149-160
    arithmetic, 102-104
    compound expressions, 157-
        158
        with **test/**[...] command,
            158-159
    file attribute expressions, 151-
        155
    integer expressions, 156-157
    string expressions, 150-151
        with patterns, 21, 150-
            151
        with **test/**[...] command,
            150
    vs **test** and [...], 160

false command, 178, 234
fc command, 73, 74-77, 134, 368
FCEDIT variable, 76, 339, 368
fg command, 90, 93, 96, 368
fi keyword (see **if** command)
field separator variable, 125, 203-
    204, 340
file attribute expressions (see
    expressions)
file creation mask, 241-242
file descriptors, 18-22, 196, 195
    checking, 160-161
    general description, 18

manipulating, 18-22, 196
reading from file descriptors,
    204-212
writing to, 196-200
file input substitution, 37, 51
file name substitution, 23-36
    disabling, 34
    general description, 23
    matching **.** files, 30
    patterns, 30, 262, 266-267
    special characters, 31, 35
    with [[...]] command, 150-152
    with the **case** command, 162-
      164
files,
    .logout file, 255
    .profile file, 5, 78, 89
    .sh_history file, 74, 125
    /dev/fd, 160-161
    /dev/null, 23
    /etc/passwd file, 4, 39
    /etc/profile file, 117, 120,
      123, 131
    /etc/suid_profile file, 139
for command, 164-168, 329
    one-line format, 168
foreground command, 90
formfeed character, 193
FPATH variable, 213, 339
function command, 209, 331
function variables, 213
functions alias, 134, 333
functions, 209-214, 331
    autoloading, 213
    debugging with **typeset**, 219
    defining, 209

displaying current, 213
exporting, 138, 211
general description, 209
local variables, 213
removing definitions, 214
returning exit status, 210-211
scope & availability, 211
using in Korn shell scripts,
    211-213

getopts command, 223-225, 369
getty process, 4
gmacs option, 78, 124, 372
group id, 235
grouping commands, 13, 330-331

hash alias, 134, 333
here documents, 23, 225-226
Hewlett-Packard, 3
HISTFILE variable, 74, 125, 245,
    350, 355
HISTSIZE variable, 74, 125, 245,
    340, 355
history alias, 75, 134, 333
history file, 74-76, 80(see also
    command-history file)
HOME variable, 38-39, 125, 245,
    340

I/O redirection (see input/output
    redirection)
if command, 168-174
    one-line format, 169
    vs **case**, 174
    vs conditional execution
      operators, 10-11

with **else** keyword, 170-172
with **elif** keyword, 172
IFS variable, 125, 203-204, 340
ignoreeof option, 126, 130
ignoring signals, 216
in keyword (see **case**, **for** commands)
in-line command substitution, 36-38, 50, 333
in-line editors, 78-84, 355-364
   differences between emacs/gmacs, 84
   emacs/gmacs edit modes, 5, 83-84
   general description, 78
   vi edit mode, 5, 78-81
   vi mode commands, 81
infinite loops, 175, 177, 231
init process, 4
inner loop, 177
input/output commands, 189-208
input/output redirection, 14-24, 348-349
   appending to file, 16, 19, 139, 348
   closing, 16, 19, 22, 52, 348
   duplicating, 20, 25, 348
   here documents, 22, 225-226
   operators, 19
   overwriting, 17, 25, 127
   preventing overwriting, 17, 25
   standard error, 18-19
   standard input, 18-19, 23
   standard output, 15-16, 19
      discarding, 16, 23
   with **exec** command (see **exec** command)

with file descriptors, 18-21, 23-25, 196
with **print** command, 196-200
with **read** command, 205-212
integer alias, 103, 134, 333
integer arithmetic (see arithmetic)
integer variables, 45, 48
integer option, 53
i/o redirection (see input/output redirection)
interrupt signal, 90

job names, 97
jobs,
   background, 90-91
      and I/O, 93-94
   checking job status, 92
   foreground, 90
   interrupting, 89
   killing, 92
   leaving stopped jobs, 98
   manipulating, 90
   names, 97
   resuming, 90
   suspending, 90
   terminating, 92
   waiting for jobs, 93, 96
jobs command, 92, 96, 369
job control, 2, 89-98, 352-354
   commands, 92-93, 96
   compared to C shell, 89
   enabling, 89
   general description, 89
justifying variables, 46-48

kbasename script, 263
kcal script, 274-284
kcalc script, 268
kcat script, 259
kdirname script, 264
keyword (**-k**) option, 373
kgrep script, 269-273
kill command, 92, 134, 369-370
    displaying signals, 96
kill signal, 216
knl script, 265
kuucp script, 261
Korn shell,
    determining version, 4
    exiting from, 148
    invocation, 378-379
    invoking separately, 5
    major features, 1-3
    options, 124-130
    performance, 1, 102, 201, 256
    restricted shell, 139
    security, 139-140
    subshells, 137-138
    vendors of, 3-4
    vs Bourne/C shells, 1-3
Korn shell scripts,
    comments, 188, 332
    compatibility with other
        shells, 1, 189
    debugging, 3, 218-223
        debug prompt, 125, 221,
            246
        options, 218
        with exit status, 172
        with **trap**, 218
    executing, 141, 208

exit status, 10-11, 52, 148,
    171
    interactive execution, 22
    making executable, 142
    return status (see exit status)
    terminating, 148
    tracing, 220
    using functions in, 211
ksh (see Korn shell)

leading zeroes, 375
left-justified variables, 46-48
let command, 99, 102, 134, 370
    vs ((...)) command, 102
line continuation character, 8, 15
line-editing (see in-line editors)
line-number variable, 221
LINES variable, 187, 340
LINENO variable, 221, 338
local function variables, 213
logging in, 4
login shell, 4
logout alias, 256
lowercase variables, 44
loops,
    endless, 175, 177, 231
    nested, 177, 178
    terminating, 179

mail, 122-123
    new mail notification
        message, 123
        creating, 123
MAIL variable, 122-123, 340
MAILCHECK variable, 122-123,
    246, 340

MAILPATH variable, 122-123, 246, 341
markdirs option, 126, 130, 373
match command, 30-33, 266-267
menus, 182-188
metacharacters, 23-35
monitor (**–m**) option, 52, 89
Mortice Kern Systems, 3

nested loops, 178, 181
newgrp command, 235, 370
newline character, 193
    and **IFS**, 203
    suppressing, 192-200
noclobber option, 17, 25, 127, 130, 373
noexec (**–n**) option, 218-220, 373
noglob (**–f**) option, 34, 124, 130, 373
nohup command, 95
nolog option, 373
non-zero exit status, 9-10, 52
nounset (**–u**) option, 127, 130, 160, 373
null command, 134, 231-232
null string, 150
    assigning, 42, 71-71, 127
    comparing, 150

OLDPWD variable, 40, 338
octal codes, with **print**, 193, 193
operators
    [[...]], 149-160, 328-331
    arithmetic, 101, 105-115
        precedence, 102
OPTARG variable, 223, 338

OPTIND variable, 223, 338
options, 124-130, 372
    command-line, 130, 372
    default settings, 128
    disabling, 124
    displaying the current
        settings, 128
    enabling/disabling, 124, 246, 372
outer loop, 178
output redirection (see input/output redirection)
overlaying programs, 202

PAGER variable, 131, 246
parameters, (see also variables)
    modifying, 143-144
    names, 41
    positional, 54, 143-147
    special parameters, 51-53, 335-336
    substitution, 42, 55-57, 332
parent shell 137-138
parentheses (see ( ) characters)
parsing command-line arguments, 156, 223
path variable, 5
PATH variable, 5, 117, 125, 139, 246, 341
    affecting performance, 120-121
    default value, 120-121
    for restricted shell, 139, 379
    with tracked aliases, 133-135
patterns,
    [[...]], 150, 163152

case 23, 162-163
file name substitution, 23-34
matching ranges, 28-29
pipes, 9, 15, 51, 328
popd function, 249-255
positional parameters, 56, 143-149
accessing, 144, 237
last, 232-234
general description, 143
manually setting, 237-238
modifying, 145
number of, 144, 237
shifting, 145-146, 237
unsetting all, 238
PPID variable, 338
precedence, operators, 101
primary command prompt, 123,
135, 245-246
print command, 21, 42, 105, 134,
189-196, 370
escape characters, 190-192
octal codes, 192, 193, 206
options, 193-196
with co-processes, 229-230,
328
writing to file descriptors,
196-200
privileged mode, 139-140, 373
privileged (**-p**) option, 140, 373
process id,
current, 55
last background command, 55
profile file,
global, 117, 122, 123, 131
local, 5, 78, 89, 117, 123, 208
sample, 244-245

suid, 139
program execution (see command
execution)
programs, Korn shell (see Korn
shell)
prompts, 135-137
customizing your command
prompt, 135
debug, 123, 221, 245
primary, 123, 135, 245
secondary, 123, 135
select, 134, 199
PS1, primary prompt variable, 123,
135, 246, 341
PS2, secondary prompt variable,
123, 135, 341
PS3, select prompt variable, 123,
183, 341
PS4, debug prompt variable , 123,
221, 245-246, 341
pushd function, 249-255
pwd command, 235, 370
PWD variable, 39, 137, 235, 333,
338

quotes, 69-71
back, 72, 193
double, 70-71
single, 69-70, 134
whitespace, 70-71

r alias, 77, 134, 333
random numbers, 115-117
RANDOM variable, 115-116, 338
read command, 22, 198, 371
options, 204-212

reading,
    co-processes, 227-229
    files, 201-202
    file descriptors, 204-212
    interactively, 206-207
    terminals, 201-202
    word separator, 203
readonly command, 235-237, 371
readonly variables, 43, 235, 236
    unsetting, 47
redirection (see input/output
    redirection)
removing,
    aliases, 134
    functions, 214
    jobs, 92
    options, 124, 245
    variables, 51
        attributes, 47
REPLY variable, 182-183, 207,
    330, 338
resetting traps, 216
resource limits, 239-241
restricted shell, 139, 327
return character, 193
return command, 182, 210-211,
    371
return status, 10, 148, 171
returning from functions, 210-211
right-justified variables, 46-48
rsh, 139, 192

scripts (see Korn shell scripts)
search path,
    commands, 117, 125, 139,
        245
    directory names, 119-120, 125

functions, 213
    mail files, 122, 123, 245
secondary command prompt, 125
SECONDS variable, 339
select command, 125, 182-187, 329
    exiting from, 182
    menu format, 187-188
    prompt, 125, 183
semicolon, 8, 12, 15, 167-169, 175
set command, 17, 34, 372-374
    displaying variable values,
        237
    enabling/disabling options,
        124
    with arrays, 67, 335
    with positional parameters,
        237-239
setenv function, 256
setting,
    aliases, 130-132
    field separator, 203-204
    file creation mask, 241-242
    functions, 209
    options, 124, 245
    positional parameters, 237-
        239
    resource limits, 239-241
    traps, 214
    variables, 42-43, 45
shell scripts (see Korn shell scripts)
SHELL variable, 5, 123, 139, 246,
    341
shift command, 145-146, 374
shifting arguments 145-146
signals, 216
    exit, 216
    ignoring, 216

interrupt, 90
listing, 96
trapping, 215-217
single quotes, 69-70, 135
source alias, 257
special parameters, 51-53
standard output (see input/output
    redirection)
standard input (see input/output
    redirection)
standard error (see input/output
    redirection)
stop alias, 134
string length, 54
stty tostop, 94
su command, 139
subshells, 137-138, 142, 330
    differences to parent shell,
       137
    exporting to, 138
substitution,
    arithmetic, 37
    command, 36-38, 50, 333
    file input, 37, 51
    file name, 24-34, 342-343
substrings, 60-61, 263-264
system error number, 53-55
system resource limits, 239-241

tab character, 193
temporary files, 52
TERM variable, 117, 124, 125,
    246
terminating commands, 8, 12, 15
test command (see [[...]] command)
testing expressions (see

expressions)
then keyword (see **if** command)
tilde substitution, 38-39
time command, 239, 331
times command, 239, 374
TMOUT variable, 121, 125, 246,
    341
trackall (-h) option, 130, 134, 373
tracked alias, 133-134
trap command, 215-218, 375
    debugging with, 218
traps, 215-218
    exit & function traps, 217
    general description, 215
    ignoring signals, 216
    precedence, 218
    resetting, 216
    signals, 216
true command, 175, 239-240
type alias, 132, 243, 333
typeset command, 42-49
    assigning variables, 43-49,
       245-246
    creating local function
       variables, 213
    debugging functions, 219
    displaying current functions,
       213
    displaying exported variables,
       234
    exporting variables, 138, 144
    exporting functions, 211
    readonly variables, 236
    with variables, 63, 64, 66,
       103-105

ulimit command, 240-241, 377
umask command, 117, 241-242, 377
unalias command, 135, 378
underscore variable, 123
unset command, 51, 214, 378
unsetting,
    aliases, 135
    functions, 214
    options, 124, 245
    positional parameters, 236-239
    variables, 51, 239
until command, 176-178, 330
    differences with **while** command, 176
uppercase variables, 44, 48

variable attributes,
    assigning, 43-49, 375-376
    displaying, 49
    multiple, 49
    removing, 48
variable expansion, 53-65
variable substitution, 42, 53-65
variables, 41-66
    accessing values, 42
    array variables, 41, 63-67
    assigning,
        and exporting, 234
        attributes, 43-49, 375-376
        file input, 53
        values, 42-43, 45
    attributes, 43-49
    checking value, 49, 58, 231

comparing to null string, 150
data types, 41
deleting left/right patterns, 60-61, 263-264
delimiting, 54
displaying values, 53, 189, 237
expansion, 53-65
exporting, 138, 144, 234
fixed length, 46-48
general description, 41
integer, 45, 103-104
justified, 46-48
length, 54
lowercase, 44, 48
names, 41
null, 42, 70, 71, 127
readonly, 44, 236-237
substitution, 42, 53-61
substrings, 60-61, 263-264
unset, 127, 130, 160
unsetting, 51, 239
uppercase, 44, 48
using alternate value, 59
using default value, 55
value in subshells, 143
verbose (**−v**) option, 219, 222, 373
version of, **ksh**, 4
vertical tab character, 193
vi option, 78, 130
viraw option, 373
VISUAL variable, 78, 125, 342

wait command, 93, 96, 378
waiting for background commands, 93, 96
what command, 4

whence command, 134, 242-243,
378
while command, 174-176, 330
differences with **until**
command, 176
one-line format, 175-176
whitespace, 71, 190
wild-card characters, 25-34

xtrace (**-x**) option, 130, 218, 220,
373

zero exit status, 10, 11, 52